Military History
and the
Military Profession

Military History
and the
Military Profession

Edited by
David A. Charters,
Marc Milner,
and
J. Brent Wilson

Foreword by Anne N. Foreman

Westport, Connecticut
London

Library of Congress Cataloging-in-Publication Data

Military history and the military profession / edited by David A.
  Charters, Marc Milner, and J. Brent Wilson ; foreword by Anne N.
  Foreman.
      p. cm.
   Includes bibliographical references and index.
   ISBN 0–275–94072–1
   1. Military art and science—History. 2. Military history.
   3. Military history—Historiography. I. Charters, David.
   II. Milner, Marc. III. Wilson, J. Brent.
   U27.M49   1992
   355′.009—dc20   92–9114

British Library Cataloguing in Publication Data is available.

Library of Congress Catalog Card Number: 92–9114
ISBN: 0–275–94072–1

First published in 1992

Praeger Publishers, 88 Post Road West, Westport, CT 06881
An imprint of Greenwood Publishing Group, Inc.

Printed in the United States of America

The paper used in this book complies with the Permanent
Paper Standard issued by the National Information Standards
Organization (Z39.48–1984).

10 9 8 7 6 5 4 3 2 1

Contents

Foreword

By way of introduction I would comment that as a lawyer who originally trained as a historian, I am frequently struck by the similarities between law and history. Both emphasize strongly the discovery, accumulation, and establishment of facts. Each views situations as fundamentally unique. Both historians and lawyers are wary of theory, and both structure their analysis on change over time, the one by sequencing events and exploring the interaction of people and forces in order to explain what occurred, and the other by emphasizing precedent and principle for the purpose of resolving controversy. Both demand rigor in the analysis: cold, cruel, hard questions and insistence on logical thought to come to conclusions based on fact. Both these disciplines are extremely useful in government, but we do not often recognize history in that role. Law, of course, appears practical and appropriate for government; after all, the rule of law undergirds the foundations of the Anglo-American form of government. History, however, is normally viewed by people in positions such as mine as something academic; it is interesting, to be sure, but not immediately relevant to the harried, pressured "real" world of decision making.

However, history is all around us, and of course we use it every day with hardly a second thought. Every person in government approaches a problem or issue at the very least, on the basis of his or her own personal experience, against which are measured the facts, the pattern of events, the people involved, the conditions, and the objectives to be sought. Almost subconsciously, our minds search for previous data or knowledge about the problem. When we ask our staffs for information or analysis, or for recommendations, they invariably produce background that comes from the past or that frames the problem in a form similar to a historical narrative.

Is such background researched with the same rigor, thoroughness, attention to detail, and comprehensiveness that historians often bring to a question? Sometimes it is—but not always. We use history and the historical method frequently, but not directly, and sometimes not well. Do the staff or principals realize they are using (or abusing) the historical method? They rarely do. To cite only one example, people constantly use reasoning by analogy. They conclude that a situation, set of facts, or problem "is just like" something else, and then go on to react as though the two were nearly identical. In their wonderful book *Thinking in Time*, Richard E. Neustadt and Ernest R. May warned us of the dangers of drawing conclusions in this manner and basing decisions on such flawed analogies. Nonetheless, how often has policy been based on analogy? The Munich example was cited repeatedly as a basis for policy decisions during the Cold War. Appeasement of totalitarian regimes, the reasoning went, leads only to disaster; their aggression must be resisted firmly, by force if necessary, whenever it occurs. Sometimes, as in the Korean War, the analogy worked to America's benefit, but just as often it turned out disastrously, as in Vietnam. Given these realities, I want to suggest three major reasons why history is crucial to decision making and leave you with a challenge to make it even more important to government.

The first is a general statement of value: History can save us from making mistakes. It can produce a sound rendering of the reality of the facts: who, what, when, where, how, and why. Historians can separate the myth from the reality. For the policy-maker, they can produce a base for action that does not depend on personal experience, inaccurate memory, or interested advocacy. History, insofar as its purpose is to recreate reality, is an important foundation on which to approach a problem.

It is particularly important to have historians in the military and in the upper reaches of the government because our officers change assignments every two to four years and our senior civilian officers in the Department of Defense average less than three years in a job. Now, there are benefits to this rotation: People do not become stale, and they bring new enthusiasm and unique experience to their posts. However, the rapid turnover of individuals, both in positions of responsibility and in staff support billets, enhances the tendencies to waste an enormous amount of time "reinventing the wheel" and to make the wrong decisions.

My own experience in trying to live with this reality is to combine my history and law training to obtain solid facts. Issues come to me with staff summary sheets condensing them and recommending a course of action. Attached are several pages, or several inches of pages, of background and documents. The next step then is to call in anybody who has coordinated, concurred, or refused to approve the recommendation and "depose" them on what they really meant, why a particular paper was included, what the situation really resembles, how carefully the issue has been considered, and similar questions. The process is iterative: sending people back for facts and then discussing the issues in depth against a backdrop of what occurred before, mistakes and successes made in the past, and previous courses of action. Staff elements in the U.S. Air Force (USAF) do keep records, draw on memory, and consult their history offices for information, facts, documents, and analysis.

During 1989–1990, the U.S. Department of Defense underwent a process known as the Defense Management Review (DMR). Much of it consisted of reassessing the current organization, searching out inefficiencies and areas to cut back, identifying missions or functions that might be jettisoned, and proposing budget reductions invited by altered world conditions or necessitated by the country's own economic situation. Time and again, the various elements of the Air Force referred to earlier drawdowns and decisions. That historical experience frequently arose in discussion, and recalling it prevented us from making errors or reinventing not just wheels, but sometimes broken wheels.

The second reason why history is valuable is that understanding the historical background prevents policy-making in a void. It provides context; it makes sense of the facts. One thing that continues to amaze me is how infrequently people are armed with the real facts of an issue or problem, phrased in such a way as to explain how the present situation evolved. Pushing for an explanation of the facts brings out the nuances and the totality of what is actually transpiring, helping people to arrive at sound conclusions.

The third value for history relates closely to the first two and contributes to sound decision making: History provides perspective. History does not simply establish facts or provide the relevant data. It provides a depth of understanding to a problem, a set of issues, or the evidence that can lead a policy- or decision-maker to a better choice than he or she might otherwise make. The process is not just avoiding mistakes, it is also being informed to the level of being comfortable—to seeing the nuances, the complexity, or a way out of a difficult jam. Alternately, it could be the realization that nothing *can* be done to solve a problem and that only a marginal improvement or the minimizing of loss is possible.

By this I am not so much suggesting the use of "lessons learned" as I am pointing out that history can support a particular course of action simply on the basis of understanding the conditions, the possibilities, and the choices. History is accumulated experience. Finding out what occurred earlier—how it came about, why, and what was done previously—stimulates the imagination and suggests new or different alternatives.

During our discussions over reducing the force, officers in the room frequently recalled times when resources were constrained and what decisions were made in those times. In the 1970s, the Air Force chose to have weapons, equipment, and people, but not the facilities, spare parts, and programs for the support of that force structure. The result came to be known as "the hollow force": still a large air force, but one less capable of going to war and winning in combat than its numbers implied. Flying hours were reduced, with the consequence that USAF pilots were not as well trained. We neglected our facilities, which led to poor living conditions and inefficiencies of storage and maintenance; some airplanes were cannibalized of parts to keep others flying, which lowered our in-commission rates and our ability to generate sorties for exercises—and in a crisis, to handle an adversary. Overall, the result was low morale, poor attitudes, and good people leaving the service: just what one might expect.

The perspective of that time clearly affects the air force's choices today. We know that others have faced the dilemma of too many requirements and too few resources. We know that it is possible to deal with the dilemma and to choose differently; we can choose less force structure. The consequence is likely to be less capability; there is no way to avoid that. However, the perspective of how that choice was made earlier not only informs the current decision, it also gives the policy-maker the confidence to go forward and the ability to explain, to those who must live with the repercussions, what the alternatives were and why a particular course of action was chosen. It can be comforting to know that others faced great difficulties, decided, and survived, and that from the present perspective those decisions were less than optimum.

At the same time, history can be a liberating force; it can free one to make changes and to see that the consequences may not necessarily be devastating. History can function as a guide. As the Air Force undergoes many of its budget exercises, I frequently hear references to the reasons why certain offices or programs exist. Senior decision-makers know the story; they will remark, "Yes, we can abolish that, or move that, but we have it or do it because . . . , and therefore, if you abandon that activity, then . . . We have reached this point because. . . . " Now occasionally one probes into the past only to find that the emperor indeed is naked; that an office was created to solve a problem that has since disappeared, because of the personalities involved, or for some other purposes no longer relevant, but that the bureaucratic structure has continued anyway and can be abolished. That, too, is consoling. In the end, history leads one to ask very tough questions, questions of "why" and "how" as well as "what," and the answers are often enormously revealing.

Finally, we need to remind ourselves about the number of times we *do not* use history. My last point is that *how* one uses history, and whether one *can* use it professionally, are issues that historians should ponder and address. We all know that history is useful. I have not mentioned the many ways in which military services find it crucial to their institutional life: for orientation, indoctrination, cohesion in units, and pride; for doctrine, operations, and planning; and for professional military education, at which the U.S. Army and Air Force are particularly effective. However, for the decision-maker, history must also be *timely*. Often in the upper reaches of government, we lack the necessary time to ponder issues as thoroughly as we might like. Because there are so many actions constantly pressing forward, because world events occur so rapidly and without much warning, and because senior staff need answers quickly, much floods onto the decision-maker's desk. There are people to see, inspections to be made, meetings to attend, leadership and representational duties to perform, and negotiations to be undertaken—all the myriad activities of individuals involved in large institutions coping with a world that constantly seems to be moving more quickly. Often we lack the time to consult with historians or to commission a study that will require three or four months of research and writing. The request must allow enough time for such work to be valuable in the process of deciding. However, if historians require time for their work, and if decision-makers lack the time, how can history help? Let me suggest three broad approaches to confronting this dilemma.

The first is to build historical analysis into the staffing process, largely as the USAF does today. If active, thoughtful professional scholars are employed on the staffs of senior policy-makers, if the staffs are practiced in using their services, and if the historians have adequate records and other materials on which to base the information and perspective, decisions can be improved and policy will be better informed. The very presence of an active historical program not only provides the leadership with a powerful tool for analysis, it also raises the consciousness of the entire organization, making it more likely to use history and integrate a sound understanding of the past into policy and decision making. In effect, the presence of energetic historians affects the culture of the organization and stimulates usage. Insofar as using history improves the organization, its further use is stimulated, setting in motion a reciprocal cycle of excellence that should provide enormous satisfaction to professional historians and, at the same time, save lives and national resources.

A second approach, which is particularly effective if practiced by a staff historical office but also possible for independent historians, is to anticipate the needs of leaders and prepare analyses and other materials in advance of demand. Such work entails risk and is difficult. Situations cannot always be predicted, work may be prepared that is never used, and historians working within bureaucracies may be questioned about how they are using their time if too many unnecessary studies are produced. Nonetheless, being prepared to aid in policy is perhaps the only way in which historians can volunteer information and analysis at that critical moment when history can make a difference to those who must decide, many of whom are too harried or are not, by education or experience, themselves inclined to inquire if history can be helpful. As a lawyer and former General Counsel of the Air Force, I practiced what I am preaching here, day to day, on issues (such as environmental pollution) that could land the institution in trouble and individuals in prison, and it worked.

A third approach combines the first two, but injects the element of mutual consultation before and during the moment when historical perspective may be needed: the policy-maker and the historian sit down together and decide what would be helpful, when, and in what form. Both sides must come to the discussion prepared to understand the other's viewpoint and willing, insofar as possible, to adjust their activity in order to gain the benefit of the relationship. The decision-maker must anticipate what he or she needs long enough in advance to provide the historian time or else must be willing to delay or suspend an action long enough to allow the historian to research and analyze the problem. From personal experience, I can say that the broader the issue and the less well-charted the territory, the more personal need I feel for historical perspective. To respond, the historian must be prepared to act quickly, cut corners in research, and, above all else, to produce a product tailored to the client: perhaps a briefing, or a two-page analysis (rather than a fifty-page monograph) that is brutally to the point, hedges as little as possible, and can be read and absorbed quickly.

In the final analysis, we know that the past is useful. Perhaps the most enduring question is how and in what circumstances can it be used for the benefit of senior decision-makers in government? Historians, like lawyers, must be prepared not to be used or to be ignored after being consulted. That is central to the client relationship, and my underlying thesis has been that the relationship between historian and decision-maker is a client, rather than an academic or pedagogical, relationship. Military historians possess considerable advantages over their colleagues in the historical profession. Those who specialize in the military possess a viable, definable field with distinct and identifiable focuses, which is both popular and useful. Students are interested; the public seems insatiable for military history, whether in the form of movies, fiction, or historical works. Moreover, unlike other historical specialties, there is a clientele in the military services and defense ministries of the world that needs and uses the perspective and analysis that historians have to offer. It is up to the historians to forge a client relationship and innovate to create the products that will prove most effective in contributing to policy and decision-making.

However, it is also up to those of us in senior positions in government to use history. I am reminded of the story, perhaps apocryphal, of the Israeli general who once accosted one of our colleagues (a medievalist, I believe). "What makes you think your studies of campaigns in the era of swords, armor, lances, and horses have any relevance to today's fast-faced, high-tech warfare?" asked the general. Replied the historian, "What makes you think, General, that you are smart enough to win the next war on the basis of your own experience alone?"

Therein may lay a lesson for us all.

Anne N. Foreman
Under Secretary of the United States Air Force

Introduction

Historians and warriors have traveled a common path throughout all recorded history. The causes, conduct, and consequences of war have affected the development of virtually all societies. Indeed, until recently, the waging of war was one of the principal executive powers and activities of governments. It is hardly surprising, then, that war was the focus of much early historical writing. The ancient "father of modern history," Herodotus, was primarily a military (or at least a diplomatic) historian.[1] His great rival, Thucydides, also wrote about war and, in the process, set the standard for modern historical methodology. Furthermore, it was Vegetius who introduced the form of military history that is the focus of this volume: the didactic, which seeks to employ history to teach the military specific things, as distinct from simply inspiring.[2] The reasons for the military's long and abiding interest in the history of war and the nature of the relationship between historians and the military are explored in the following chapters. Also examined is the nexus between the historical method of research and writing and the use the military makes of history itself.

In doing so, this volume offers a "snapshot" of the state of the art in military history at the beginning of the last decade of the twentieth century. The various essays illuminate those subjects that historians deemed worthy of exploration in recent years. They also explore specific ways that the military profession has used (or could use) history as a training and educational tool. These subjects are examined across a number of national perspectives, which highlight both what is unique and what is common across national barriers. The three environments— land, sea, and air—are represented in individual chapters, as are a number of specialized subjects, such as the place of intelligence in military history. Cutting across the national, environmental, and specialized categories are the assessments of the state of the field of study in these categories, as well as case studies that illustrate the utilitarian dimensions of applied history, both in method and example. The result of this is, hopefully, a portrait of the whole field of military history that is greater than the sum of its parts.

Why is such a study needed at this time? After all, there are many historians who doubt that military or war history has anything worthwhile to say to any audience. Others would argue with even greater force that it has nothing of value to teach the modern military, which is oriented to a high-technology warfare that was the stuff of dreams mere decades ago. Indeed, as recently as thirty years ago, Walter Millis, himself a noted American military historian, speculated that military history had reached the end of its useful life insofar as the military profession was concerned. "It is the belief of the present writer," Millis wrote, "that military history as a specialty has largely lost its function." He argued that popular military history, with its "panache," would survive, as would "old tales of war and battle and generalship." However, reflecting the spirit of the age, Millis doubted if the study of history was of much use in the nuclear era:

The old tales are increasingly irrelevant to modern politics, to modern war and modern citizenship. . . . It is not immediately apparent why the strategy and tactics of Nelson, Lee or even of Bradley or Montgomery should be taught to young men who are being trained to manage the unmanageable military colossi of today.[3]

In asserting this, Millis was completely in step with both the historians and the military of time. The former had come to challenge the long-held belief that wars were a driving force of history. Instead, wars increasingly came to be seen as short-term "blips" on a scale dominated by long-term social or economic trends. For many contemporary historians, who were interested in the lives of ordinary people, social determinism, and the role of groups or classes in history, wars came to be seen as an external factor visited on and endured by their subjects, much as were drought and the plague. The didactic methodology and the romanticism of "drum and trumpet" military history, not to mention the impolitic nature of war itself, pushed military history to the margins of the historical profession. Academic military history outside the military colleges and the official historical services remained the preserve of a select (some would say isolated) few, who were ignored and even distrusted by their colleagues.

Likewise, the military of the 1960s and 1970s and their political overloads seemed to take Millis to heart. The advent of nuclear weapons was thought to signal the end of the era of the large-scale conventional wars that had provided the stuff of military history for centuries. Consequently, if even the experience of World War II was rendered obsolete by the concept of nuclear war, what reason was there to think that earlier wars were worth studying for viable operational lessons or principles? Both government and the military rejected the past as prologue and turned enthusiastically to an intensive study of the present. They embraced the social sciences that Millis had argued were required to supplant the critical and systematic study of history. The new "military-strategic studies'' curricula at staff and defense colleges, which focused on the present with ''models'' and prescriptions, offered the military the kind of solutions that the moment seemed to demand.

However, to paraphrase Mark Twain, reports of the death of military history were ''greatly exaggerated.'' Indeed, much has happened since Millis wrote its obituary. Academic military history had experienced tremendous growth since the 1960s. A measure of that growth is described in Don Higginbotham's essay, but it is also apparent in the assessments of the field that are appearing more frequently in anthologies, journal articles, and monographs as well as at conferences.[4] The reason for such growth is that academic military historians chose to practice the part of Millis's preaching that the military had overlooked. He had, in fact, urged historians to take a more catholic view of the field—to broaden and redefine it as ''war history,'' which could encompass the whole range of human endeavors, not just the activity in the last 400 meters of the battlefield. The result has been a rich and diverse blend of military, economic, social, and political history, which is often now referred to as ''the new military history.''

If this approach represented a healthy development in methodology and historiography, it nonetheless remained almost exclusively an academic pursuit, divorced from the military profession. Yet, in spite of their penchant for strategic studies, the military had ''rediscovered'' military history in the late 1970s. This reflected changing perceptions of the nature of modern war. As the balance of nuclear deterrence revived the utility of conventional deterrence (and hence, of conventional war) as a means of keeping the nuclear threshold out of reach, the mechanized battles of World War II and those of the more recent Middle Eastern wars became subjects worthy of study.[5] Thus, history, as institutional memory and a source of tactical and operational doctrine, had regained respectability within the profession and was once again central to the education and training of military professionals.

It was with a view to examining the state of these two strands of historical endeavor—their commonalities, mutual utility, and relation to each other—that the editors commissioned these essays. This inquiry was a direct outgrowth of our own academic experience. The Centre for Conflict Studies and the Military and Strategic Studies Programme at the University of New Brunswick, Canada, combine the study of contemporary military affairs with a strong historical perspective that is rooted in the analysis of training, doctrine, and other fundamental components of preparing forces for operations. Moreover, long-standing ties with the professional military have given us a foot in both the academic and military camps and an awareness of concerns on both sides of the civil-military divide. This unique position convinced us that these two historical approaches had much in common and much to learn from each other. From the academic point of view, military history may be approaching an important crossroads. Indeed, the essays in this volume suggest a new synthesis: a merging of the two methodologies to create the ''*new* new military history.'' This would retain the breadth of approach acquired by academic historians over the last two decades, while reinjecting war—as the military understands and studies it—back into the analysis.

Such an approach could be quite useful for the military profession which, with the end of the Cold War period, may be entering a new era. As the war in the Persian Gulf demonstrated, history did not end with the collapse of the post–1945 world order, as some speculated.[6] Nor will the past ever be irrelevant to our present circumstances. As Anne Foreman's very thoughtful foreword indicates, studies of the past will always be useful to guide military forces through the present and into the future. Their greatest value, Dominick Graham insists, will lie not in the examples they teach, but in the extent to which they fulfill Michael Howard's criteria: making both professions "wise forever."

NOTES

1. See, for example, John Boardman, Jasper Griffin, and Oswyn Murray, eds., *The Oxford History of the Classical World* (New York: Oxford University Press, 1986), p. 188.

2. Vegetius, *De Re Militaria*, pub. c. A.D. 400.

3. Walter Millis, *Military History*, Service Centre for Teachers of History Publication no. 39 (Washington, DC: American Historical Association, 1961), p. 18.

4. John Whiteclay Chambers II, "The New Military History: Myth and Reality" [Conference review essay], *Journal of Military History* 55, no. 3 (July 1991): pp. 395–406.

5. See, for example, Lt. Col. J. A. English, Maj. J. Addicott and Maj. P. J. Kramers, eds., *The Mechanized Battlefield* (Washington, DC: Pergamon-Brassey's, 1985); John A. English, *A Perspective on Infantry* (New York: Praeger, 1984); Stephanie G. Neuman and Robert E. Harkavy, *The Lessons of Recent Wars in the Third World*, 2 vols. (Lexington, MA: Lexington Books, 1985–87); Anthony H. Cordesman and Abraham R. Wagner, *The Lessons of Modern War*, 3 vols. (Boulder, CO: Westview/Marsell, 1990).

6. Francis Fukuyama, "The End of History," *National Interest*, Summer 1989, pp. 3–18.

Part I

Military History: The State of the Field

1

American Military History: Clio and Mars as "Pards"

ALLAN R. MILLETT

Although a quote from Carl von Clausewitz usually precedes a serious discussion of military history, that soldier-philosopher of the American Civil War, Corporal Josiah Klegg, seems the proper authority to explain the union of Clio and Mars. Late in the war the governor of Indiana offered Si a lieutenant's commission, but Si refused because he would have to leave his "pard," Shorty. As Si told Shorty: "Seemed ter me I wouldn't 'mount ter shucks without you, 'n' that settled it."[1] Like the bonding of Si and Shorty, the study of history (Clio) and the study of war (Mars) have become inseparable "pards," even though their partnership has not always been congenial. The military history of the United States, as written by Americans, dramatizes the uneasy balance between the demands of the armed forces for "usable" history and the ambivalent interest of the professoriate in allowing the study of military history in American universities and colleges.

There are at least five kinds of military history. Risking simplification, military history is the history of warfare and military institutions. This history may be served up in different forms. It may appear as printed historical fiction, narrative and interpretative history, epic poetry, film, song, and oral tradition. The media, however, is not the message. It is the intent of the author and the expectations of the reader that matter. The first kind of military history is humanistic; in other words, the purpose of the author is to reveal universal truths about the condition of humanity as these attitudes, values, and behaviors appear under the trauma of war and the stress of military service. The second kind of military history emphasizes the military nature of membership in the collective community, whether that community is a modern nation-state or a primitive tribe. The intent in this case is to use the martial past as a way to impress the young with their military obligations and indoctrinate them in the past sacrifices of the soldiers of their community. It is military history as the inculcation of the commitment to survival. The third type of military history is antiquarian: the love of the material culture of military activity and a fascination with relics (or reproductions) that provide vicarious entertainment. It reflects a taste for the particularistic and arcane aspects of past military activity.[2]

Although one can find examples of these first three types of military history in every form of social organization, the fourth and fifth types reflect the interests of two complex institutions, the military establishments of modern nation-states and the systems of higher education that produce the intelligentsia of modern nations. Both types of military history assume some sort of utility to learning beyond personal satisfaction and entertainment. Learning must be turned to occupational or functional purposes. These types of military history are military-utilitarian and civilian-utilitarian military history, and they are defined by the military profession and by the academic profession, respectively.

Both military-utilitarian and civilian-utilitarian military history come in several subspecies, which complicates the taxonomy. Military organizations use history for several purposes. One is to legitimize their existence, which is especially important in societies that are not predisposed to grant their soldiers much status or institutional autonomy. Military history—usually positive accounts of military performance in wars that are crucial to national survival—stress that the availability of armed forces is a prerequisite for state status and that the maintenance of appropriate armed forces is part of the price of independence and national identity. Such military history may be specific in terms of prescribing policy, usually by the selective use of the past to argue for or against a particular strategic vision or policy such as "command of the sea" or universal military service. In the writing of American military history, two examples should suffice: Emory Upton, *The Military Policy of the United States* (1904) and Alfred Thayer Mahan, *The Influence of Sea Power upon History, 1660–1773* (1890). In this case, the audience is both internal and external, namely, the military leadership and the civilian political elite. The other types of military-utilitarian military history have an internal audience alone. One type might be called *regimental history* and plays an important role in socializing soldiers to organizational expectations and norms. It is designed to foster esprit, a sense of identification with group achievements, and a commitment to the highest standards of soldierly conduct, especially in war.[3]

The second internal utility of military history is the training and education of the officer corps. Military history becomes a principal way to extend learning beyond one's own experience, to enlarge the intellectual imagination through the study of others' experiences, whether command in war, the successful management of complex organizations, the conduct of campaigns, the creation and refinement of strategic principles and operational doctrine, the special difficulties of combined and joint operations, the tyranny of logistics and communications, the optimal use of technology, or the importance of unit cohesion and esprit. Military history becomes the laboratory for the scientific side of officership as well as a pallet of colors for the artistic elements of military leadership.[4]

Civilian-utilitarian military history proceeds from far different concerns than military-utilitarian military history; these concerns are sometimes antithetical in intent, sometimes complementary, and sometimes simply irrelevant. For a university-based academic military historian, the reason to study military history may simply be a way to investigate the characteristics of a particular historical experience. For example, a Turnerian historian might study the role of the U.S. Army in the expansion of the frontier, not because its activities explain the nature of the army, but because the army helps define the impact of the frontier experience on American history. If one accepts the proposition that military institutions mirror the larger society, then the study of military history may provide important clues about how a particular society functions; how it decides, for example, who serves and who does not in terms of social class, race, and gender. Some academic military historians have, in fact, argued that their mission is to provide a military history that exposes the limiting assumptions of military-utilitarian military history, that "demilitarizes" the accounts of the past that serve the armed forces' special purposes. In other words, civilian military history should perform the same intellectual service that populist political history ("the people's history") performs as an antidote for elitist political history.[5]

The final type of civilian-utilitarian military history focuses on the study of war as an intellectual pathway to establishing peace. The purpose of the investigation is to discover how humankind may reduce the threat or reality of war in the conduct of human affairs. Although this academic inquiry is not limited to historical studies, it has produced some influential works in the field. There is considerable irony in the study of military history as part of peace studies education because it often turns academics away from historical inquiry and toward other types of rational and nonrational study. The irony is that one can often build a convincing case that any specific war could have been avoided, could have been ended sooner and at less cost, and could have produced a better world if it had been followed by more enlightened peacemaking. However, the study of war in human affairs shows it to be a social phenomenon that has resisted every change in human political organization and every improvement in our material culture and ability to control our physical environment. Civilian academics, who tend to be more optimistic that most individuals about the possibility of human progress, find little comfort in studying the historical persistence of warfare.[6]

MILITARY-UTILITARIAN MILITARY HISTORY

The study of military history within the American armed forces grew in two distinct and sometimes conflicting ways, and that conflict has shaped the character of military-utilitarian military history. In an institutional sense, the dual tradition is reflected in each of the four services by the existence of a central historical office, usually a center or division in the service central headquarters, and by a system of schools for officers. It is important to know that the latter predates the former, for the perceived needs of officer education, as developed in the nineteenth century, tended to define military history in ways not always compatible with the establishment of the historical divisions in the twentieth century. As civilian historians struggled to find a place for themselves in the armed forces after World War II, their eloquent pleas about the value and objectivity of their work seemed aimed at their peers in academic life (and so they were), but the "official historians" were also fighting a more critical battle for survival and influence within their services at the same time. Their problem was that they worked for senior officers whose vague notions of the utility of military history had been shaped by experiences far different from those of the civilian historians. The tension between the dominant perspectives of the civilian historians in military employ and the military's senior leadership stemmed from different views on the utility of history to the armed forces, not its impact on the historical profession in the universities and colleges.[7]

Since the middle of the nineteenth century, the officer corps—or that small minority that reads serious books—defined military history in two ways. The first, which flourished after the Civil War, was *regimental history* written for veterans of the war and those who followed them. Like much of the literature on the army, writing on the U.S. Navy drew its inspiration from the experiences of individual officers, ships or squadrons, and commercial sponsors. The first real organizational histories of the navy were C. B. Boynton, *History of the Navy during the Rebellion* (2 vols., 1867) and three books on squadron operations commissioned by Scribners and written by Daniel Ammen, J. R. Soley, and Alfred Thayer Mahan. Both services also collected and published the documents known as *The War of the Rebellion: A Compilation of the Official Records of the Union and Confederate Armies* (128 vols., 1878–1901) and *Official Records of the Union and Confederate Navies in the War of the Rebellion* (30 vols., 1894–1922). Although these editorial projects marked the first commitment to organizational history, they did not produce agencies with this mission, and the histories of the war with Spain, even those by senior participants, came from commercial publishers and tended to be the work of journalists and politicians, not serving officers. Even the modest efforts at organizational history for internal use did not take root in the service headquarters until after World War I.[8]

The greatest attention to military history came instead in the army and navy's school systems and reflected the belief that the study of past campaigns and battles provided future leaders with the intellectual tools needed to wage war. One should not exaggerate the history-consciousness of the military schools—the United States Military Academy and the United States Navy Academy, for both stressed mathematics, science, and engineering in the classroom and minor tactics in the field. With the exception of the work of Dennis Hart Mahan at West Point and J. R. Soley at the Naval Academy, history-based instruction was virtually nonexistent. Instead, military history took root at two additional schools founded in the 1880s, the Army Infantry and Cavalry School (later called the School of the Line and Staff College) at Fort Leavenworth, Kansas and the Naval War College at Newport, Rhode Island. At Ft. Leavenworth, the army's officers studied the European campaigns of the Germans and the French, as well as the Civil War; at Newport, the students learned from Alfred Thayer Mahan that the greatness of the British Empire rested on God-given cultural superiority and the Royal Navy. In the army's experience, military history elucidated the concepts known as the *principles of war*, while the navy learned that sea power and a battlefleet-in-being provided national economic growth and security for maritime powers like the United States. Military history developed operational doctrine and strategic vision within the officer corps, although in Mahan's case the historical work had an external policy-prescriptive function as well. Service-sponsored history, including research and publication, should be the servant of officer education, not the basis for organizational action.[9]

The idea that military history might serve a more ambitious purpose than military socialization and officer education flourished in the reforms of the Progressive period. Like other Progressives, army and navy officers learned that historical analysis could pay political dividends. The creation of the War Department General Staff and the varied proposals to build a land force reserve rested on historical justification, whether it came from the writings of Upton or John McAuley Palmer. General Leonard Wood, a Progressive Chief of Staff, agreed to a proposal from Robert M. Johnston of Harvard University, the first academic military historian, that Johnston would join his staff should Wood lead an expedition against Mexico in 1914. By the end of World War I, the War Department General Staff had a historical section prepared to mount a postwar campaign to prove that the American Expeditionary Forces had won World War I: "That it was easily the decisive factor in ending the war hardly requires to be argued."[10] By 1920 the army and navy, as well as the U.S. Marine Corps, had established historical offices in Washington, D.C., whose principal mission was to support service policy-making and administration, not just unit morale and officer education.[11]

The creation of permanent central historical offices for the American armed forces did not bring any dramatic changes, however, until World War II. The dominant personalities in each office tended to be regimental historians. The service school officer-faculty tended to set the terms for historical study, which meant officer education and doctrinal development. Both the army air corps and the marine corps, for example, saw historical research as an apt method to illuminate assumptions about air power and amphibious warfare that were closer to religious faith than empirical argument. For the army ground forces officers, trained and educated at the Infantry School and at Ft. Leavenworth, military history became a vast reservoir of experience from which to pluck either tactical "lessons learned" or broad concepts of operations that could accept changes in technology without destroying an appreciation of the Clausewitzian elements of friction, chance, human error, and will. At the Naval War College, naval service officers absorbed not only Mahanian sea power concepts, but also worked through the hypothetical difficulties of a war with Japan in the Pacific.

Without disparaging the scope of the intellectual effort, one should appreciate that the interwar period benefits from a post hoc aura derived from the performance of American officers, selectively remembered, in World War II. Admiral Chester W. Nimitz, for example, testified that his Naval War College education made him a better Commander-in-Chief, Pacific (CINCPAC), but Nimitz's finest moments came from his prudent character, not his Newport experience. Whatever the source of their inspiration, the senior American military leaders of World War II believed that their study of military history had sharpened their skills as commanders. Ironically, this enthusiasm for military history did not match the goals of the civilian historians who had flooded into the army and the army air forces during World War II. They had not donned uniform or come into government service as civilians simply to gild the reputations of senior military officers. Rather, they had joined the war effort to celebrate the experience of the United States as a nation in arms.[12]

Riding the crest of their successful World War II historical projects, the service historical offices persevered and survived the completion of those projects and the departure of the generation of historians who carried the burden of researching and writing them. The historical divisions differ in size and the methods they use to perform their missions, but their orientation is strikingly similar. It is shaped to a large degree by the values of their work force of civilian historians. Although the service historical divisions claim that they write for their service clienteles, usually the central staffs and the school systems, their publications also serve a civilian audience outside the military establishment. If this were not so, then why do they bother to publish their books by the tens of thousands through the U.S. Government Printing Office or commercial presses? Why is there such sensitivity to scholarly reviews? The key is that the World War II generation of official historians did not come from the officer corps (although many served as wartime officers), but from universities and graduate programs. They retained civilian values; not just those of academia, but those of the nation's political and intellectual elite. They believed that an enlightened electorate and the public officials who made up the federal government needed to know more about a democracy's conduct of war; not just in the operational sense (where democracy hardly mattered), but also in civil-military relations, the formation of national policy and strategy, coalition diplomacy, manpower and material mobilization, the application of civilian science and technology to war, and the financial and economic problems of waging total war. Since the Cold War simply extended many of these questions past 1945, the service historians saw no reason to change their interests. If anything, they argued that historical study should be part of an emerging field of *national security policy studies*. Not surprisingly, the army and air force history offices—staffed by hundreds of civilian professional historians—lead the way in turning service-sponsored historical study outward toward the civilian world, but even the navy and the marine corps gave increased emphasis to the external mission, the use of history to legitimize the function of military defense, and the existence of large and expensive postwar armed forces.[13]

The institutionalization of the central service historical agencies has several important implications. First, it created a second major focus within the armed forces—the other remained the officer education system—for historical study. In addition, this dual structure inevitably leads to competition with the service senior leadership over resources, attention, and authority. Who, for example, speaks for military history within the U.S. Army, the head of the department of history at the Military Academy or the chief of Military History? They both do, along with the head of the Combat Studies Institute, the director of the U.S. Army Military History Institute, and the senior historian of the Training and Doctrine Command, which supervises the Reserve Officers' Training Corps (ROTC) and the army educational system (West Point and the intermediate and senior service schools excluded).[14] With some simplification, this competitive—and collaborative—relationship exists within all the services and ensures continued debate about *which* type of military history the service should stress. While such pluralism may confuse outsiders and appear redundant to organizational experts, it ensures intellectual stimulation within the armed forces history communities and provides a wide variety of publications and historical services. It also ensures that the faculties of the historical divisions and schools will remain open to external influence from military and civilian sources. The senior officers of all the services have, on occasion, appeared discomfited because there is no *doctrine* for historical study and because the practicing historians sometimes give short shrift to questions of socialization and officer education or show considerable distaste for marshaling historical examples to support existing strategic preferences or operational doctrine. As long as the armed forces see any value in historical study, they will have to accept a certain amount of disarray in their historical programs. If official history becomes nothing more than sophisticated regimental history or a superficial exploration into the thoughts of the "great captains," it will lose whatever real utility it has developed.

CIVILIAN-UTILITARIAN MILITARY HISTORY

An alternative focus to military-utilitarian military history developed slowly in American universities and probably dates from the 1930s with the development of group studies of warfare and military affairs at the University of Chicago and Princeton University. The intellectual touchstone of these American academics—those who were historians—was probably the German scholar Hans Delbrück, whose own exposure to the military history of the Prussian army made him progressively uneasy about the intellectual sterility and narrowness of the military's military history. In one sense, Delbrück simply wrote operational history better through assiduous research and careful analysis; in another sense, he rejected the primacy of didactic operational history and argued for the study of state policy and strategy and for the relationship between civilian and military institutions. Like other fields in American history, legitimacy for the inquiry into warfare came from the "scientific school" of Continental historical scholarship. While the scholars of the 1930s laid the intellectual foundations for academic military history, World War II gave an entire generation of historians the experience of war and taught them that its study could be a legitimate interest for an academic historian.[15]

Just as military history within the armed forces developed a dualistic—and sometimes contradictory—character, military history in American universities and colleges grew within an environment that reflected several warring intellectual assumptions about the field. One crosscurrent, as perceived by aspiring military historians, was that their colleagues in the professoriate had a liberal bias against warfare and military organizations, and even against the study of war and military organizations. No doubt this charge of bias was, and is, true, but it varies from campus to campus and time to time. The question of active philosophical and political opposition to the study of military history cannot in itself explain the slow growth of this specialization in academic history departments. It stems primarily from the character of historical curricula in postwar universities, which divided advanced history courses into distinct geopolitical and periodized categories. Military history began to flourish with the rise of specialized topical courses—a reflection of expanded specialties, the demands of graduate and undergraduate student populations, enlarged faculties, and a cultural environment that requested that historical knowledge be arranged on lines of subject matter, not periods. This movement peaked by the 1970s and fundamentally reshaped the way in which courses entered the curriculum.

In military history, one other factor influenced the creation of courses, and sharpened the intellectual debate over the appropriate focus of military history in civilian universities. That influence was the effort by the army and navy to have its ROTC cadets and midshipmen receive their coursework in military history from academic historians, not officer-instructors. As ROTC programs flourished in the 1950s and 1960s because of the demand for junior officers in the Cold War armed forces, the army and navy perceived an opportunity to add more intellectual content (and legitimacy) to their precommissioning programs by requesting that academic departments offer undergraduate military history courses which, of course, would be open to all undergraduates. The ROTC proposals predated the collapse of history enrollments in the 1970s. The navy's plan even predated campus upheavals of the Vietnam War period, which sharpened army sensitivity to the future existence of its own ROTC program. The fusion of ROTC students and the modest civilian student interest in military history, accelerated by the Vietnam War, created an intellectual challenge to academic historians.[16]

The same questions of definition that arose in the armed forces historical community affected the development of military history on campuses. The ROTC directors wanted military history courses to stress learning tactics and operations by historical example, and they wanted courses to portray service history in peace and war in the regimental history tradition. Civilian historians, even veterans and reserve officers, found such proposals intellectually uninteresting, irrelevant, or beyond their competence. Such military history simply changed the teachers, not the subject. Instead, military historians in university teaching positions—which may have reached as many as 400 by the 1970s—looked for an intellectual foundation for their research and teaching that did not depend on the military-utilitarian tradition.

Academic historians drawn to military history for whatever reasons found that they, like their compatriots in other emerging topical fields such as women's history or the history of technology, had to establish a new intellectual basis for their work without any meaningful historiographical tradition, except the one established by the military-utilitarian writers. The void was never complete, however, for specialists in American history, where scholarship in two of the nation's most important wars, the American Revolution and the Civil War, had not faltered since the nineteenth century.[17] What historians wanted, but which could not be satisfied by the rich historiography of two specific wars, was some general interpretation of the role of military affairs in American history that was not driven by military-utilitarian history. They needed no warmed-over version of Upton, Mahan, Palmer, Treror Dupuy, or E. B. Potter, but rather a type of military history that put the *history* before the *military*. Two significant books at least provided a point of debate: Walter Millis, *Arms and Men* (1956) and Russell F. Weigley, *The American Way of War* (1973), which were complemented by a significant product of the official history community of the army, *American Military History* (1969) edited by Maurice Matloff. Two important articles stressed the meaning of its military past to American political and intellectual culture: John Shy, "The American Military Experience: History and Learning" (1971) and David M. Kennedy, "War and the American Character" (1975).[18] As important as these general interpretations were, academic military historians also began to show, at the monographic level, a major effort to write scholarly history of American military affairs from within the context of the more general problems of the nation's history, including sectionalism, westward expansion, the growth of maritime-commercial activity and the creation and liquidation of an overseas empire, the creation of national industrial and transportation systems, the history of immigration, race relations, the reforms of the Progressive period, and, of course, the history of American foreign policy. In other words, American historians had plenty of historiographical tradition for their military history if they looked in the right places.[19]

One source of intellectual inspiration to which some military historians turned proved of limited value: the social sciences. Part of the attraction was the search for contemporary "relevance" in an era in which nuclear weapons had supposedly rendered the lessons of military history obsolete; another was the "quaint lust" of academic intellectuals for influence on policy-making. Social science specialists in international relations and American government claimed the intellectual high ground as academic consultants to the national government, and historians tried to follow their point patrols to the White House, the Pentagon, and Capitol Hill, even though they were largely elbowed aside in the 1950s and rediscovered only in the 1980s. Part of the attraction of social science for historians involved the application of general theories and quantitative methods to historical problems; many historians did not seem to realize that the theories and the methods did not necessarily change history into policy-prescriptive analysis or even approach scientific replication. A third attraction of social science was its orientation toward liberal-progressive reform politics and noninterventionist foreign policy, along with an emphasis on comparative, transnational analysis. A fourth advantage, which proved more lasting, was that social scientists recategorized military affairs into topical subjects, all of which, of course, had historical dimensions. One of the most influential reviews of military literature divided military affairs into five basic areas: the profession of arms, military organizations, military systems, civil-military relations, and war and warfare.[20] All these factors eventually proved closer to prostitution than inspiration, but they did provide some mental ferment in the academic military history community that sharpened its own definition of its interests in contrast with military-utilitarian military history and policy-prescriptive behavioralism. It reinforced the conviction that historical study could be useful to civilian policy-makers in the national security establishment, but that such useful history—which was largely cautionary and prudential—had to be history qua history, and not the artful and dishonest manipulation of selected historical data with social science assumptions and preexisting biases.[21]

The search for historiographical roots and flirtation with the "policy sciences" did, however, combine to create "the new military history," a label that came into general usage in the 1960s. In a negative sense, "the new military history" meant history that was not oriented to the study of the conduct of war, especially at the operational and tactical levels. "New" military historians did not write "drum and trumpet" history sour with the stench of gunsmoke and redolent with the imagined thrills of victory and the agonies of defeat. Rather, they wrote social history of the military (often critical), institutional and organizational history (but not in the regimental vein), and the intellectual history of theorists of warfare (but not "great captains"). As one of the "new military historians" later observed, he and his academic brethren almost wrote combat out of military history and often overlooked the fact that military institutions usually had some passing interest in their basic function, the preparation for and the conduct of warfare. Some "new military historians" did indeed use social science methodology, and others used social science concepts like professionalization to frame historical questions. Some even dabbled in psychohistory or attempted to advance general theoretical propositions about the dynamics of organizational change through historical analysis.

The accomplishments of three generations of military historians are real enough in several ways: Academic military history attained a legitimacy in the professional academic community that it did not have in the 1950s, traditional historical research and its philosophical assumptions enjoyed greater repute in the national security studies community than they had in the age of behavioralism, and the armed forces historical community became more open to the research of university-based military historians, even if the vote is still out among the military's senior officers. Academic military history has not, however, swept the field of all its critics, and its influence on the writing of comprehensive American history (if textbooks are any example) has been modest. Nevertheless, the "new military history" produced a place for military history in American universities that is independent of ROTC patronage and not wed to any special need to serve the interests of the armed forces. Even if some academic historians fret about the specialty's weak historiographical roots and the unholy alliance with the policy sciences, academic military history does have a character of its own.[22]

BRIDGING THE GAP BETWEEN CLIO AND MARS

At the risk of conjuring up a great Hegelian synthesis in order to celebrate the coming of a "*new* new military history," the historians of the armed forces and the universities have bridged the gap between military-utilitarian and civilian-utilitarian military history, drawing intellectual stimulus from both genres and blurring the distinctions between them. Even military history designed for officer education and organizational socialization shows the considerable influence of the fusionist trend in military history. From the older military history tradition comes a returned emphasis on the special problems of waging war and fighting battles as well as the role of professional military education (including historical study) in the preparation of officers for operational and high leadership responsibilities. The precise way in which operations and internal military developments are defined and studied, however, draws much inspiration from academic military history.

There are ample examples of the fusionist movement. Three recent examinations of the relationship between aviation history and air force history, for example (all completed by past or present civilian historians of the Office of Air Force History), reported that air force history needed to pay far more attention to aviation history, which would free it from its self-imposed insularity. In fact, at least two publications from the Office of Air Force History show how far that office has advanced from regimental organizational history, and a third recent book, a history of the air national guard, won a national prize for the best book written by a public historian. The air force also established a new curriculum at the Air University schools to study air warfare through the historical case study method and to enlarge its faculty with civilian historians. In addition, the service initiated a grass-roots historical study program, "Project Warrior," to teach institutional history as part of the general history of warfare.[23]

In the navy, the new "Contributions to Naval History" series will publish scholarly monographs that deal with the historical background of issues of contemporary policy interest; the first two monographs, which dealt with postwar navy thinking on containment and naval policy and the development of the Office of the Chief of Naval Operations, were both written by civilian professional historians, as will be the next two monographs, which will deal with submarine development and the political struggle over naval aviation.[24] The most publicized fusionist history event in the navy, of course, was the creation in 1972 of the "Strategy and Policy" core course at the Naval War College, a history-based introduction to strategic thought, albeit with a coating of salt-spray. The same trend influenced instruction in the navy's ROTC program, in which midshipmen received a far more challenging course in naval history than a history of the navy in the regimental tradition.[25] The other naval service, the U.S. Marine Corps, redefined its historical program so that its multivolume history of the Vietnam War would include studies of significant nonoperational issues like the administration of the Uniform Code of Military Justice in a pacification campaign. In addition, the Marine Corps Training and Education Center introduced a "battle studies" program that forced the students to investigate the implications of organizational policies on operational performance.[26]

At every level of activity in military history in the army, the fusionist trend influences how the subject is taught and learned. The Center of Military History, for example, defined its multi-volume series on the Vietnam War to accommodate two separate projects, a series of Vietnam monographs written by senior officer-participants and another designed to follow the path of the scholarly World War II official history. In addition, the army created the Combat Studies Institute in 1979 to produce publishable studies not just on operations but also on the question of how doctrine is written and translated into training. In addition to the respected Leavenworth Papers series, the Combat Studies Institute organized a major assessment of land combat doctrine and training for commercial distribution: Charles E. Heller and William A. Stofft, *America's First Battles, 1775–1965* (1986), which studied the dynamics of army adaptation to operational experience. The army school system remains a key locus of historical study. Although the historians at the Military Academy remain officers, all the other advanced, intermediate, and senior-level schools have mixed civilian-military history faculties with doctoral degrees and strong ties to the academic community. The Combat Studies Institute and the Army War College, prodded by the collocated Army Military History Institute, have been especially successful in organizing anthologies, conferences, and visiting lectureships that bring army officers and academic military historians together on a continuing basis.[27]

Champions of the traditional military-utilitarian military history may believe that the "civilianization" of the armed forces historical divisions and officer education system is just another unreciprocated disaster, but, in fact, the older definitions of military history have affected the work of academic historians, who now show more interest in doing research on subjects of special interest to professional officers and civilian policy-makers. Academic military historians have produced a corpus of biographical literature on American senior officers— especially the leaders of World War II—that is impressive in its quality, its quantity, and its nonadulatory (but sympathetic) tone. These "great captains" have flaws and blind spots, and they represent special systems of selection and assignment that must be understood in order to appreciate the way in which these admirals and generals functioned. These officers are not blessed individuals as much as products of the military profession and their times.[28] In addition, academic military historians have assumed the task of writing the institutional history of the armed forces—and their work is accepted as authoritative, even though their books do not pay special homage to "battles and leaders" or trumpet the special contributions of the services to national greatness.[29]

In one sense, academic military historians have not shifted from the traditional focus on the three "Cs"—the causes, conduct, and consequences of warfare. They recognize that they have no "camping rights" to any of the "Cs," although their expertise in the history of the conduct of warfare is paramount. In addition, the study of the American Revolution and the Civil War continues with a vitality all its own, only marginally influenced by the "new military history." However, even the study of these two wars shows the new intellectual cement contributed by academic military historians and armed forces historians: the linkage between effectiveness in the campaign and battlefield and the cultural environment that produces military organizations and conditions their behavior.[30]

The institutional-cultural approach to military history—another way to describe the fusionist trend—does not invalidate the other types of military history, which have also flourished. It does, however, provide a common intellectual foundation that can be shared by the armed forces historians and the academic historians, since both groups have the common mission of public education, not just for personal amusement and occupational goals but for civic leadership as well. The mission of education for public service is a goal worthy of government and higher education, and in the study of national security policy, military historians have an important role to play.

NOTES

1. Wilbur F. Hinman (Late Lt. Col., 65th Ohio Volunteer Infantry), *Corporal Si Klegg and His "Pard,"* 11th ed. (Cleveland, OH: N. G. Hamilton Publishing, 1898), p. 553.

2. Although I know of no other description of the five types of military history, the categories are implicit in the following essential discussions of the field: Charles Francis Adams, "A Plea for Military History," a paper read at the 1899 meeting of the American Historical Association and printed in the author's *Lee at Appomattox and Other Papers* (Boston: Houghton Mifflin, 1903), pp. 337–75; Charles Oman, "A Plea for Military History," ch. 9 in his *On the Writing of History* (London: Dutton, 1939), pp. 159–75; and Col. Thomas E. Griess, "A Perspective on Military History," in Col. John E. Jessup, Jr., and Robert W. Coakley, eds., *A Guide to the Study and Use of Military History* (Washington, DC: Center of Military History, U.S. Army, 1979), pp. 25–40. For my own earlier evaluations of scholarship in American military history, see Allan R. Millett, "American Military History: Over the Top," in Herbert J. Bass, ed., *The State of American History* (Chicago: Quadrangle Books, 1970), pp. 157–82, "American Military History: Struggling through the Wire," ACTA of the International Commission on Mil-

itary History (Manhattan, KS: University Press of Kansas, 1977), pp. 528–37; and "The Study of American Military History in the United States," *Military Affairs* 41 (April 1977): 58–61.

See also the brief statements by Michael Howard, Brian Bond, David Chandler, J.C.A. Stagg, John Childs, John Gooch, Geoffrey Best, and John Terraine in "What Is Military History?" *History Today* 34 (December 1984): 5–13.

3. For discussion of the military's military history and its special characteristics, see especially Michael Howard, "The Use and Abuse of Military History," [1961 lecture to the Royal United Services Institute (RUSI)], reprinted in *Parameters* 11 (March 1981): 9–14; Stefan T. Possony and Dale O. Smith, "The Utility of Military History," *Military Affairs* 22 (Winter 1958–59): 216–18; Maury Feld, "The Writing of Military History," *Military Affairs* 22 (Spring 1958): 38–39; Benjamin Franklin Cooling III, "Military History for the Military Professional," *Parameters* 1 (Winter 1972): 28–35; Stanley Sandler, "History and the Military," *Military Review* 52 (January 1972): 26–31; John Gooch, "Clio and Mars: The Use and Abuse of Military History," *Journal of Strategic Studies* 3 (December 1980): 21–36; Gen. John A. Wickham, Jr., "The Professional Soldier and History," *Army Historian* 4 (Summer 1984): 1–2; Department of the Army, *The Writing of American Military History: A Guide*, Pamphlet no. 20–200, (Washington, DC: Department of the Army, 1951).

4. Lt. Col. John F. Votaw, "An Approach to the Study of Military History," in Jessup and Coakley, *Guide to the Study and Use of Military History*, pp. 41–56; Allan R. Millett, "Military History and the Professional Officer," *Marine Corps Gazette* 51 (April 1967): 51; Brooks E. Kleber, "History and Military Education: The U.S. Army," *Military Affairs* 42 (October 1978): 136–41; K. A. Loughrey, "A Letter to My Brigadier—An Essay on Formal Training in Military History as a Necessary Part of Officer Development," *Defense Force Journal* 40 (May–June 1983): 56–60. The current relationship between officer education and military history is described and justified in detail in U.S. House of Representatives, Committee on Armed Services, Hearings before the Panel on Military Education, "Professional Military Education," 100th Congress, 1st and 2d sess., 1987–1988 (House Armed Services Committee [HASC] 100–125). See also Richard A. Preston, "Perspectives in History of Military Education and Professionalism," in Lt. Col. Harry Borowski, USAF, ed., *The Harmon Memorial Lectures in Military History, 1959–1987* (Washington, DC: Office of Air Force History), pp. 269–301.

5. Ronald H. Spector, "Military History and the Academic World," in Jessup and Coakley, *Guide to the Study and Use of Military History*, pp. 431–37; Louis Morton, "The Historian and the Study of War," *Mississippi Valley Historical Review* 48 (March 1962): 599–613; Peter Paret, "The History of War," *Daedalus* 100 (Spring 1971): 376–96; Peter Karsten, "Demilitarizing Military History: Servants of Power or Agents of Understanding?" *Military Affairs* 36 (October 1972): 88–92; Arthur A. Ekirch, Jr., "Military History: A Civilian Caveat," *Military Affairs* 21 (Summer 1957): 49–54; Alfred Vagts, *A History of Militarism* (New York: Norton, 1937), pp. 21–36.

6. Paul J. Scheips, "Military History and Peace Research," *Military Affairs* 36 (October 1972): 92–96; Walter Millis, *Military History*, Service Center for Teachers of History Publication no. 39, (Washington, DC: American Historical Association, 1961).

7. Kent Roberts Greenfield, *The Historian and the Army* (New Brunswick, NJ: Rutgers University Press, and Port Washington, NY: Kennikat Press, 1954); M. C. Helfers, "The United States Army's History of World War II," *Military Affairs* 19 (Spring 1955): 32–36; Hugh M. Cole, "Writing Contemporary Military History," *Military History* 12

(Fall 1948): 162–67; Tyson Wilson, "The Case for Military History and Research," *Military Affairs* 21 (Summer 1957): 54–60.

8. Col. John E. Jessup and Robert W. Coakley, "A Century of Army Historical Works," in Jessup and Coakley, *Guide to the Study and Use of Military History*, pp. 285–302; Romana Danysh, "Military History and the Department of Defense," in Jessup and Coakley, *Guide to the Study and Use of Military History*, pp. 401–13. See also Carol Reardon, *Soldiers and Scholars: The U.S. Army and the Uses of Military History, 1865–1920* (Lawrence, KS: University Press of Kansas, 1990); for trends in naval history, see James M. Merrill, "Successors of Mahan: A Survey of Writings on American Naval History, 1914–1960," *Mississippi Valley Historical Review* 50 (June 1963): 79–99.

9. Col. Thomas E. Griess, "Dennis Hart Mahan: West Point Professor and Advocate of Military Professionalism, 1830–1871" (Ph.D. dissertation, Duke University, 1968); Jay Luvaas, "The Great Military Historians and Philosophers," in Jessup and Coakley, *Guide to the Study and Use of Military History*, pp. 59–88; Robert Seager II, *Alfred Thayer Mahan* (Annapolis, MD: Naval Institute Press, 1977), pp. 160–90; Henry Barnard, *Military Schools and Courses of Instruction in the Science and Art of War* (Westport, CT: Greenwood Press, 1969; repr. 1972), pp. 715–935; John I. Alger, *The Quest for Victory: The History of the Principles of War* (Westport, CT: Greenwood Press, 1982).

10. Historical Section, War Department General Staff, "The American Military Factor in the War," November 1918, Major General George Van Horn Moseley Papers, Manuscript Division, Library of Congress.

11. R. M. Johnston to the Adjutant General, USA, 24 April 1914, and Gen. L. Wood to Sec War L. Garrison, 24 April 1914, General Leonard Wood Papers, Manuscript Division, Library of Congress, Russell F. Weigley, *Towards an American Army* (New York: Columbia University Press, 1962), pp. 177–222. See also James L. Abrahamson, *America Arms for a New Century* (New York: Free Press, 1981).

12. On the nineteenth-century officer corps and its educational background, see Edward M. Coffman, *The Old Army: A Portrait of the American Army in Peacetime, 1784–1898* (New York: Oxford University Press, 1986), pp. 42–103, 215–86; Peter Karsten, *The Naval Aristocracy* (New York: Free Press, 1972); James L. Morrison, Jr., *"The Best School in the World": West Point, the Pre-Civil War Years, 1833–1866* (Kent, OH: Kent State University Press, 1986); Ronald H. Spector, *Professors of War: The Naval War College and the Development of the Naval Profession* (Newport, RI: Naval War College Press, 1977); Timothy K. Nenninger, *Leavenworth Schools and the Old Army; Education, Professionalism, and the Officer Corps of the United States Army, 1881–1918* (Westport, CT: Greenwood Press, 1978). For the extension of nineteenth-century military education, see Boyd L. Dastrup, *The U.S. Army Command and General Staff College: A Centennial History* (Ft. Leavenworth, KS: U.S. Army Command and General Staff College, 1981); Col. Harry P. Ball, USA (Ret.) *A Responsible Command: A History of the U.S. Army War College* (Carlisle, PA: Alumni Association of U.S. Army War College, 1983); Michael Vlahos, *The Blue Sword: The Naval War College and the American Mission, 1919–1941* (Newport, RI: Naval War College Press, 1980); Lt. Col. Donald F. Bittner, USMCR, *Curriculum Evolution: Marine Corps Command and Staff College, 1920–1988* (Washington, DC: History and Museums Division, Headquarters Marine Corps [HQMC], 1988); Robert T. Finney, *History of the Air Corps Tactical School, 1920–1940*, USAF Historical Studies no. 100 (Montgomery, AL: Air University, 1951).

On the official history movement, see Rear Adm. Ernest M. Eller, USN (Ret.), "The Navy's Historians," *United States Naval Institute Proceedings* 89 (April 1963): 96–109;

Martin Blumenson, "Can Official History Be Honest History?" *Military Affairs* 25 (Winter 1963): 153–61; Stetson Conn, "The Pursuit of Military History," *Military Affairs* 30 (Spring 1966): 1–8; William James Morgan and Joyce L. Leonhart, *A History of The Naval Historical Center and the Dudley Knox Center for Naval History* (Washington, DC: Naval Historical Foundation, 1983); Theodore Ropp, "A Generation of the Center of Military History," CMH seminar, 11 May 1977; Robert W. Coakley, "The United States Army in World War II," in Robin Higham, ed., *A Guide to the Sources of United States Military History* (Hamden, CT: Archon Books, 1975), pp. 378–403; Robert Frank Futrell, "The U.S. Army Air Corps and the United States Air Force, 1909–1973," in Higham, *United States Military History*, pp. 404–29; Dean C. Allard, "The Navy, 1941–1973," in Higham, *United States Military History*, pp. 514–46.

13. For statements of these views by distinguished participants, see Louis Morton, "Historia Mentem Armet: Lessons of the Past," *World Politics* 22 (January 1960): 261–75; and Maurice Matloff, "The Present State and Future Directions of Military History," *Army Historian* 2 (Winter 1984): 7–11. The contemporary service historical offices are described in U.S. Government Accounting Office Report GAO/NSIAD–86–139FS, *Historians: Information on Historian Programs in the Department of Defense*, July 1986.

14. See, for example, U.S. Army Center of Military History, *U.S. Army Historical Directory 1990* (Washington, DC: Center of Military History, 1990).

15. Gordon A. Craig, "Delbrück: The Military Historian," in Edward Mead Earle, ed., *Makers of Modern Strategy* (Princeton, NJ: Princeton University Press, 1943), pp. 260–83; Felix Gilbert, "From Clausewitz to Delbrück and Hintze: Achievements and Failures of Military History," *Journal of Strategic Studies* 3 (December 1980): 11–20; Dexter Perkins and John L. Snell, with the Committee on Graduate Education of the American Historical Profession, *The Education of Historians in the United States* (New York: McGraw-Hill, 1962), pp. 74–77, 123; W. Stull Holt, "Historical Scholarship," in Merle Curti, ed., *American Scholarship in the Twentieth Century* (Cambridge, MA: Harvard University Press, 1953), pp. 83–110; Theodore Ropp, "War, From Colonies to Vietnam," in W. H. Cartwright and Richard L. Watson, Jr., *The Reinterpretation of American History and Culture* (Washington, DC: National Council for the Social Studies, 1973), pp. 207–26; John Higham, *History: Professional Scholarship in America*, rev. ed. (Baltimore, MD: Johns Hopkins University Press, 1989).

16. Richard C. Brown, *The Teaching of Military History in Colleges and Universities of the United States*, USAF Historical Studies no. 124 (Maxwell Air Force Base, AL: Air University, 1955); John K. Mahon, "Teaching and Research in Military History in the United States," *Historian* 27 (February 1965): 170–84; Department of the Army, Ad Hoc Committee on the Army Need for the Study of Military History, *Report and Recommendations*, 4 vols., (Manhattan, KS: *Military Affairs* and Kansas State University, 1971), vol. 1.

For a description of many of the new topical fields and their historiographical challenges, see Stanley I. Kutler and Stanley N. Katz, eds., *The Promise of American History: Progress and Prospects* (Baltimore, MD: Johns Hopkins University Press, 1982), a special issue (December 1982) of *Reviews in American History*.

17. Allan Nevins, James I. Robertson, Jr., and Bell I. Wiley, eds., *Civil War Books: A Critical Bibliography*, 2 vols. (Baton Rouge, LA: Louisiana State University Press, 1967); Don Higginbotham, "American Historians and the Military History of the American Revolution," *American Historical Review* 70 (1964): 18–34; Don Higginbotham, "The Early American Way of War: Reconnaissance and Appraisal," *William and Mary*

Quarterly 44 (April 1987): 230–73; E. Wayne Carp, "Early American Military History," *Virginia Magazine* 94 (July 1986): 259–84.

18. Walter Millis, *Arms and Men* (New York: Putnam's, 1956); Russell F. Weigley, *The American Way of War* (New York: Macmillan, 1973); Maurice Matloff gen. ed. *American Military History* (Washington, DC: U.S. Army Center of Military History, 1969); John Shy, "The American Military Experience: History and Learning," *Journal of Interdisciplinary History* 1 (Winter 1971): 205–28; David M. Kennedy, "War and the American Character" *Stanford Magazine* 3 (Spring-Summer 1975): 14–18, 70–72.

19. For a comprehensive bibliography, see Higham, *United States Military History*, with two supplements edited by Higham and Donald J. Mrozek and also published by Archon Books in 1981 and 1986. For scholarship in the form of doctoral dissertations, see Allan R. Millett and Benjamin Franklin Cooling III, *Dissertations in Military Affairs* (Manhattan, KS: Kansas State University Library, 1972), with annual supplements in the journal *Military Affairs*, now the *Journal of Military History*.

20. Kurt Lang, *Military Institutions and the Sociology of War* (Beverly Hills, CA: Sage Publications, 1972).

21. For the early optimism, see Harvey A. DeWeerd, "Military Studies and the Social Sciences," *Military Affairs* 9 (Fall 1945): 187–92; Theodore Ropp, "Military History and the Social Sciences," *Military Affairs* 30 (Spring 1966): 8–13; and Eugene Lyons and Louis Morton, *Schools for Strategy: Education and Research in National Security Affairs* (New York: Praeger, 1965). The diminished interest in historical research with the study of national security policy can be traced in the 1952–1965 annual reports of the Social Science Research Council, and I discuss the issue in *Academic Education in National Security Policy* (Columbus, OH: Mershon Center, Ohio State University, 1977). The passing of the advisory "honeymoon" can be sampled in Committee on Foreign Affairs, U.S. House of Representatives, *Hearings* and *Reports*: "Behavioral Sciences and the National Security," 89th Congress, 1st sess., 1965; and Colin S. Gray, *Strategic Studies: A Critical Assessment* (Westport, CT: Greenwood Press, 1982). For guidance on the useful, if limited, wisdom that historical analysis provides civilian policy-makers, see Richard E. Neustadt and Ernest R. May, *Thinking in Time: The Uses of History for Decision Makers* (New York: Free Press, 1986).

22. Martin K. Gordon, "American Military Studies," *American Studies International* 15 (Fall 1976): 3–16; Reginald C. Stuart, "War, Society, and the 'New' Military History of the United States," *Canadian Review of American Studies* 7, no. 1 (Spring 1977): 1–10; Peter Karsten, "The 'New' American Military History: A Map of the Territory, Explored and Unexplored," *American Quarterly* 36 (Summer 1984): 389–418; Edward M. Coffman, "The New American Military History," *Military Affairs* 94 (January 1984): 1–5. For an example of the genre, see especially Richard H. Kohn, "The Social History of the American Soldier: A Review and Prospectus for Research," *American Historical Review* 86 (June 1981): 553–67. The critique of the genre is Dennis E. Showalter, "A Modest Plea for Drums and Trumpets," *Military Affairs* 39 (April 1975): 71–74. For a critique of the residual historiographical challenges, see Walter E. Kaegi, Jr., "The Crisis in Military Historiography," *Armed Forces and Society* 7 (Winter 1981): 299–316. For a more optimistic assessment of academic military history, see Paul Kennedy, "The Fall and Rise of Military History," *Yale Journal of World Affairs* 1 (Fall 1989): 12–19.

23. Stanley L. Falk, "Gaps in the Published History of the Air Force: Challenge for Historians," *Historian* 44 (August 1982): 453–465; Richard P. Hallion, *The Literature of Aeronautics, Astronautics, and Air Power* (Washington, DC: Office of Air Force

History, 1984); Michael Gorn and Charles J. Gross, "Published Air Force History: Still on the Runway," *Aerospace Historian* 31 (Spring/March 1984): 30–37. The three books are Maurer Maurer, *Aviation in the U.S. Army, 1919–1939* (Washington, DC: Office of Air Force History, 1987); Jacob Neufeld, *Ballistic Missiles in the United States Air Force, 1945–1960* (Washington, DC: Office of Air Force History, 1990); and Charles J. Gross, *Prelude to the Total Force: The Air National Guard, 1943–1969* (Washington, DC: Office of Air Force History, 1985). On Program for Military Excellence (PME), see Air Command and Staff College and Air War College, "A Curriculum Proposal, 1987," author's possession.

24. Michael A. Palmer, *Origins of the Maritime Strategy: American Naval Strategy in the First Postwar Decade* (Washington, DC: Naval Historical Center, 1988); Thomas C. Hone, *Power and Change: The Administrative History of the Office of the Chief of Naval Operations, 1945–1986* (Washington, DC: Naval Historical Center, 1989).

25. "Syllabus, Strategy and Policy Course, 1985–1986," Naval War College, Newport, RI; Naval War College, *Naval War College Self Study 1989* (Newport, RI: Naval War College, 1989); John B. Hattendorf, B. Mitchell Simpson III, and John R. Wadleigh, *Sailors and Scholars: The Centennial History of the U.S. Naval War College* (Newport, RI: Naval War College Press, 1984); Chief of Naval Education and Training, ROTC, "Sea Power and Maritime Affairs, Naval Science 202," 1984, provided by the project director, Kenneth J. Hagan, U.S. Naval Academy.

26. Gen. A. M. Gray, Jr., Commandant of the Marine Corps, to Lt. Gen. George C. Axtell, USMC (Ret.) president of the Marine Corps Historical Foundation, 8 December 1987, drafted by the author and copy in his possession; Annual Reports of the Director, History and Museums Division, to the commandant of the Marine Corps, FY 1986–FY 1990 (M & MD Bulletin 5520), author's possession; Col. A. R. Millett, USMCR, to the Assistant Commandant and Chief of Staff, subject: Status of Military History in the U.S. Marine Corps, 2 March 1989, author's possession. The book cited is Lt. Col. Gary D. Solis, USMC, *Marines and Military Law in Vietnam: Trial by Fire* (Washington, DC: History and Museums Division, HQMC, 1989). From 1984 to 1988 the author served as deputy director (mobilization-designate) of the Marine Corps History and Museums Division and during 1973–1978 and 1984–1988 was as an adjunct faculty member, Marine Corps Command and Staff College.

27. David F. Trask, "The 'New Military History' and Army Historians," *Army Historian* 5 (Fall 1984): 7–10; Ronald H. Spector, "Getting Down to the Nitty-Gritty: Official History and the American Experience in Vietnam," *Military Affairs* 38 (February 1974): 11–12; J. Rod Paschall, "The Army Historian and Combat Developments," *Army Historian* 5 (Fall 1984): 5–6; Maurice Matloff, "Government and Public History: The Army," *Public Historian* 2 (Spring 1980): 43–51; Roger H. Nye, "The Army Historians: Who Are They?" *Army Historian* 1 (Fall 1983): 6–8; U.S. Army Center of Military History, *Historical Analysis Agencies Directory* (Washington, DC: Center of Military History, 1985). For examples of the Combat Studies Institute's work, see Charles E. Heller and William A. Stofft, *America's First Battles, 1776–1965* (Lawrence, KS: University Press of Kansas, 1986); and Maj. Paul H. Hebert, USA, *Deciding What Has to Be Done: General William E. DePuy and the 1976 Edition of FM 100–5. Operations* (Ft. Leavenworth, KS: Combat Studies Institute, 1988).

28. Forest C. Pogue, *George C. Marshall*, 4 vols. (New York: Viking Press 1963–87); D. Clayton James, *The Years of MacArthur*, 3 vols. (Boston: Houghton Mifflin, 1970–85); Allan R. Millett, *The General: Robert L. Bullard and Officership in the United*

States Army, 1881–1925 (Westport, CT: Greenwood Press, 1975); Stephen E. Ambrose, *Eisenhower: Soldier, General of the Army, President-Elect, 1890–1952* (New York: Simon and Schuster, 1983); E. B. Potter, *Nimitz* (Annapolis, MD: Naval Institute Press, 1976); Thomas B. Buell, *Master of Seapower: A Biography of Fleet Admiral Ernest J. King* (Boston, MA: Little, Brown, 1980); Barbara Tuchman, *Stilwell and the American Experience in China, 1911–1945* (New York: Macmillan, 1970); Martin Blumenson, *Patton* (New York: William Morrow, 1985); Donald Smythe, *Guerrilla Warrior: The Early Life of John J. Pershing* (New York: Charles Scribner's Sons, 1973); Donald Smythe, *Pershing: General of the Armies* (Bloomington, IN: Indiana University Press, 1986); Elting E. Morison, *Admiral Sims and the Modern American Navy* (Boston, MA: Houghton Mifflin, 1942); Gerald E. Wheeler, *Admiral William Veazie Pratt, U.S. Navy* (Washington, DC: Naval History Division, 1974); Paolo E. Coletta, *Admiral Bradley A. Fiske and the American Navy* (Lawrence, KS: Regents Press of Kansas, 1979); John F. Shiner, *Foulois and the U.S. Army Air Corps, 1931–1935* (Washington, DC: Office of Air Force History, 1983); Phillip S. Melinger, *Hogt S. Vandenberg* (Bloomington, IN: Indiana University Press, 1989); Hans Schmidt, *Maverick Marine: General Smedley D. Butler and the Contradictions of American Military History* (Lexington, KY: University Press of Kentucky, 1987); Norman V. Cooper, *A Fighting General: The Biography of Gen. Holland M. "Howlin' Mad" Smith* (Quantico, VA: Marine Corps Association, 1987).

29. Russell F. Weigley, *History of the United States Army* (New York: Macmillan, 1967); Allan R. Millett, *Semper Fidelis: The History of the United States Marine Corps* (New York: Macmillan, 1980); Kenneth J. Hagan, *In Peace and War: Interpretations of American Naval History, 1775–1978* (Westport, CT: Greenwood Press, 1978); Kenneth J. Hagan and William R. Roberts, eds., *Against All Enemies: Interpretations of American Military History from Colonial Times to the Present* (Westport, CT: Greenwood Press, 1986).

30. See, for example, Charles Royster, *A Revolutionary People at War: The Continental Army and American Character, 1775–1783* (Chapel Hill, NC: University of North Carolina Press, 1979); Robert Middlekauff, *The Glorious Cause: The American Revolution, 1763–1789* (New York: Oxford University Press, 1982); E. Wayne Carp, *To Starve the Army at Pleasure: Continental Army Administration and American Political Culture, 1775–1783* (Chapel Hill, NC: University of North Carolina Press, 1984); James M. McPherson, *Battle Cry of Freedom: The Civil War Era* (New York: Oxford University Press, 1988); Richard M. McMurry, *Two Great Rebel Armies* (Chapel Hill, NC: University of North Carolina Press, 1989); Edward Hagerman, *The American Civil War and the Origins of Modern Warfare* (Bloomington, IN: Indiana University Press, 1988); Gerald Linderman, *Embattled Courage: The Experience of Combat in the American Civil War* (New York: Free Press, 1987); Herman Hattaway and Archer Jones, *How the North Won* (Urbana, IL: University of Illinois Press, 1983); Richard E. Beringer, Herman Hattaway, Archer Jones, and William N. Still, Jr., *Why the South Lost the Civil War* (Athens, GA: University of Georgia Press, 1986).

2

The Development of British Military Historical Writing and Thought from the Eighteenth Century to the Present

TIM TRAVERS

THE EIGHTEENTH-CENTURY TRADITION

Sir Michael Howard argued that military history only starts when a country is at peace; thus, classical history was not military history because war was so much a part of society. According to Howard, therefore, military history only emerged in Britain in the eighteenth century, when presumably clear-cut distinctions and contrasts between the conditions of war and peace also occurred. Howard seems to have a point, since it was in the eighteenth century that William Penn, Jean-Jacques Rousseau, and Immanuel Kant all drew up plans for achieving world peace, even if Kant, for example, still assumed that war was the natural state of humanity and felt that conflict could only be abolished through the specific establishment of peace.[1] On the other hand, the historian John Gooch claimed that military history with its penchant for providing norms and precepts as a guide for the training of soldiers and the conduct of operations, really emerged as a result of the development of two factors in the late 1700s. One was the growth of the idea that war was a technical profession, whose practitioners required specialized knowledge in order to conduct operations, while the other factor was the resurgence of the military aristocracy, participating in the reforms of the time, which placed much greater emphasis on intellectual capacity, as reflected in the creation of the new military academies of the later eighteenth century.[2]

Both Howard and Gooch made good points, but a recent discussion by Azar Gat, in his book *The Origins of Military Thought, From the Enlightenment to Clausewitz*, provides an even more convincing explanation. "The middle of the eighteenth century," wrote Gat, "marked a revolutionary growth in military productions." This was caused by the upsurge of the intellectual activity of the Enlightenment. In particular, wrote Gat, "the ideal of Newtonian science excited the military thinkers of the Enlightenment and gave rise to an ever present yearning to infuse the study of war with the maximum mathematical precision and certainty possible.'' At the same time, the military thinkers of the mid-eighteenth century also inherited the Aristotelian neoclassical tradition, which allowed for artistic genius and creativity. Thus, while the military thinkers of the 1700s believed that ''the art of war was also susceptible to systematic formulation, based on rules and principles of universal validity which had been revealed in the campaigns of the great military leaders of history,'' they also allowed room for the creativity of the military leader.[3]

Indeed, it seems to be from the eighteenth century on that the two mainstream, original traditions of British military history emerged. One tradition was the *narrative campaign* style of military history, which basically described campaigns in a chronological way; these were usually derived from personal experience and often written in the form of a memoir. The other tradition may be called the *analytic-utilitarian* style, which tended to emphasize the lessons, principles, and rules of war as deduced from campaigns or applied to history in an a priori manner. These traditions were not necessarily mutually exclusive, but they did emerge from different sources, with the narrative tradition stemming from memoir literature and the analytic-utilitarian tradition arising from Enlightenment ideas.

Looking first at the narrative tradition, it would seem that although there were previous military histories such as the Earl of Clarendon's study of the English Civil War, they were largely political, and it apparently took the campaigns of the Duke of Marlborough to produce the first narrative campaign histories. Hence there were a number of narrative campaign accounts of Marlborough's wars, usually by participants, such as that of John Millner, a sergeant in the Royal Regiment of Foot of Ireland, who entitled his opus *A Compendious Journal of all the Marches, Famous Battles, Sieges, And other most note-worthy heroical and ever memorable actions of the Triumphant Armies, of the ever glorious Confederate High Allies, in their late and victorious war against the Powerful Armies of proud and lofty France, in and on the confines of Holland, Germany, Flanders, so far as our successful British troops extended in Conjunction therein, Digested into Twelve Campaigns, begun AD 1701, and ended in 1712.* There were also other eighteenth-century Marlborough campaign volumes by such individuals as John Deane, William Bishop, Brigadier Richard Kane, and Captain Robert Parker, who all followed the mixed narrative campaign/memoir tradition. Kane, for example, tended to focus on the doings of Marlborough and the Comte de Tallard and on details of battles, strategy, and tactics. He did, however, criticize Marlborough for changing plans at the battle of Ramillies (1706) and for causing unnecessary casualties by trying to force the village of Blenheim instead of waiting outside and firing into it. Parker, on the other hand, wrote a rather mundane account of Marlborough's wars, with each chapter describing one campaign. More lively were the other rank accounts, such as that of Matthew Bishop, who stressed the ideal of fame rather than personal gain. Bishop was predictably horrified by the actions of his fellow soldier John Jones, whose practice was to go around the battlefield searching for spent cannon balls and then sell them back to the same artillery that originally fired them![4]

It was from this mixed memoir/campaign history, therefore, that the narrative campaign tradition emerged. In addition, a particular characteristic of British (and perhaps other) military histories also now seemed to appear, namely, the tendency of wars to stimulate, in chronological sequence, first the campaign narrative accounts, and only second, the analytic-utilitarian military history versions. Hence, the narrative-memoirs of the Marlborough wars were followed later in the century by the works of the outstanding British military historian and analyst of the period, Henry Lloyd (c. 1718–1783). Lloyd may be said to be the originator of the analytic-utilitarian military history tradition, and in his work there can be found certain important ideas concerning military history that remained remarkably constant in regard to the British experience of writing military history until perhaps quite recently. First, according to Lloyd there are specific rules, principles, laws, and lessons that can be deduced from a study of past military campaigns. Second, there will nevertheless always be areas of military operations that rely on accident, creativity, or genius. (Here it is of interest to note that, as Azar Gat pointed out, while military historians and thinkers of the 1700s generally believed that the details, organization, and deployment of armies were mechanical and systematic matters, the conduct of operations required the genius of generals. In contrast, military historians and analysts of the nineteenth and twentieth centuries argued the reverse, feeling that strategy could be reduced to principles and laws, while tactics were open to constant change.)[5] Third—and of application to both traditions of British military history—the experience of Lloyd in the eighteenth century suggests very strongly that military thought, including military history, is not written in a vacuum, but rather derives from the prevailing intellectual trends of the time as much as from the particular campaigns being described or analyzed.

Lloyd was well educated in a Jesuit school and then entered the clergy. Undeterred by his original profession, Lloyd managed to serve in several armies, namely those of France, Austria, Prussia, the Duke of Brunswick, Count Schaumberg-Lippe, and Russia (in whose army he was promoted to the rank of major-general). Following this he was engaged as a secret agent by the British Government (he had already spied on Britain for the French, disguised conveniently enough as a clergyman). Therefore, Lloyd had had much military experience; he was also very well acquainted with the philosophers of the Enlightenment, particularly Baron de Montesquieu, and had also evidently read the memoirs of Marshal de Saxe.

Lloyd commenced his best-known work, *The History of the Late War in Germany: Between the King of Prussia, and the Empress of Germany and her Allies*, by declaring that there were two kinds of authors on war, didactical and historical. The former were of limited use, while the latter were clearly the best. However, by *historical*, Lloyd meant those who had actually experienced war and had then written about it, such as Xenophon, Polybius, Caesar, and Arrian. These historians' works "will ever be regarded by military men in particular, as a pure spring from whence the general principles of war may be deduced." However, Lloyd complained of the "moderns, who have undertaken to write the history of different wars, or of some renowned commanders, [but] being chiefly men of learning only, and utterly unacquainted with the nature of military operations, [they] have given us indeed agreeable, but useless productions." Nevertheless, not even the historians with military experience had yet properly explained the operations of war. To do this it was necessary to describe *all* aspects of a campaign, and Lloyd would undertake this task. Lloyd, therefore, set out to describe the principles of war, the plan of operations, a military description of the seat of war (i.e., the location of the relevant fortresses, camps, positions, etc.); the geography of where the events occurred, the actual conduct of operations, and the maneuvers attempted.[6]

In the fashion of the day, Lloyd stated that the art of war has "certain and fixed principles, which are by their nature invariable; the application of them only can be varied; but they are in themselves constant." Lloyd meant that the preparations for war were mathematical and mechanical, although the application of the principles of war required the genius of a commander. Thus, for example, referring to the mechanical preparation for war, Lloyd criticized Frederick the Great's system of clothing and training his Prussian troops, whereby they suffered from "short cloaths, little hats, tight breeches, high heeled shoes, and an infinite number of useless motions." On the other hand, Lloyd criticized some ignorant generals who did not know the principles of war and so could not apply them, one example being that they often gave battle because they did not know what else to do. Lloyd then went on to describe the campaigns of 1756 and 1757, drawing lessons from each; for example, stressing the great importance of speed in maneuver, or declaring that a wood or a mountain, if taken, must be occupied entirely or that sieges, like that of Prague, should only be undertaken as a last resort. Interestingly, Lloyd tended to quote contrasting accounts of a particular battle, such as that of the battle of Kollin (1757), where he first cited the Count of Vienna, then a Prussian account, and finally a French account, in order to try and reach an objective conclusion. Lloyd also provided brief biographies of prominent generals to give greater context. Finally, Lloyd was the first, to this author's knowledge, to draw sequential, accurate maps of a battle in order to give a fluid view.[7]

In his next volume, dealing with the campaigns of 1758 and 1759, Lloyd laid out more clearly his mechanistic position regarding armies:

War is a state of action. An army is the instrument with which every species of military action is performed; like all other machines it is composed of various parts, and its perfection will depend, first, on that of its several parts; and second, on the manner in which they are arranged; so that the whole may have the following properties, viz., strength, agility, and universality; if these are properly combined, the machine is perfect.

By this Lloyd meant that the way in which troops were armed and ranged produced strength, the speed of an army produced agility, and the formations of an army, by which it could meet any eventuality, produced universality. All this, of course, was the mechanical aspect of military history, and reflected such Enlightenment mechanistic thinkers as Julien Offroy de La Mettrie and Baron d'Holbach.[8]

Then, however, Lloyd went on to look at the application of this mechanism, and here he acknowledged that while any army is a machine, its parts have passions. The general must be the first to look at the passions of his soldiers. Drawing on utilitarian psychology, Lloyd believed that a general must understand that his soldiers behave according to the springs of pain and pleasure, which are themselves derived either from sensual or animal wants or from social causes. Once the animal wants are satisfied (fear, self-preservation, etc.), then the social causes of honor, shame, glory, ambition, and desire for superiority should be encouraged in order to spur soldiers and officers on to greater efforts in the field. Lloyd also followed de Saxe in urging armies to make use of music: "It were to be wished some able musician and philosopher would make experiments, by executing different pieces, to a promiscuous audience of men and women of different ages, soldiers in particular; the result would show what species of harmony was most adapted to raise courage in the troops."[9]

In other words, Lloyd recognized the psychology of war and saw that the mechanistic analogy also required an understanding of human behavior. Nevertheless, he obviously felt that if a general could correctly calculate and operate the springs of human action, then soldiers and officers would simply become automatons: a more perfect part of the machine. In other words, Lloyd's psychology was not part of the creative application of the principles of war, but was still part of the mechanistic preparations for war.

Lloyd's ideas, derived from his historical study of Frederick the Great's campaign and from the war in America, really related to the peculiarly eighteenth-century problems of time, space, and logistics. This required a new way of looking at war, and so, anticipating Napoleon, Lloyd continually emphasized the combination of speed, logistics, and the prior conceptualization of an entire campaign. He stated clearly that "time is everything in war", and, if allied with a correctly chosen line of operations, then all would be well. Thus, "the final success of a war must chiefly depend on the length and nature of the line of operation; if this is well chosen and directed to some capital object, success will in general attend it, but if ill chosen, victory itself will lead to nothing."[10] No doubt, too, the use of fluid maps by Lloyd enabled him to apply a visual sense of time and space to the history of warfare.

Finally, Lloyd borrowed from Montesquieu to point out that the outcome of a war depended not only on the mechanism of an army, its passions, and the application of the principles of war, but also on the resources and nature of a country. Lloyd argued that "it is impossible to calculate, with any degree of probability, the duration and event [outcome] of a war, unless we are acquainted

with the political system, principles of government, and resources of the con-
tending powers.'' Lloyd claimed that nations depended particularly on the size
of their population and the quantity of their industry to produce revenue, and
thus to field armies and fleets. He emphasized the importance of the five key
resources of a country—agriculture, manufactures, commerce, fisheries, and
population—and demanded the appointment of five professors to study and report
on each area! By this time (the early 1780s), Lloyd was also stressing a blue
water global strategy for Britain, through which seapower would mean "power,
glory, and political influence." Frightened by France's efforts to build a superior
fleet, Lloyd declared rather rashly that land forces were nothing for Britain,
while marines were everything.[11] In all this, it is clear that Lloyd's historical
researches had shown him that military success depended on far more than speed
and the calculation of the passions on the battlefield.

Although Lloyd was a rather typical eighteenth-century figure in his wide
interests, he was most unusual in British military thought of the day in applying
Enlightenment ideas to warfare. However, he set the stage for future British
military historians by using historical examples to discover rules and laws of
warfare (e.g., his line of operations concept), as well as in seeking historical
justification for previously established principles (e.g., his understanding of the
army as a machine). Lloyd's histories of Frederick the Great's campaigns were,
therefore, very closely linked to his analyses of strategy and the production of
his lessons and principles of warfare. In addition, Lloyd left space for creativity
and genius, and above all, his views closely reflected the prevailing intellectual
trends of the Enlightenment. In all these ways, Lloyd presaged much of what
was to come in nineteenth- and twentieth-century British military history. Indeed,
it seems that the eighteenth century largely set the rules for what was to come
in both the narrative and analytic-utilitarian traditions of military history.

THE NINETEENTH-CENTURY TRADITION

Following the Napoleonic wars, there appeared many British military memoirs
and campaign narratives, such as those of Captain John Henry Cooke, Sir Richard
Henegan, Lieutenant J. W. Dunbar Moodie, and John Green. Simultaneously
with these came the 6 volumes of W.F.P. Napier's *History of the War in the
Peninsula* which was begun in early 1828. Although Napier appreciated the
French-Swiss analyst of Napoleonic war, Antoine-Henri Jomini, and agreed with
the latter's principle that the mass of the army should be directed at the decisive
point, Napier did not produce principles of his own. Instead, by and large his
work continued the narrative tradition of the campaign-memoirs of the Marlborough wars and simply described chronologically the relevant battles and
sieges. Occasionally, Napier produced precepts, for example, on the financial,
logistical, and geographical limitations of war. Alternately, he would draw conclusions such as, "There is no operation in war so certain as a modern siege,
provided the rules of art are strictly followed, but, unlike the ancient sieges in

that particular, it is also different in this—that no operation is less open to irregular daring, because the course of the engineer can neither be hurried nor delayed without danger." All in all, however, Napier tended much more to the view that war was an art and not a science.[12]

Beyond this, Napier reflected the romanticism of the early nineteenth century in his vivid, sometimes melodramatic, prose and in the manner in which he emphasized moral forces, personal genius, and chance. In this respect Napier moved beyond Lloyd, who had certainly appreciated the creativity of generals in applying principles but did not place the same emphasis on individual personality, perhaps because he had not lived to see Napoleon's campaigns nor to feel the subjective appreciation of romanticism for the creative genius. Consequently, Napier provided much livelier portraits than did Lloyd. Similarly, Napier's descriptions of battle have a melodramatic quality that was absent from the memoir histories of the eighteenth century.

If Napier can be firmly placed in the narrative tradition, the next British military historian, who was significant because of his establishment of a genre rather than because of any erudition, really belongs to the analytic tradition. Sir Edward Creasy's volume *The Fifteen Decisive Battles of the World* was first published in 1851, and by 1877 it had already gone through twenty-eight editions. Creasy reflected the mid-Victorian positivist belief in the existence of laws of nature and behavior and of chains of cause and effect that influence all future generations. Thus if the actions of one individual were significant because they set the pattern for the future like ripples spreading from a stone thrown into a pond, then how much more significant would earth-shaking battles be for future history. Therefore, Creasy stated that decisive battles "have for us an abiding and actual interest, both while we investigate the chain of causes and effects, by which they helped to make us what we are; and also while we speculate on what we probably should have been, if any one of those battles had come to a different termination." Later, Creasy assured his readers that the effect of these collisions was not limited to a single age, "but may give an impulse which will sway the fortunes of successive generations of mankind." In accord with this belief, it was no wonder that the Victorians took life so seriously and indulged in so many books of morality and correct behavior. Certainly, Creasy believed that laws regulated life, including military history: "But when I speak of Causes and Effects, I speak of the obvious and important agency of one fact upon another. . . . I speak of those general laws only, by which we perceive the sequence of human affairs to be usually regulated." Creasy, therefore, introduced nothing of interest in his descriptions of battles, but his importance lay partly in his introduction of a new genre—the decisive battle—and partly in the value that he ascribed to those decisive battles and, by implication, to military history, for all humankind.[13] Once introduced by Creasy, this genre of the decisive conflict as the centerpiece of military history became firmly established, and it continued into the twentieth century with similar titles by Field Marshal Montgomery and J.F.C. Fuller, even including the March 1990 issue of *Journal of Strategic*

Studies, which was devoted to the "Decisive Campaigns of the Second World War."

Creasy's Victorian sense of the importance of studying facts in order to discover the chains of cause and effect that influence all life was carried over by another mid-Victorian military historian, Edward Hamley. In his celebrated book, *The Operations of War Explained and Illustrated*, Hamley specifically rejected rules and principles of war in favor of fact and reason alone. All that was necessary was to relate the history of various campaigns and then to deduce lessons from this material based on the facts. This was merely the favorite Victorian method of deriving the laws of nature from facts, as Charles Darwin had done, and then learning to adapt to those laws. The difference with Hamley was that he chose to apply the system to military history; hence, "the reader will be convinced that military science is not mere pedantry, but a reality of vast importance." The military leader need not be a genius, since "the conditions of success are attainable and capable of demonstration[;] . . . the preparation of study and thought is essential to skill in war." All that was required was "sound sense, clear insight and resolution."[14] This was the typical Victorian ideal, enshrined similarly in Samuel Smiles's best-seller *Self-Help* (1859), that since facts were open to all, any individual could, by hard work and study, discover the facts of life for him- or herself and succeed. Some of Hamley's facts and lessons were sensible, such as the caution that new firearms had increased the power of the defense, although this had not made the attack obsolete. However, other assertions were questionable even then, an example being the argument that it was better to break a front rather than attack a flank. However, Hamley also covered himself with the puzzling statement that strategy is "a flexible science."[15]

Hamley's work lay within the analytic-utilitarian tradition, and his book, with its representative campaigns each illustrating a deduced lesson or fixed principle of war, became the standard in service academies and Staff College examinations, almost until the end of the nineteenth century. Hamley was not an innovator; he simply put received and accepted wisdom into an agreeable form for the general reading public, as well as for the military officer struggling to pass exams, and found examples to illustrate what was already known. In fact, he simply carried over into military history the mid-Victorian belief in the existence of laws of nature and of society. Thus, he had strongly reinforced the eighteenth-century concept of the existence of fixed principles of warfare, although Hamley concentrated on strategic principles rather than tactics. Henceforward, this belief in the existence of fixed strategic principles was so firmly entrenched that it would not be dislodged, especially since it "proved" the validity of military science and enhanced the reputation of the officer corps in society.

WRITINGS AT THE TURN OF THE CENTURY

Not surprisingly, therefore, Hamley's great stress on lessons was continued by the avowedly utilitarian military historian C. E. Callwell. In his classic study of guerrilla warfare and the methods of defeating irregular groups, Callwell stated concisely that the great masters of the past, plus the experience of wars in America and Europe, "have established certain principles and precedents which form the groundwork of the system of regular warfare today. Certain rules of conduct exist which are universally accepted. Strategy and tactics alike are in great campaigns governed, in most respects, by a code from which it is perilous to depart." Callwell was sure that he could find similar principles in small wars as well, and he proceeded to do so: The chief principle was to overawe the enemy by bold initiative and resolute action. Only in the case of nocturnal counterattacks did he admit defeat, reluctantly conceding that rules in this case could not be laid down.[16] Understandably, Callwell was far more cautious about rules in 1919, after the terrible problems of World War I, when he published his volume in the "Campaigns and Their Lessons" series, dealing with the Dardanelles. In this volume Callwell declared that the lessons he advanced were suggestive and not didactic. Some amphibious landings succeeded and some did not. Moreover, the great size of modern armies made such landings hazardous.[17] Callwell drew many lessons from Gallipoli, but his confidence in the existence of immutable principles, which he had inherited from the mid-Victorian period, had definitely come apart by 1919, although his analytic-utilitarian approach was to continue.

Another historian who at least started in the analytic tradition at the end of the 1800s was Colonel G.F.R. Henderson. He was later an influential figure at the Staff College but, partly because mid-Victorian scientific certainties had become undermined by the 1890s, Henderson became a rather transitional figure. He looked backward to Napoleonic campaigns, as many did, but toward the end of his career also apprehensively began to accept the decisive impact of firepower. He vacillated on the question of the laws or principles of war, sometimes writing that war was not a mechanical art and that "war . . . is no exact science, it has no fixed code of rules." However, Henderson also contradicted himself by asserting that there *were* established principles, that there were a few great principles, that two great principles of command existed (destroy the enemy's army and achieve decisive success), or that there were two great principles of war (mystify, mislead, and surprise the enemy and never give up the pursuit as long as one's army's strength lasts). However, the title of his important 1903 book of essays and lectures, *The Science of War*, indicates that he at least hoped, or wished, that war could be reduced to a set of law-like principles.[18]

Nevertheless, Henderson was also clearly influenced by the late-nineteenth-century trend toward antipositivism, which rejected the mechanistic laws of nature and society and emphasized the subjective and often irrational qualities of humans and society. Hence, his earlier book, *Stonewall Jackson and the American Civil War* (1898), tended to stress character, instinct, and morale as much as strategy, and his lectures at the turn of the century also focused a great deal on instinct and morale. Borrowing from Social Darwinism, Henderson stated that Austria in 1866 did not lack in virile qualities, although it was deficient in strategy. He stressed the need for "national spirit" in modern war and felt that armies were living organisms. Moral force in war is most important, he wrote, and he claimed that when Napoleon studied Alexander, Hannibal, and Caesar, "he found in these campaigns a complete study of human nature . . . [and] learned from history the immense value of the moral element in war." Indeed, the influence of morale and individual character was the true way of studying military history, claimed Henderson.[19] It may also be that Henderson's confidence in the rules and principles of war were badly shaken by his experience during the Boer War where, while serving as director of intelligence to Lord Roberts, he broke down after the Modder River battle and was sent home.[20] Henderson was, however, mentally flexible and did change his mind, especially as firepower negatively influenced close order infantry, the cavalry, and offensive strategies. His ambivalent attitudes were a response to the rapidly changing battlefield, but they also very much reflected contemporary cultural and intellectual trends. In this sense his ideas pointed to the future.

THE TWENTIETH-CENTURY TRADITION

The new century ushered in a new group of military writers, including the celebrated J. W. Fortescue. It is true that Fortescue wrote his well-known history of the British army in the narrative campaign tradition and that he followed Napier's lead in confirming the notion of British military superiority and in reinforcing the growing self-regard of the British army and its individual regiments. However, when he came to actually consider the nature of warfare, it was a different story. In his book *Military History*, published in 1914, Fortescue made some good points, for example arguing that the Peninsula campaign was one of logistics and attrition. However, his military history was submerged in Social Darwinian analogies and reflected the whole Edwardian atmosphere of moral reform. Thus, he argued that the law of nations was the law of force and that this was largely moral force. Young, vigorous, and virile communities would defeat effete nations, declared Fortescue, thinking perhaps of the Boer War. The rise and fall of civilizations had nothing to do with peace, societies, or commerce, but rather occurred through the subjection of inferior nations by superior nations, and this was really achieved by moral force, which came through self-discipline and self-sacrifice. Fortescue had also inherited late-nineteenth-century racial ideas, for he believed that the Mughal Empire of India came to an end through intermarriage with Hindu women, thus diluting the stern Tartar blood, "which weakened and ruined the Mogul Emperors." Fortescue essentially focused on the moral health of the nation and empire, and in typical Edwardian terms, he concluded, "Military history is not the history of physical but of moral force."[21]

Fortescue really belonged to the narrative campaign history tradition, for he did not enunciate laws or principles, and he is best known for his history of the British Army. However, he did consistently stress the moral factor in war, and in 1928 he was still arguing that moral force was the key to success in war.[22]

Fortescue's Edwardian-style arguments led on to the work of Sir Charles Oman, who still expressed the antipositivism of the 1890–1930s period. In 1929 Oman advanced the argument that history was not logical or progressive, but rather was subject to the irrational irruptions of what he called *cataclysmic figures*. These figures were very often military figures; hence, it was necessary to study military history with some care. "I look upon war as merely the greatest of the influences that make history 'cataclysmic,' " wrote Oman. These military personalities of "unusual endowments," such as Mohammed, could alter the fate of kingdoms or even continents, and so, "Military history must be studied because it gives the explanation of many of the great cataclysms which break up the annals of the world into separate epochs." Sometimes it was not just the "heroic individual figure" that affected the history of the world, but a school or succession of leaders applying a system of tactics and organization, such as the Mongols. Oman then went on to argue that if history was indeed the result of cataclysmic military personalities (and he was not far wrong in 1929), then military history must be studied as carefully as economic history and must not be left to professional soldiers, because civilian ministers had the ultimate responsibility in understanding the art of war.[23]

Oman certainly expressed the irrationalism of the 1930s in his work, but he can also be seen as leaning toward the analytic tradition in that he obviously believed that cataclysmic military personalities were part of a fixed law of military history: they were the ones who invariably made history. Oman was also particularly concerned to defend military history from those who saw history as part of an inevitable world movement (the Marxists), from the false optimism of those who believed in happy progress, and from those who debunked military history and its hopeless "drum and trumpet" practitioners.[24] Of course, Oman was fighting the post–World War I reaction against warfare and its historians, and it is sometimes surprising to read books published at the same time as Oman but with very different viewpoints. One such book was the amusing debunking of military history, *1066 And All That*, which actually first appeared in 1930, one year after Oman wrote his defense of military history.[25]

However, just at the time when military affairs and history were under attack, appeared the work of Basil Liddell Hart and J.F.C. Fuller. So much has been written concerning these two figures, and their production was so extensive, that it would be foolish to do more than make one or two points concerning their relationship to the traditions of military history. Therefore, it is worth noting that both individuals continued the tradition of Lloyd in their efforts to establish principles of war and in the way that their concepts reflected the prevailing intellectual currents. This was particularly true of Fuller, who, as is well known, followed Herbert Spencer's Social Darwinist and biological ideas, which were common currency in the late 1800s and early 1900s as part of the antipositivist movement. Stimulated by these ideas, Fuller published *The Foundations of the Science of War* in 1926. In this book, Fuller finally reduced warfare to two main principles, the law of the economy of force and the principle of velocity. Because

Fuller was a biological thinker, he was able to think in terms of tactical principles as well; in other words, the analogy of body, brain, and soul led to stability, activity, and cooperation, or, more usefully, stability, activity, and mobility. Unfortunately, Fuller was able to generate principles of war at will; thus, for the 1924 edition of the *Field Service Regulations*, he included four principles: objective, offensive, mobility, and security; and he supplemented these with four means to apply them: surprise, cooperation, concentration, and economy of force. Fuller was unusual in applying rules and principles to both strategy and tactics, but he was reminiscent of Lloyd in his intellectual breadth of interests. Unfortunately, Fuller tended to find principles and trinities of truth under every stone and then locate examples to support them, so that in the end his stimulating insights were often devalued.[26]

Fuller's analytic-utilitarian approach was partially echoed by B. H. Liddell Hart. Liddell Hart was motivated by the deadlock of the Western Front, and his analytic works sought escape from the problems of that style of warfare. Liddell Hart believed that the British generals of World War I had totally ignored military history and had, therefore, disregarded the key principles of surprise and concentration. He felt that the past was a mirror for the present and that it could teach utilitarian military lessons for the future. However, the strategic principles that he claimed to find in history, such as the strategy of the indirect approach, have an a priori feel to them and it is significant that his book, *The Strategy of Indirect Approach* (1941), actually began life as *The Decisive Wars of History* (1929). It is also the case that he became more pessimistic as World War II approached, and he began to doubt that lessons could be learned from history at all, since he now believed that the truth was camouflaged by history, especially regarding strategy and ways of dealing with aggression. Hence, Liddell Hart belonged, at least initially, to the analytic tradition of military history, as did Fuller, and like Fuller he was willing to find a number of lessons at the tactical level ("the expanding torrent").[27]

In the late 1920s, however, the classic memoirs of the Western Front began to appear, and following shortly after them, as might be expected, came the classic histories of World War I, especially Liddell Hart's *The Real War* (1930) and Charles Cruttwell's *A History of the Great War, 1914–1918* (1934). With these works a third tradition in British military history arrived on the scene: the *objective military history* tradition. This combined an analytic and narrative approach with a critical (meaning objective) use of archival sources, and it employed a thesis or argument, but without the stress of fixed principles and rules of war and without the purely descriptive chronology of the narrative campaign tradition. The military history of this objective tradition was often, but by no means always, written by academics, it was only partially developed in the interwar period, and it did not fully evolve until after the 1950s. Dealing only with Liddell Hart's work, it seems that he was able to switch from the analytic-utilitarian style when writing purely military history. Thus, his 1930 history of World War I selected various battle fronts and campaigns to provide an objective sketch of the whole war, including air and sea fronts. He was suspicious of the British high command, but relied to a considerable extent on inside information supplied by J. E. Edmonds, the British Official Historian, and by other senior officers. He also depended on the published British official histories, and so the later chapters were weaker because in 1930 the official history had chronologically only reached as far as the Somme. Therefore, Liddell Hart's grasp of original sources may not have been extensive, and his understanding of the French language also was apparently not as good as he claimed. Nevertheless, the book remains valuable as one of the few overviews of the war, as does the work of Cruttwell, who was equally unkind to the British high command, but in his case also criticized the command style of all armies. Liddell Hart perhaps never escaped his own World War I experience, and his views appeared to mirror the critical view of the high command engendered by the memoir literature of the late 1920s and early 1930s. Moreover, according to the political scientist John Mearsheimer, Liddell Hart's originality and influence on European military thought may not be as great as initially believed.[28]

The emergence of a third, objective tradition in British military history in the 1930s seems to have been a response not only to World War I, and to the memoirs of that war, but also to the intellectual currents of the time, an example being the new strictly analytic and rational spirit in British intellectual life created by A. J. Ayer and the logical positivists. Liddell Hart and Cruttwell's histories were no doubt also stimulated by the growing professionalism of the British army and its expectations of, and preparations for, war in the 1930s. However, World War II put a temporary end to the development of this objective tradition.[29]

Judging by the experience of previous wars, one might anticipate that after World War II there would first appear a series of British war memoirs before a subsequent upsurge in British military history. This indeed occurred with the memoirs of the late 1940s and the 1950s, followed by the military history "boom" of the 1960s and 1970s. However, this boom actually required certain preconditions before it could be fully realized. First, there were the war memoirs, already mentioned; second was the need for an audience, partially created by the media, including television, theater, film, and publishers; third was the influence of what may be called a prevailing war culture; fourth was the availability of sources, archives, and archivists; and last was the involvement of academia. Moreover, even before dealing with these preconditions, there was the special quality of World War II itself.

The historian John Keegan was surely right to draw attention to the "historiographical heritage of the Second World War". Because of the impact of the war on the many civilians caught up in it, a more humane, interesting and popular military history developed. World War II, therefore, had a vitalizing and diversifying effect on military history generally. The personal accounts came first. In 1947 Alex Bernstein (actually Alex Baron) published *From the City, from the Plough*, which enjoyed huge sales. Hard on the heels of this success came R. Grenfell's dramatic *The Bismarck Episode* (1948) and then in 1949 appeared

Eric Williams's *The Wooden Horse*, which was a runaway best seller. This was followed by Fitzroy MacLean's *Eastern Approaches* (1949), which went into seven printings, and then came Vladimir Peniakoff's *Popski's Private Army*, published in 1950, which also sold extremely well. The Popski book was not unlike MacLean's *Eastern Approaches*, and in fact, when a section of MacLean's book was bound into 100 copies of the Popski book by mistake, only a handful of readers noticed. A trans-Atlantic success was Herman Wouk's *The Caine Mutiny* (1951), which resembled Nicholas Monsorrat's *The Cruel Sea* (1951) both of which had heavy sales (the former selling 100,000 copies in two years). By helping to develop an audience and a consciousness of military history, these memoirs and best-sellers were *one* of the key ways in which the ground was prepared for the remarkable awakening of military history that took place a very few years later.[30]

Another ground-breaker was the media, which also helped to create an audience. In this context an important event occurred in 1963, when the British Broadcasting Corporation (BBC) decided to mark the fiftieth anniversary of the outbreak of World War I with a television series dealing with the Western Front. As the producer, Toney Essex, wrote to one enquirer: "Because this momentous event is now passing into history, the BBC has decided to make a series of programs" which would be "the fullest visual history ever undertaken." This "Great War" series was, in fact, BBC-TV's first offering on the new Channel 2 network, and was made for a sum of £150,000, being supported by 20th Century Fox, a U.S. and a Canadian company, and the Imperial War Museum.[31]

It is impossible to quantify the effect of this BBC program, or the media as a whole, on the writing of British military history, but there must have been a very considerable impact on the audience for, and the promotion of, World War I histories, and military history generally. The demographics of the audience for military history, via the media, the stage, the cinema, and the reading public, are probably significant here, for there were now two audiences in the 1960s: the veterans of World War I, who were anxious to tell and hear their stories before time ran out, and the younger generation, who had experienced World War II as civilians or veterans. It cannot be claimed, however, that it was only the 1964 BBC series or the media generally that started the revival of interest in the history of World War I, for Leon Wolff's *In Flanders Fields* was already published by 1959, and Alan Clark's *The Donkeys* in 1963; and in regard to World War II, Corelli Barnett's *The Desert Generals* appeared in 1960. What the media actually seems to have done was to crystallize the public's interest in military history. Moreover, as a specific link between the media and history, it is relevant to note that military historian Max Hastings originally worked on the BBC "Great War" series as a researcher, and that another well-known military historian, Corelli Barnett, wrote the series script.

The audience and interest now existed for military history, and it is not surprising that a fourth tradition in British military history emerged at this point, alongside the narrative, utilitarian-analytic, and objective military history traditions. This was the new *popular military history*, which derived from, and resembled, the original narrative campaign history in style and content. Like the narrative memoirs of the Marlborough, Napoleonic, and Crimean wars, popular military history was defined by its function as popular reading for the literate public of the day. However, popular military history differed from the narrative tradition in two ways. At one end of the scale it resembled objective military history; for example, it drew extensively on a variety of sources (sometimes archival, but often secondary sources or personal accounts, such as oral history interviews), a trend that stemmed from the 1960s radical popular culture and the new academic history, where "history from below" had become a significant force. At the other end of the scale, where it most resembled the narrative tradition, popular military history simply told a descriptive story. On the whole, popular military history was defined by its market and by a narrative style rather than an analytic mode. Utilizing the popular military history market, publishers now adapted the pocket book of World War II, and produced cheap paperback editions, such as Penguin and Pelican. Jonathan Cape introduced its Jackdaw compilation series for the younger and general market in December 1963, with the first title being *The Battle of Trafalgar*. This series had small sales at first but soon took off, and Jonathan Cape did its best to cash in on the popular military history market, scoring particularly well with a blockbuster novel, Len Deighton's *Bomber*, in 1970.[32]

It also appears that the conflict-laden 1950s and 1960s helped to create an atmosphere that may be called a war culture: the third precondition for the military history boom. This war culture encouraged the general public, which was seeking an understanding of why these conflicts existed and how the interminable nuclear threat had developed, to read military history. It was against this background that the Institute of Strategic Studies was founded by Alastair Buchan in 1959, with Ford Foundation money, and ironically opposed by Whitehall. In addition, National Service in Britain, which continued through this period and was only ended by the National Service Act of 1957, helped to maintain a generation that was familiar with military affairs and wanted to know more.

The arrival of objective military history, and to some extent the popular variety, also required archives, archivists, and sources in order to flourish. These, too, were forthcoming in the 1960s. For example, the Imperial War Museum received its first significant set of papers in the late 1950s, these being the papers of World War I general Sir Ivor Maxse. Then, in 1965, the German archives from the Cabinet Office were sent over after the completion of the World War II Official History volumes. In 1969, the Department of Documents opened up in the somewhat inaccessible "Bedlam" tower, and in the same year the Imperial War Museum Sound Archives commenced. Also in the late 1960s, the Liddell Hart Centre for Military Archives was opened at King's College, London University, and later, other archival centers were unveiled at Churchill College, Cambridge, and the National Army Museum. Peter Liddle also began his own personal archive collection. It was in the mid–1960s, too, that the Public Record

Office reduced its fifty-year rule to thirty years, thus opening up most of the World War I records for serious researchers (apart from Court Martial and Shell Shock files). That this was an important step was noted by the author Robert Rhodes James, who in the late 1960s remarked that the tidal wave of books on World War I then rolling across the country was remarkable for the "smallness of the contribution made by professional [academic] . . . historians.'' James explained this situation, to a large extent, by the fact that the British official archives had only just opened. Until this time, claimed James, most books on World War I were merely reassessments of already published material.[33]

Together with audience, demography, publishers, popular military historians, books, archives, sources, and a war culture went a final part of the puzzle required to explain the postwar resurgence of British military history. This was larger-scale university involvement and the emergence of greater numbers of scholars who began to write objective military history in the 1960s and 1970s. The one individual who all agree seems to have spearheaded this effort was Michael Howard. In the late 1950s Howard pioneered the War Studies curriculum at King's College, and in 1956 he wrote a Historical Association paper entitled "Military History as a University Study." Then, in 1961, he delivered a paper to the Royal United Service Institute in which he argued that military history must be studied in width (i.e., comparatively), in depth (i.e., going to the sources and discovering the real experience), and in context (i.e., as a reflection of society as a whole). This was, in fact, the whole burden of Howard's approach: military history must go beyond the analytic-utilitarian tradition of lessons and principles and beyond the narrative-memoir tradition, (commonly known as "drum and trumpet" history) and instead be "directed by human curiosity about wider issues and by a sense of its relevance to the nature and development of society as a whole." Military historians should particularly aim at studying "how and perhaps why societies organize themselves for and conduct war."[34] According to two current British historians, Howard was extremely influential in that he made military history respectable in Britain, he made it relevant and important, and he put it into a social context.[35] Howard's example was followed by perhaps the next best known British military historian, John Keegan, whose celebrated book *The Face of Battle* was published by Johnathan Cape in 1976. This book again put military history into a social context by asking the wider questions of why and how people fought and how the experience of battle changed people?

With military history beginning to enter the mainstream of university studies in Britain in the 1960s, it was to be expected that graduate students would now become increasingly attracted to the subject.[36] Here, an analysis of graduate student theses in British universities should be able to chart the changes in the field. In the 1940s and early 1950s, graduate theses tended to concentrate almost exclusively on medieval and classical military topics and were often obtained from Oxford and Cambridge. There is, however, one startling exception, and this was Noble Frankland's Oxford Ph.D. in the 1950–1951 year, which concerned the planning of the Bomber Offensive in World War II, and which was by far the earliest World War II thesis written in Britain. In contrast, in the mid- and late 1950s came a number of theses on nineteenth-century wars and colonial warfare, and in 1959–1960, doctoral candidates Alan Milward, Peter Paret, and M. E. Mallett obtained their Ph.D.s (two from Oxford and one from London). The real turning point seems to have come in the year 1961–1962 when fifteen advanced degrees in the military area were obtained. These were earned from a wider variety of British universities, and included the future military historians Brian Bond and Christopher Duffy. A large number in that year, five, concerned naval history, although none dealt with twentieth-century warfare. This last aspect did not change until the mid- to late 1960s when World War I topics became frequent, under the influence of King's College, London University, and when World War II topics, often produced from the London School of Economics, became standard. Finally, in the 1970s, military history Ph.D. theses became so frequent that by 1977, a new separate heading in the *Index to Theses* was introduced, simply entitled "History: Military Studies."[37]

Therefore, with the ground prepared in the 1950s and 1960s by the various aspects discussed above, and with the proliferation of graduate study in military history at a wide variety of British universities, this *should* mean that military history had definitely entered the British academic mainstream, but had it? In 1984 the journal *History Today* published a forum on military history, and two reactions became clear. The first was that military history still had the odor of the battlefield about it, and that therefore, military historians were still not viewed as academically mainstream and respectable. Second, following from this came the curious admission that while many historians were putting warfare into the wider social context (i.e., the war-and-society approach), nevertheless, by doing this they could not be seen as real military historians! Thus, the historian of eighteenth-century military affairs, John Childs, argued that military history had been rescued from the "drum and trumpet" school of ex-military officers by the Chichele professors at Oxford and by King's College, but the study of civil-military relations, war and society, and similar topics was not actually military history. Military history, Childs argued, was strictly the study of armed forces, institutions, methods, and operations of war. A similar line was taken by Geoffrey Best, the editor of Fontana's "War and Society" paperback series, who declared that military history only concerned itself with "Battles and how to fight them, Campaigns and how to conduct them, and the ways armed forces gear themselves up." All the rest of war studies (Michael Howard), war-and-society studies (Arthur Marwick), and armed forces and society studies (Morris Janowitz), "is not military history proper, and even the best of it may not include any proper military history at all." Because of this situation, Best himself set out to include what "the warriors" left out, namely, psychology, culture, economics, and similar subjects. It seems that this approach was to define military history quite narrowly and then suggest areas that had been left out by military historians.[38]

In fact, following Michael Howard's calls for a wider military history, that is exactly what did happen in Britain. World War II, and the prevailing intellectual currents that persuaded scholars to look at history from below, plus the impact of the social science, social structure, *Annales*-type history of the 1960s and 1970s, all entered and enlivened military history to a very great degree. For example, Shelford Bidwell's interesting book *Modern Warfare* (1973) covered a wide range of subjects and predated John Keegan's *Face of Battle* in its interest in war and psychology. Arthur Marwick's books looked at the relations between war and society and the impact of war in actually changing society; Michael Mallett analyzed the relations between mercenaries and society in Renaissance Italy; and World War I historiography experienced a renaissance with books ranging from the social history of J. M. Winter to David French's strategic studies, Dominick Graham's path-breaking work on the influence of technology, and the recent controversial book, *Haig's Command* (1991), in which Denis Winter reexamined the much vexed problem of the British high command in a different manner. This growing list indicates that both objective and popular military history are well established in Britain.

Indeed, the two contemporary streams of objective and popular military history are well represented in publishers' lists, even if there is some rationalization going on among academic publishers who are reportedly losing money, an example being the 1991 takeover of Harper Collins Academic by Routledge. However, for the near future, writing in British military history appears to be going principally in the direction of grand strategy, operations, intelligence, biography, and popular history. With the removal of Sir Michael Howard to Yale University, John Keegan remains perhaps the best known military historian in Britain. Consequent on his stern rejection of the social science approach to military history—''I am a historian, not a social scientist''—we can expect further volumes from him in the narrative campaign and battle/commander analysis mode, and thus the continuation of the popular history model.[39]

CONCLUSION

In summary, a few conclusions can be tentatively drawn. First, the origin of modern British military history appeared in the eighteenth century. In that century the *analytic-utilitarian* tradition, with its desire for principles, lessons, and laws, emerged with Henry Lloyd. This tradition continued with historians such as Creasy, Hamley, Henderson to some extent, Callwell, Oman, Fuller, and Liddell Hart. The analytic-utilitarian tradition then underwent a significant division in the twentieth century, in which one branch became *objective military history*, starting with Liddell Hart and Cruttwell, and leading into the post-1950s rejuvenation of critical military history, but without the previous era's principles and lessons. The other branch led into the modern strategic studies analysts, who were not historians but who retained the original Enlightenment concept of principles and lessons.

Somewhat earlier in the eighteenth century occurred the *narrative campaign* tradition, emerging from the personal memoirs of the Marlborough wars and stimulated by a reading public that was willing to buy an average of 3,000 copies per memoir. The memoir tradition continued after each major British war, including World Wars I and II, but this stream was particularly distinguished by the narrative campaign volumes of Napier, Fortescue, and others. Looking back to this tradition came a new invention of the twentieth century, which was consequent on a large and willing reading public: the *popular military history*. This was also generally campaign-oriented but paid greater attention to sources, although sometimes without the critical attention to archival sources and analyses of the academically related objective military history. Thus, altogether, four traditions of British military history have been suggested; the *analytic utilitarian*, the *narrative campaign*, the *objective history*, and the *popular history*.

Second, it is necessary to be cautious about the internal logic and variety inherent in the question of principles, laws, and rules of the analytic-utilitarian school. In some cases, these were meant to be fixed and rigid rules or laws, particularly as they applied to strategy in the nineteenth and twentieth centuries and tactics in the eighteenth century, but in other cases they were meant to be much more flexible or offered only as guides to action. However, if there is a theme that follows military history all the way through from the 1700s to the present, it is the tendency to see warfare either as an art or a science, and sometimes, like Napier and Henderson, to end up somewhere in between. However, it seems to be particularly in the mid-nineteenth century that British military history started to establish the concept of fixed principles of war. This may have reflected the influence of thinkers such as Jomini, but it was much more likely an expression of the mid-Victorians' confidence in their ability to discover and apply natural and social laws, in this case, to the history of warfare.

Third, British military history seems to reflect fairly closely the prevailing intellectual and social trends of the day more than the actual wars and campaigns that it seeks to portray. This was the case, for example, with Henry Lloyd, the mid-Victorians Creasy and Hamley, the irrational antipositivist trend of the 1890s to the 1930s, and the war-and-society interest of the 1960s. Fourth, military histories of the analytic-utilitiarian, objective, and popular traditions normally follow, chronologically, the memoir literature of the war that they go on to discuss. They are also influenced by that memoir literature. This is more true, however, of the nineteenth and twentieth centuries than of the eighteenth century. Fifth, the post–World War II rejuvenation of British military history was very much a product of the experience of World War II by all civilians as well as by the military, and therefore it assumed a wider-ranging, deeper, more complex, and more humane approach to war than previous military history. In addition, and more speculatively, the resurgence of post–1950s, British military history seemed to require a number of key preconditions before it could really take off, and these related to such matters as audience, demography, media, publishers, authors, archives, sources, university involvement, and the existence, in some form, of a war culture.

Finally, in ending, it appears to this author that a great deal has been left out of what must be a tentative sketch of three centuries of British military history and that what has been included is often reviewed in a necessarily limited or speculative manner. However, it is possible to take comfort from St. Augustine, who in concluding his massive, multivolume *City of God*, wrote, "I am done. . . . From all who think I have said either too little or too much, I beg pardon."[40]

NOTES

1. Michael Howard, "What is Military History?" *History Today* 34 (December 1984): 5; Immanuel Kant, *On History*, ed. Lewis W. Beck (Indianapolis: Bobbs-Merrill, 1963), p. 92.

2. John Gooch, "Clio and Mars: The Use and Abuse of Military History", *Journal of Strategic Studies*, 3, (December 1980): 21.

3. Azar Gat, *The Origins of Military Thought, From the Enlightenment to Clausewitz*, (Oxford: Clarendon Press, 1989), pp. 26–29.

4. John Millner, *A Compendious Journal* . . . (London, 1733); Brigadier Richard Kane, *Campaigns of King William and the Duke of Marlborough; with Remarks on the Strategms by which every Battle was won or lost, from 1689 to 1712* (London, 2d ed., 1747), pp. 68, 51; Captain Robert Parker, *Memoirs of the most Remarkable Military Transactions, From the Year 1683 to 1718* (Dublin, 1746; London, 1747). It has been suggested that perhaps Parker copied Kane, or vice versa, or even that both copied an earlier source, *The Life and Adventures of William Bishop of Deddington in Oxfordshire* (London, 1744), pp. 224, 210, 216.

5. Gat, *Origins of Military Thought*, p. 113.

6. Henry Lloyd, *The History of the Late War in Germany; between the King of Prussia, and the Empress of Germany and her Allies* (London, 1766), vol. 1, preface, pp. B1–2.

7. Ibid., no page numbers [p. D2]; *History of the War of 1756*: pp. xxff.; *History of the War of 1757*, pp. 75, 105.

8. Major General Lloyd, *Continuation of the History of the late War in Germany, between the King of Prussia and the Empress of Germany and her Allies. Illustrated with a number of Maps and Plans*, part 2 (London, 1781), pp. 1–2.

9. Ibid., pp. 69, 77, 80–81, 84, 96.

10. Major General Lloyd, *History of the late War in Germany, between the King of Prussia and the Empress of Germany and Her Allies, Containing the campaigns of 1758 and 1759* (London, 1790), vol. 2, pp. 89, 87.

11. General Lloyd, *A Political and Military Rhapsody on the Invasion and Defence of Great Britain and Ireland* (London, 1790), pp. 1, 93–94, 10–13, 16.

12. William Napier, *History of the War in the Peninsula*, ed. and abridged by Charles Stuart (Chicago, 1979), p. 236. See also the excellent chapter on Napier in Jay Luvaas, *The Education of an Army: British Military Thought, 1815–1940* (Chicago: University of Chicago Press, 1964). However, it seems to the present author that Napier was not so much halfway between art and science as Luvaas concluded, but was actually closer to art. Luvaas, *Education of an Army*, p. 27.

13. *The Fifteen Decisive Battles of the World: From Marathon to Waterloo* (London, 1851; 28th ed., 1877), pp. viii-x.

14. Edward Bruce Hamley, *The Operations of War Explained and Illustrated* (London: Blackwood, 1866), pp. 58, 419, 421. Again, see Luvaas's very good analysis in *Education of an Army*, ch. 15, especially the stress on Hamley's acceptance of already existing rules. The present author differs mainly in trying to put Hamley in his intellectual context.

15. Hamley, *Operations of War*, pp. 390, 204, 419.

16. C. E. Callwell, *Small Wars: Their Principles and Practice* (London: Her Majesty's Stationery office, 2d edition, 1899), pp. 3, 4, 434.

17. Major General C. E. Callwell, *The Dardanelles* (London: Constable, 1919), pp. vii, 5, 335.

18. Colonel G.F.R. Henderson, *The Science of War: A Collection of Essays and Lectures: 1891–1903* (London, 1903, 3d printing, Longmans 1908), pp. 367, 45, 43, 47.

19. Ibid., pp. 4, 24, 20, 173–74. For the widespread antipositivist movement, see Roland Stromberg, *European Intellectual History since 1789* 5th ed. Englewood Cliffs, New Jersey: Prentice-Hall 1990), esp. ch. 5.

20. Lord Roberts, "Introduction", in Colonel G.F.R. Henderson, *Stonewall Jackson and the American Civil War* (London: Longmans, Green, 1898), p. xxxvii. Once more, Luvaas's outstanding interpretation of Henderson in *Education of an Army*, chapter 7, lacks only the intellectual and cultural context, although Luvaas did say that after World War I the emphasis shifted to strategy, morale, and psychology of command.

21. J. W. Fortescue, *Military History* (Cambridge, 1914), pp 12, 14, 17–19, 149, 152, 45.

22. J. W. Fortescue, *Six British Soldiers* (London, 1928), p. 271.

23. Charles Oman, "A Defence of Military History," in his *Studies in the Napoleonic Wars* (London, 1929), pp. 25–36, reprinted with some changes in Charles Oman, *On the Writing of History* (New York, 1939; 1969).

24. Oman, *Studies in the Napoleonic Wars*, pp. 25–26.

25. W. C. Sellar and R. J. Yeatman, *1066 and All That* (London: Methuen 1930; repr. 1980), pp. 121–22.

26. See the useful biography by Brian Reid, *J.F.C. Fuller, Military Thinker* (New York: St. Martin's, 1987), esp. ch. 4.

27. Captain B. H. Liddell Hart, *Reputations* (London: Little, Brown, 1928), p. 94; B. H. Liddell Hart, *Through the Fog of War* (London: Faber, 1938), pp. 9, 343ff.; and B. H. Liddell Hart, *Why Don't We Learn from History?* (London: Allen & Unwin, 1944); Gooch, "Clio and Mars," p. 32; Hew Strachan, "The British Army and 'Modern' War: The Experience of the Peninsula and of the Crimea," in John Lynn, ed., *The Tools of War* (Urbana, Illinois: University of Illinois Press, 1990), p. 220.

28. Personal communication with Hew Strachan; Gooch, "Clio and Mars," p. 33; John Mearsheimer, *Liddell Hart and the Weight of History* (Ithaca, NY: Cornell University Press, 1988), ch. 8.

29. One wonders how much military history really suffered from the antiwar sentiment of the 1930s, since the public was buying war memoirs in quantity; for example, T. E. Lawrence's *Revolt in the Desert* (New York: George H. Doran 1927) quickly had a print run of 90,000 copies. See Michael S. Howard, Jonathan Cape, Publisher (London: Cape, 1971), pp. 92–93.

30. John Keegan, "The Historian and Battle", *International Security* 3 (1978–1979), pp. 140–42; Howard, *Cape*, pp. 233–44.

31. BBC-TV "Great War" Series Correspondence Files, volumes AAR-ALL, ALL-ANT, Imperial War Museum.

32. Howard, *Cape*, pp. 295, 300.

33. Robert Rhodes James, "Britain: Soldiers and Biographers," in W. Laquer and G. Mosse, eds., *The New History* (New York, 1967), p. 211.

34. David Skaggs, "Michael Howard and the Dimensions of Military History," *Military Affairs* 49 no. 4 (October 1985): 181–82.

35. Interviews with David French, London, 31 July 1990, and Anthony Verrier, Calgary, 2 September 1990. I am indebted to Anthony Verrier for some suggestions concerning the latter stages of this chapter. I am also grateful to Brain Bond for several comments on the current state of the military history profession.

36. Gerald Jordan would date this assimilation a little later, to the early 1970s; see his "Introduction", in *British Military History: A Supplement to Robin Higham's Guide to the Sources* (New York: Garland, 1988), p. 1.

37. *Index to Theses accepted for Higher Degrees* (London: Aslib 1950–1970, 1977).

38. John Childs, Geoffrey Best, et al., "What is Military History?" *History Today* 34 (December 1984): 9–12.

39. John Keegan, *The Mask of Command* (New York: Viking, 1987), p. 1.

40. St. Augustine, *City of God* (abridged Image ed., New York, 1958), book 22, p. 545.

3

"Naked Truths for the Asking": Twentieth-Century Military Historians and the Battlefield Narrative

DONALD E. GRAVES

"Fighting," stated von Clausewitz, "is the central military act; all other activities merely support it."[1] The study of battles is central to military history and has dominated it from the time of Thucydides until well into the present century. To popular historians, battles *are* military history, as the never-ending flow of "drum and trumpet titles" on publishers' lists demonstrate. To the professional historian, military actions, with their confusion, terror, and violence, are extremely difficult subjects of study.

The problems of writing battlefield narratives are well known. Most participants possess only a limited view of the action, and their evidence is often biased and unreliable. This is especially true if the action is far removed in time, as the more participants reflect, the more distorted their recollections are likely to become. Ian Hamilton said, and said well, that "on the actual day of battle naked truths may be picked up for the asking; by the following morning they have already begun to get into their uniforms."[2] Limited, conflicting, and unreliable evidence forces historians to reconstruct actions using informed conjecture, and they must do so with extreme caution. Battles are also traumatic events, and historians must keep a firm grip on their emotions, for a battlefield, Robert Rhodes James reminded us, "is a sombre place for the person with imagination," and the "perils of sentimentality are as grave as those of cynicism."[3]

Over the past two centuries, the difficulties inherent in the study of battles have led English-speaking historians to evolve a highly artificial format for the battlefield narrative. The origins, composition, and shortcomings of this format were masterfully set forth by John Keegan in his 1976 book, *The Face of Battle*. Keegan concluded that this format, which he called the "battle piece," is "so strong, so inflexible and above all so time-hallowed that it exerts virtual powers of dictatorship over the military historian's mind."[4] He identified four major elements of the traditional battlefield narrative: extreme uniformity of human behavior, abrupt or discontinuous description of movement, stereotyped characterization, and an oversimplified depiction of human behavior.[5]

It is significant that three of these four elements are concerned with human nature, for although weapons and tactics have evolved, humanity has not changed greatly, and our "reaction to stress and danger, to isolation, to great leadership, to victory and defeat remain reasonably constant."[6] Keegan argued that an understanding of the psychology of soldiers under stress is essential to the understanding of the nature of battle, but he was aware that this psychology could not, as one veteran of trench warfare put it, be learned "as one learns mathematics" but rather "must be sensed."[7] The problem, as Keegan pointed out, is that historians have tended to ignore or simplify the human face of battle and have, instead, concentrated on those aspects of warfare that are more susceptible to traditional methodology.

The result is that, prior to the twentieth century, much of the history of warfare has been the history of generals, not of soldiers. In the last seventy years, however, there has been an increasing willingness on the part of professional military historians to examine battles from the ground up as well as from the top down: to search for the "naked truths" of battle as opposed to its gaudy uniforms. This trend can be traced back at least to the official histories of World War I.

The official war histories of Great Britain and Australia present a study in contrasts. The British history was prepared under the direction of Brigadier General Sir James Edmonds, an engineer officer who had coauthored a popular book on the American Civil War. Edmonds personally drafted the eight books of the fourteen-volume series that dealt with the Western Front, and he was always careful to describe himself as a compiler rather than an author. Edmonds had a fairly narrow definition of his task: it was intended "to provide with reasonable compass an authoritative account, suitable for general readers and for students at military schools."[8] His books are characterized by intensive research, a clear and concise writing style, and an almost total absence of interest in the behavior or fate of the common soldier. Battles are presented like chess games, and Edmonds betrays little interest in the fate of the pawns. "The atmosphere of reality is completely wanting," observed J. F. C. Fuller; "as a matter of fact, one gets a far better psychological picture of the last war from novels than from Edmonds."[9] To John Keegan, the British official histories "are so little informed by the humane spirit of general historiography that they might have been written by what the advance men for science fiction movies like to call 'alien life forms.' "[10] What is more, we now know that Edmonds, for all his marshaling of masses of data, did not hesitate to suppress or falsify records when it suited his purposes.[11]

In contrast to the narrow and sterile view of battle presented by Edmonds is the work of the Australian official historian, C.E.W. Bean. Bean had the advantage of being a war correspondent with the Australian army and, with two exceptions, either observed every major action fought by the Australian infantry or was on the field the next day, examining the terrain, conducting interviews, and making sketches. He was thus in an ideal position to get the "naked truths" of battle, and his copious personal records became one of the major sources for the writing of the Australian history.[12] Unlike Edmonds, Bean *was* concerned with the individual soldier, and he determined that his work would view the war

from the front line as well as from the rear, and that, as far as possible, the responsibility for the events described should be attributed to the men actually responsible—at least sufficiently to prove that the responsibility for important decisions, which the official reports tend to lay unduly on commanders, was in fact constantly taken also by subordinates.[13]

Bean included the names of junior officers and noncommissioned officers (NCOs) who played a prominent part in action and, unlike Edmonds, he did not refrain from criticizing senior officers if he felt criticism was due. Thus, the Australian history has a humanity, intimacy, and honesty completely lacking in the British effort.

To some degree, Bean's interest in the common soldier is present in all the official histories of World War II, and nowhere more so than those of the U.S. Army. During the conflict, the War Department assigned 300 officers and men to collect information for the historical program, and their efforts produced battlefield narratives that are accurate, detailed, and empathetic to the common soldier. The U.S. Army also successfully experimented with *field* history detachments; by the time of the Korean conflict, these detachments became a fixture at every level of command from the theater down to the division.[14]

It was somewhat ironic that just as the battlefield narrative was achieving new standards of comprehensiveness and depth in the immediate postwar period, the whole discipline of military history was reshaped by new developments. With the emerging doctrine of deterrence rather than combat and the advent of the systems analysts who made military study the realm of the mathematician, physicist, and social scientist, the behavior of men in battle was increasingly regarded as irrelevant. Finally, there was the inception of a "new military history" focused on institutions, society, and thought rather than action.[15]

Against these trends—either toward warfare as a mathematical abstract or away from it entirely—stood the work of S.L.A. Marshall. While theorists were proclaiming the demise of the traditional soldier in the nuclear age, Marshall sought "to understand the essential nature of fear, or conversely, of courage, with all that it implies as to individual and group effectiveness under ordeal."[16] A journalist with very little real military experience, Marshall used the knowledge he gained as a member of one of the U.S. Army's historical detachments both to devise a methodology to pierce the confusion surrounding battles and as a base on which to construct a theory of the nature of combat.

Marshall served as a historian in the Makin campaign in the Pacific in 1943. Frustrated by his inability to reconstruct actions using traditional methods, he hit on the idea of conducting a group interview of all the men who had participated in an action, immediately after it had occurred. This approach was basically derived from Marshall's journalism background: he was an expert at collecting the conflicting statements of different witnesses, synthesizing them, and "narrating complicated and violent stories as simply and dramatically as he could."[17] The technique proved successful, and Marshall took it with him when he was transferred to the European theater in 1944. During the last ten months of the war, he claimed to have conducted group interviews of 400 American rifle companies, approximately one-third the rifle companies serving in the theater.[18]

Marshall's methodology was not entirely new; he had nineteenth-century forerunners. In 1830, the British army commissioned Captain William Siborne to construct a model of the battle of Waterloo at the height of the action and, in order to get information, Siborne circulated a letter to all the surviving British officers who had participated.[19] A few decades later, Colonel Charles Ardant du Picq of the French army, who was determined to obtain more precise information about the nature of battle, sent questionnaires to his fellow officers asking them to relate their experiences during the Crimean and Franco-Austrian wars.[20] Both Siborne and Ardant du Picq, however, restricted their queries to officers and conducted them long after the event had taken place. What was novel about Marshall's approach was that he questioned *all* the participants in a group *as soon as possible* after combat.

In 1947, Marshall published a small book entitled *Men against Fire*.[21] Written in a forthright and provocative style that, depending on the reader, has "the flavor of social science prose" or represents the intuitive "distilled truths of a searching mind," it was well received.[22] Marshall believed a battle was composed of a series of small combats in which the proper use of firepower was the guarantor of success. He reduced the entire tactical art to a simple prescription: Bring enough firepower to bear, and you will achieve victory.[23] As Marshall saw it, this simple truth had not been realized in the wartime American army; even worse, he stated that based on his research, only 15 percent of the men in an "average" infantry company fired their weapons in action while, "in the most aggressive," only 25 percent, one man in four, would fire at the enemy.[24]

This was an astounding claim to make, but the forcefulness of Marshall's argument and his assertions that it rested on extensive statistical data gathered in interviews with combat soldiers soon gave it the authority of gospel. The American army accordingly revised its training methods to try to increase the number of men firing in combat, the so-called *ratio of fire*. Although there were a number of Americans who had doubts about the validity of Marshall's claims, few were prepared to risk official disapproval by openly voicing them.[25] Marshall was also widely read throughout the Western military world, and those armies that did not agree with him did not stridently oppose him. With one exception, no one seems to have publicly questioned S.L.A. Marshall's theories on the behavior of men in battle.

The exception was Major General Howard Kippenberger of the New Zealand army. Kippenberger was an infantry veteran and editor-in-chief of the New Zealand history of World War II. Shortly after *Men against Fire* was published,

Kippenberger, wishing "to know whether the well-authenticated conclusions reached by the author were of equal application to the New Zealand soldier," sent a detailed questionnaire, based on Marshall's book, to fifty veterans who had seen service in the New Zealand infantry during the war.[26] The completed questionnaires were analyzed by Colonel L. W. Thornton, who compiled a report that was later published as an official pamphlet.

The responses of the New Zealanders are illuminating. So strongly did they reject Marshall's dictum that, in combat, three men out of four will not fire even when they have the opportunity, that Thornton was forced to accept the idea that there must be a "fundamental difference between the U.S. and N.Z. soldier."[27] To Marshall's claim that "in an attack, half the men are in terror and the other half are unnerved," one respondent asked, "Which half won the War?"[28] The opinions of the New Zealanders were at such a variance from Marshall's theories that Thornton concluded:

There can be no doubt that there are marked differences between the reaction of a New Zealander and an American in battle assuming that Marshall presents a true picture, which does not appear to have been seriously contested in [the] USA. Even allowing for the effect of time (and nostalgia) on the recollections of our Infantry commanders, it is clear that the New Zealander in action is more dour, more objective, and more constantly aware of his place in a mutually reliant "team" than is his American counterpart.[29]

The operative phrase is whether Marshall was presenting a "true picture" of the behavior of the American soldier in combat. In fact, he was not. More than four decades after *Men against Fire* first appeared, Roger Spiller proved that not only did Marshall not conduct the interviews he claimed he had conducted, he rarely, if ever, asked soldiers whether they had fired their weapons. There is no record that Marshall ever collected the statistical data necessary to devise the precise ratio of fire about which he wrote in *Men against Fire*: the data were an invention, as was the ratio itself.[30]

The importance of S.L.A. Marshall's writings does not lie in his pseudo-scientific and incorrect prognostications on the behaviour of men in battle; rather, he was an innovator in other areas. He pioneered the use of the postaction interview, he helped develop an understanding of the working relationship between fear and fatigue, and he initiated the scientific investigation of the soldier's burden.[31] However, his true genius lay in the fact that, following the lead provided by Bean, he focused the study of battles on their lowest but most important denominator: the individual soldier. In Keegan's words, Marshall looked "at the forest and saw the trees."[32]

Marshall illuminated a different kind of military history, a soldier's history. This is the history of combat, an immediate and personal experience that is full of Hamilton's "naked truths." Paul Fussell, himself a veteran infantry officer, defined combat as being about survival, and it's about killing in order to survive, and one forgets the presumed ideological motives when one is performing these operations. You're captured by combat, and the only way to get out of the capture is to reduce the threat to your own personal safety, which is to kill the enemy.[33]

Although the two terms are usually used interchangeably, it is important to note the difference between *combat* and battle: They occur simultaneously, but at different levels. Roger Spiller has formulated a useful working distinction: To Spiller, "battle" belongs "to the province of the professional . . . and the higher military commander; the term expresses their ambitions, which are spelled out in the orderly terms of strategies and tactics." "Combat," on the other hand, "is preeminently the domain of the soldier on the fighting line and may or may not correspond to his commanders' ambitions for victory."[34]

Historians, especially official historians, have tended to concentrate on the study of battle as opposed to combat, because battles leave a "paper trail" of plans, orders, returns, and reports, and are therefore much more susceptible to traditional methodology. Herein lies a danger because, as Spiller warns us, one can spend a lifetime studying the "causes and consequences, strategies, tactics, weaponry and personalities of war, only to find at the end of it all he knows very little more about combat than when he began."[35]

Furthermore, the study of combat is important. John English has remarked that wars are fought and won "by platoons and squads. . . . Good sections make good platoons and companies, which, in turn, make the difference on the battlefield."[36] What he is referring to is more than the intervention of blind chance that occurs when a small unit or individual soldier is, or is not, in the right place, or takes the right action at the right time, and influences the outcome of an engagement. Any military formation is an aggregate of small groups, and the outcome of even the largest operation will inevitably turn on the performance of one or a few small groups.

Consider the attack of the New Zealand Corps against the German paratroop battalion holding Monte Cassino in March 1943. When stripped to its basic elements, this operation resolves itself into two companies of New Zealand infantry (about 150 men, given the average strength of a rifle company at that time) fighting a similar number of well-entrenched Germans.[37]

Consider the attack made by the 1st Canadian Corps against the Hitler Line south of Rome in May 1944. The battle plan deployed one infantry division, reinforced with armored units and able to call on 800 artillery pieces, against four weak German battalions. Again, reduced to its basics, the actual attack saw three Canadian infantry battalions committed on a 2,000-yard front that, if analyzed using the strength of the units involved and the tactics of the time, meant 200 Canadian infantrymen, or 1 man for 10 yards of front, pitted against 800 well-entrenched Germans supported by tanks and self-propelled guns. The result was the heaviest Canadian casualty rate during the Italian campaign for a single day's fighting.[38]

Finally, take 2nd Canadian Corps's attack toward Falaise from Caen on 8 August 1944: the second phase of Operation TOTALIZE. This time, besides all the normal military resources available to an Allied general in this late stage of the war, the corps commander obtained the use of 700 four-engine bombers from the 8th Air Force. However, in 4th Canadian Armored Division's sector, the operation resolved itself into an attack along an extremely narrow front by one squadron of tanks and an attached company of infantry.[39]

I have taken some trouble to belabor what may seem to be a rather obvious point—that the actions of small units and individuals profoundly influence or determine the outcome of engagements—because I believe that too often, historians pay it lip service while following the traditional, comfortable, and well-worn path of analyzing operations by using extant records and interviewing senior officers. This will provide a battle narrative; however, it will not sustain a combat narrative.

As a case in point, the Canadian official history acknowledges the ferocity of the fighting during the attack on the Hitler Line, but you have to read it very carefully to learn that, within two hours and forty minutes of the attack going in, the four companies of one of the assaulting battalions, the Seaforth Highlanders of Canada, were reduced to a rump of 100 men under the command of a major.[40] We are informed that, by the end of the day, the fighting strength of another battalion, the Princess Patricia's Canadian Light Infantry (PPCLI), was down to 77 all ranks; this is bad enough, but no mention is made of the fact that they probably started the action with a fighting strength of between 375 and 400 men.[41]

Despite these casualties, the 1st Canadian Division's attack on the Hitler Line was a success as a "battle," as defined in the terms of generals' wars. At least, the commander of the 8th Army thought it was successful; he described it as "extremely well laid on, very well supported and brilliantly executed."[42] However, as a "combat" experience, in the terms of soldiers' history, the attack on the Hitler Line, especially for the Seaforths and Princess Pats, was anything but a victory.

The recent resurgence of interest in the experience of the fighting man—and a new appreciation of the pioneer work of Siborne, Ardant du Picq, Bean, and Marshall—grew in part from the American experience in Vietnam. That conflict demonstrated the inadequacies of systems analysis as a basis for military decisionmaking and sparked an investigation of the meaning of operational efficiency. This was coupled with the fact that, until very recently, the Warsaw Pact nations possessed a superiority in conventional forces, which generated, in the words of Dennis Showalter, a "new commitment to battle as a craft, whose outcome is determined on the front lines as well as in the factories and the schools."[43] This reevaluation of the purpose of armies was given both impetus and a sound literary direction by the publication in 1976 of Keegan's *Face of Battle*.

The result, I feel, has been an exciting new literature that shows the influence of the intellectual broadening of frontiers that the profession has experienced at the hands of the so-called "new military historians." Although much of this new literature is not specifically concerned with either battles or combat, its common denominator is its recognition that fighting is the principal function of armies and, in this, appears to differ from what is normally termed the "new military history." In other respects, it is almost indistinguishable, as its authors show by their interest in the psychological, sociological, and economic elements of warfare and their investigation of the social, cultural, and intellectual patterns demonstrated by the education and training of armies and the evolution of doctrine.

This literature is rich in its diversity, and although any selection of titles is necessarily subjective, I should like to mention a few of what I regard as the more notable examples. Tim Travers set out to find the reasons behind the organized butchery on the Western Front in 1916–1917 and, in doing so, has left a perceptive and literate portrait of prewar British military thought and shown that British senior commanders were constrained by attitudes and hampered by technological limitations.[44] In attempting to account for the behavior of men in action, Terry Copp and Bill McAndrew investigated Canadian military attitudes to neuropsychiatric casualties during the World War II and have helped us to understand that the uniformity of behavior in battle is a myth.[45]

The evolution and development of tactical doctrine and theory have been the subject of excellent works by Shelford Bidwell and Dominick Graham, John English, Timothy Lupfer and Bill McAndrew.[46] Finally, in a category of its own, there is Gerald Linderman's excellent *Embattled Courage*, which deals with the gap between expectations of combat and the reality of combat during the Civil War period and with the efforts of returning veterans to reintegrate themselves into postwar society.[47] There are still good battlefield narratives of the traditional type being produced—witness the work of Coox, D'Este and Pfanz—but their authors display a level of scholarship and a breadth of vision that place them in the forefront of academic endeavor.[48]

It is clear that in recent times, professional historians have moved beyond the stifling bounds of the "battle piece" that Keegan identified fourteen years ago. Their approach to the study of Clausewitz's "central military act" is evolving and maturing, and the battlefield narrative, the oldest historical form, has a bright and relevant future.

NOTES

1. Carl von Clausewitz, *On War*, ed. Michael Howard and Peter Paret (Princeton, New Jersey: Princeton University Press, 1984), p. 227.

2. Ian Hamilton, *A Staff Officer's Scrap-Book during the Russo-Japanese War*, 2 vols. (London: E. Arnold, 1906), I:v; quoted in Jay Luvaas, "Military History: An Academic Historian's Point of View," in Russell Weigley, ed., *New Dimensions in Military History* (San Rafael, CA: Presidio, 1975), p. 33.

3. Robert Rhodes James, "Thoughts on Writing Military History," *RUSI Journal* (May 1966): p. 100.

4. John Keegan, *The Face of Battle* (New York: Viking, 1976), p. 36.

5. Ibid., pp. 36–38.

6. Corelli Barnett, Shelford Bidwell, Brian Bond, and John Terraine, *Old Battles and New Defences: Can We Learn from Military History?* (London: Brassey's, 1986), p. iii.

7. Adolf Von Schell, *Battle Leadership: Some Personal Experiences of a Junior Officer of the German Army with Observations on Battle Tactics and the Psychological Reactions of Troops in Campaign* (Fort Benning, Ga.: *Benning Herald, 1933; repr. 1962, Marine Corps Association), p. 19*.

8. Jay Luvaas, "The First British Official Historians," in Robin Higham, ed., *Official Histories: Essays and Bibliographies from around the World* (Manhattan: KS: Kansas State University Library, 1970), p. 493.

9. J. F. C. Fuller to B. H. Liddell Hart, 14 June 1929, quoted in Luvaas, "First British," p. 504.

10. John Keegan, "The Historian and Battle," *International Security* 3, no. 3 (Winter 1978–79): p. 144.

11. See David French, " 'Official but Not History'? Sir James Edmonds and the Official History of the Great War," *RUSI Journal* 131, no. 1 (March 1986): 58–63; Timothy Travers, *The Killing Ground: The British Army, the Western Front and the Emergence of Modern Warfare, 1900–1918* (London: Allen and Unwin, 1987), pp. 203–249, and Timothy Travers, "Allies in Conflict: The British and Canadian Official Historians and the Real Story of Second Ypres (1915)," *Journal of Contemporary History* 24 (April 1989): 301–25.

12. C.E.W. Bean, "The Writing of the Australian History of the War of 1914–1918: Sources, Methods, and Some Conclusions," in Higham, *Official Histories*, p. 71.

13. Ibid., p. 70.

14. Robert K. Wright, "Clio in Combat: The Evolution of the Military History Detachments," *Army Historian* 6 (Winter 1985): 3–6.

15. On these postwar developments, see Weigley, *New Dimensions*, pp. 3–5; Edward M. Coffman, "The New Military History," *Military Affairs* 48 (January 1984): 1–5; and Dennis E. Showalter, "Of Decisive Battles and Intellectual Fashions: Sir Edward Creasy Revisited," *Military Affairs*, vol. 52 (October 1988): 206–8.

16. S.L.A. Marshall, *Bringing Up the Rear: A Memoir* (San Rafael, CA: Presidio, 1979), p. 202.

17. Fredric Smoler, "The Secret of the Soldiers Who Didn't Shoot," *American Heritage*, March 1989, p. 44.

18. Roger J. Spiller, "S.L.A. Marshall and the Ratio of Fire," *RUSI Journal* 133 (Winter 1988): p. 64.

19. The replies were published by Siborne's son, see H. T. Siborne, ed., *Waterloo Letters*, 2 vols. (London: Casssell, 1891).

20. On Ardant du Picq, see [Charles] Ardant du Picq, *Battle Studies: Ancient and Modern Battle* (Harrisburg, PA: Military Service Publishing Co., 1958); and Stefan T. Possony and Etienne Mantoux, "Du Picq and Foch: The French School," in Edward Mead Earle, ed., *Makers of Modern Strategy: Military Thought from Machiavelli to Hitler* (New York: Athenaeum, 1966), pp. 206–33.

21. S.L.A. Marshall, *Men against Fire* (New York: William Morrow, 1947).

22. Smoler, "Secret," p. 40; John G. Westover, "Marshall's Impact," *Newsletter of the S.L.A. Marshall Military History Collection*, no.13 (Summer 1986).

23. Spiller, "Ratio," p. 63; Marshall, *Men against Fire*, pp. 53–56.

24. Marshall, *Men against Fire*, p. 56.

25. In private it was another matter; see David Hackworth and Julie Sherman, *About Face* (New York: Simon and Schuster, 1989), pp. 547–86, for a vicious indictment of Marshall's personal and professional qualities.

26. *Infantry in Battle: Notes on the Training and Command of New Zealand Infantry Units* (Wellington, NZ: Army Headquarters, 1950), p. 4.

27. Thornton to Kippenberger, 29 Mar 1949, IA 77/38, Kippenberger Papers, National Archives of New Zealand Wellington.

28. Ibid.

29. Ibid. I am indebted to my colleague, W. J. McAndrew, for bringing this material to my attention.

30. Spiller, "Ratio," p. 68.

31. See F.D.G. Williams, "The Labors of Sisyphus: The Writings of S.L.A. Marshall," *Defence Analysis* 2, no. 2 (1986): 167–72, for a summary of Marshall's work.

32. Keegan, "Historian and Battle," p. 146.

33. Roger J. Spiller, "The Real War: An Interview with Paul Fussell by Roger J. Spiller," *American Heritage*, November 1989, p. 131.

34. Roger J. Spiller, "The Thousand Yard Stare: Psychodynamics of Combat in World War II" (Paper presented to the meeting of the Organization of American Historians in Washington, D.C., March 1990). I am indebted to Roger Spiller for permission to quote from this unpublished paper.

35. Roger J. Spiller, "The Tenth Imperative," *Military Review*, 69, no. 4 (April 1989): 6.

36. John English, *On Infantry* (New York: Praeger, 1981), p. 218.

37. N. C. Phillips, *History of New Zealand in the Second World War, 1939–1945. Italy*, vol. 1, The Sangro to Cassino (Wellington, N.Z.: 1957) War History Branch, Department of Internal Affairs, pp. 267–79.

38. G.W.L. Nicholson, *Official History of the Canadian Army in the Second World War*, vol. 2, The Canadians in Italy, 1943–1945 (Ottawa: Department of National Defence, 1957), pp. 412–26.

39. C. P. Stacey, *Official History of the Canadian Army in the Second World War*, vol. 3, The Victory Campaign (Ottawa: Department of National Defence), pp. 222–31.

40. Nicholson, *Canadian Army*, pp. 422–23.

41. Ibid., p. 423.

42. Leese to Vokes, 28 May 1944, quoted in ibid., p. 426.

43. Showalter, "Decisive Battles," p. 207.

44. Travers, *Killing Ground*.

45. Terry Copp and Bill McAndrew, *Battle Exhaustion: Soldiers and Psychiatrists in the Canadian Army, 1939–1945* (Montreal: McGill-Queens, 1990).

46. Shelford Bidwell and Dominick Graham, *Fire-Power: British Army Weapons and Theories of War, 1904–1945* (London, 1982); John English, *On Infantry* (New York: Praeger, 1981); Timothy Lupfer, *The Dynamics of Doctrine: The Changes in German Tactical Doctrine during the First World War*, Leavenworth Paper no. 4 (Fort Leavenworth, KS: Combat Studies Institute, 1981); Bill McAndrew, "Fire or Movement? Canadian Tactical Doctrine, Sicily—1943," *Military Affairs* (July 1987): 140–45.

47. Gerald Linderman, *Embattled Courage: The Experience of Combat in the American Civil War* (New York: Free Press, 1987).

48. Alvin D. Coox, *Nomonhan: Japan against Russia, 1939*, 2 vols. (Stanford, CA: Stanford University Press, 1985); Carlo D'Este, *Decision in Normandy: The Unwritten Story of Montgomery and the Allied Campaign* (London: Collins, 1983); Harry Pfanz, *Gettysburgh: The Second Day* (Chapel Hill: University of North Carolina Press, 1987).

4

The Soldier and the Battle

BILL McANDREW

"To look at old facts through new glasses, then to make use of the facts in order to gain a better understanding of those glasses-that, after all, is what makes history worthwhile."

Martin Van Creveld, *COMMAND IN WAR*

On 10 August 1944, just south of Caen in the Normandy bridgehead, a twenty-year-old Canadian infantryman shot himself in the left foot with his Bren gun. One of four soldier brothers, another of whom had been killed in Italy a few months before, he had fought well for two months. After a week's rest, his battalion was moving back into the line when it was bombed by friendly aircraft, taking about 100 casualties. Badly shaken, he moved forward where, two days later, a report on his case observed: "Two enemy tanks were bringing fire to bear on his position and had killed men in the immediate vicinity. This was too much for him and he lost his nerve and shot himself." He was hospitalized and then court-martialed, and was sentenced to two years' imprisonment with hard labor.[1]

This soldier's fate was unusual only in the classic structure of its catch-22. Because he was able to make a rational choice between unpalatable alternatives, presumably he was of sufficiently sound mind not to be considered a battle exhaustion casualty. Had his shaky condition been acknowledged earlier, instead of prison he could have been given a job in his unit's rear echelon. Alternatively, he might have been medically evacuated to his unit medical officer, and then, perhaps, to a field psychiatrist in No. 1 Canadian Exhaustion Unit. From there he could have been sent to Britain for further therapy or to a Special Employment Company for laboring jobs behind the front line. In this way, his record would not have been stained with a dishonorable discharge.[2]

This by no means isolated case prompts several questions about the behavior of men in battle. How typical was this soldier's situation? Was that normal or aberrant behavior? What alternatives were available for soldiers who succumbed to intolerably stressful conditions? What distinguished disciplinary from medical responses to noneffective soldiers? What was the relationship between actual soldierly behavior and operational doctrine and performance? On the assumption that there is as much to learn from examining a snowflake as in scanning the universe, the Canadian Army's World War II experience may offer a useful microcosm for exploring universal questions about men in battle.

SOLDIERS IN BATTLE

The first point to note is that we do not know much about how soldiers, Canadian or otherwise, actually performed. Anyone without direct experience who tries to participate vicariously in battle through a spectrum of contradictory sources will soon be bewildered. Generally there is more, or sometimes less, than meets the eye. Few Canadian historians have probed beyond romanticized notions of heroic warriors. Campaign and operational histories generally assume effective behavior, and regimental accounts naturally exclude all but the exemplary. Fewer Canadian social scientists have displayed an interest in how their countrymen reacted to combat. If they thought about the topic at all, Canadian academics simply extrapolated from American and British research. Roger Spiller's comment that "the competition between science and military tradition to explain the human dimension of combat makes clear that knowledge, after 3,500 years of recorded military history, is still very crude" applies even more so in Canada.[3] A few novels and memoirs offer hints but, however informative, their slim slices of reality are necessarily idiosyncratic. Donald Pearce, a subaltern in the North Nova Scotia Highlanders, recalled how individual battle experiences were just that. "No one else has really been in the same places as anyone else," he wrote "and I refuse to play the game of comparing experiences. The whole war seems to be a quite private experience; I mean for everyone. Each man talks about a quite different war from mine, and ultimately everyone is separated from everyone by layers of privacy or egoism."[4]

The impossibility of describing endless layers of realities may account for a certain reluctance to probe further. To cite Spiller again, he remarked that "because the soldier's history of war does not readily submit to the orderly requirements of history, and because, when uncovered, it often challenges the orderly traditions by which military history has shaped our understanding of warfare, the soldier's war has been the great secret of military history."[5] Like military commanders, historians prefer tidy, not chaotic, battlefields. Most mistrust individual recollections and differ over how many it takes to form a theory. Anecdotal evidence, however, can add much to incomplete war diaries and sometimes self-serving after-action reports that are confidently cited. Perhaps their most valuable insight is to warn against easy generalizations that presume the average soldier's thoughts and moods. A certain skepticism may be in order, for example, when a corps commander writes that his exhausted troops were "keen to get into battle again," or about a historian's equally remarkable conclusion that "the reward of General Patton's efforts was the confident enthusiasm with which his soldiers willingly put their lives on the line to help him achieve his destiny."[6]

Front-line fighters are seldom as bloodthirsty as distant commanders, or theorists, but it is a curious, not to say unrealistic, fact that correct and effective soldierly behavior is commonly taken for granted. This is especially puzzling in an age when the behavioral sciences have been mobilized to explain the diversity of human reactions to stress. Nonetheless, strategic analyses, operational accounts, and tactical narratives proceed as if soldiers who have to implement tidy map plans expose themselves more or less casually to mutilation and death. Self-sacrifice invariably prevails over self-preservation, an extraordinary proposition that is explained as the natural result of training or inherent courage. To the extent that this did occur, it likely demanded a certain suspension of belief. After all, it was hardly rational for a soldier to break cover and advance toward hostile machine guns. One platoon commander has described how his role in battle was

essentially histrionic[,] . . . to feign a casual and cheerful optimism to create an illusion of normality and make it seem as if there was nothing in the least strange about the outrageous things one was asked to do. Only in this way could he ease the tension, quell any panic and convince his men that everything would come out right in the end.[7]

It was not always possible to establish an illusion of normality. While most soldiers performed their unenviable tasks doggedly, and some, with exceptional courage, a significant minority found ways to avoid the stress of battle. Some straggled, ran, or hid; some became medical and others, disciplinary cases. There was nothing new in this, nothing unusual about individuals losing their will or self-control. The wonder is that more did not. A northerner at Antietam captured the essence of the fighting soldier's dilemma when he wrote:

The truth is when bullets are whacking against tree trunks and solid shot are cracking skulls like egg shells, the consuming passion in the heart of the average man is to get out of the way. Between the physical fear of going forward, and the moral fear of turning back, there is a predicament of exceptional awkwardness, from which a hidden hole in the ground would be a wonderfully welcome outlet.[8]

It is impossible to know how many soldiers in any battle, in any war found "hidden holes." In his persuasive description of World War I trench life, Tony Ashworth concluded that informal agreements between opposing front-line troops to live and let live were sufficiently common to be considered normal.[9] It is reasonable to suppose that widely dispersed World War II battlefields offered more, not fewer, holes, and scattered evidence suggests that the outcome of many clashes was decided by relatively few fighters. It seems natural that soldiers would find ways to avoid stressful situations. Although records are incomplete, some, particularly those accounting for what may ironically be termed aberrant behavior, suggest an understandably diverse range of human responses to the terrors of battle.

The first are those concerned with battle exhaustion or neuropsychiatric casualties. Like other World War II armies, Canadians at first ignored their "shell shock" experience of World War I. When finally forced to acknowledge the phenomenon once more, commanders and medical staffs reacted much as they did with venereal disease: They were never quite sure whether to call military police for a disciplinary problem or doctors for a medical one. Despite reservations, however, an army psychiatric establishment evolved during the war. A psychiatrist landed in Sicily with 1st Division, others joined him in Italy, and even more accompanied the troops to Northwest Europe (NWE).[10]

These psychiatrists had an active practice which fluctuated in intensity with the course of battle. Psychiatric cases consistently tracked physical casualties at a rate of one to four, three, or even two. In Italy the two-division Canadian Corps had just over 5,000 cases in nineteen months. In NWE, three divisions had a like number between D and VE days. The numbers reflect only soldiers diagnosed in the medical evacuation system and exclude those looked after in their units, undetected psychosomatic cases, and dysfunctional soldiers killed after they lost their self-control.[11]

The second category of aberrant behavior for which there is some statistical evidence is that of military crime. Self-inflicted wounds were difficult to prove, but more than 230 incidents were reported in Normandy, and the Italian rate was comparable. Courts-martial numbers were more detailed. There were 4,383 Field General Courts-Martial (FGCM) in NWE in 1944–1945: 2,088 in Italy in 1944 and the first quarter of 1945 before the corps moved to Holland. A large proportion heard charges of desertion, cowardice, or leaving a reinforcement draft while proceeding to the front. Disciplinary screws were tightened severely in the final winter of the war. During the last six months in Italy, FGCMs averaged between five and ten a day. With the death penalty unavailable as a deterrent, courts awarded exemplary sentences of two to five years' imprisonment with hard labor as a matter of policy. Severe sentences may have deterred some soldiers, but the possibility of losing wartime credits for postwar gratuities was probably an even more effective control on unsoldierly behavior.[12]

Battle exhaustion and disciplinary losses together presented a serious drain on limited manpower resources. The Italian theater offers a convenient measure of its scale and scope. When 1st Canadian Corps left Italy in the spring of 1945, its consultant psychiatrist, Lieutenant-Colonel Arthur Doyle, conducted a survey of Canadians in the military prison system. He found about 1,600. Most were infantrymen, and many had been previously evacuated as physical or psychiatric casualties. In addition, there were at least another 1,300 noneffectives reassigned from combat units to labor companies. Most, also, were infantrymen. Placing these numbers in perspective, there were seldom more than 75 fighters in an operational rifle company; that is, 300 in a battalion. The nine battalions of an

18,000-man infantry division, then, might deploy around 3,000 riflemen. The total was about equivalent to the number of noneffectives.[13]

Medical and disciplinary behavioral explanations merged because, except for extremes, it was difficult to define a reasonable line between them. Especially late in the war, it became largely a matter of random circumstance whether a soldier who could no longer function effectively in combat ended up peeling potatoes in his company kitchen, loading trucks with ammunition, staying in the hospital, or doing hard time. In action a soldier might be reported as being "useless and demoralizing to other men," "shaky and weak in action. Froze to slit trench," or as "jeopardizing the lives of other men in the platoon. Stays in slit trench all the time, except during shelling, when he runs around everywhere." If he could not regain his self-control with the help of his mates or unit medical officer, the soldier would be channeled to a forward field psychiatrist. One recalled that these soldiers presented

a rather monotonous and anything but dramatic picture—dejection, fatigue, and apathy being the outstanding features, with varying degrees of tremors, unshaven faces, dull eyes and muddy uniforms completing the "beat up" appearance. The complaints were also sterotyped—"I just can't take it anymore; I can't stand those shells; I've had it."[14]

Unit medical officers and psychiatrists faced perplexing diagnostic challenges. Very few of their patients presented symptoms of classic mental disorders. The incidence of schizophrenia or psychosis was no greater than in a comparable civilian environment. Some were clearly dysfunctional, with physical impairment having a psychological cause for example, paralysis, blindness, or aphonia which required medical intervention. Were the others more properly dealt with by doctors or military policemen? The psychiatrists were in an unenviable position. Conscious of their dual responsibilities—to their individual patients who wanted out of battle and to the army who wanted them back at the front, the field psychiatrists found effective guidance for restoring broken psyches in rediscovered World War I handling principles of immediacy, proximity, and expediency. However, for their soldier patients, recovery meant returning to the milieu organized for their violent death which had caused the problem in the first place. The psychiatrists whose medical specialty in this era hovered only on the fringes of medical respectability, faced a most delicate dilemma. Surviving records reflect a most conscientious search for a pragmatic balance between tough-mindedness and humane concern which is remarkable under the circumstances. They returned to their units those with the most promising prognosis, sent others to noncombat laboring jobs, and evacuated the rest for more intense treatment in base hospitals.[15]

In time the doctors detected patterns of incidence. The great majority of psychiatric as well as physical casualties were infantrymen. Soldiers who were new to battle were vulnerable. If they survived initial shocks, individuals might acquire protective battle experience, but too much fighting eventually wore out even the strongest. Virtually everyone had his breaking point. Precipitating causes might be battle stress or personal distress, which could sap will, motivation, and morale and, as British General Frank Richardson aptly remarked, the psychiatric casualty is "the last stage in the failure of a man's personal morale."[16]

Morale and motivation dictated how soldiers would behave on the battlefield, but they were beyond the control of psychiatrists. "The psychiatric problem was always in two parts: the symptoms of neurosis and the morale of the man," the official medical history observed. "In a soldier who failed the test of battle, the neurosis was first treated and then morale was considered. In short [the psychiatrists were] dealing with two distinct problems long differentiated by the vulgar but accurate terms 'nerves' and 'guts.' "[17] The psychiatrists saw the results of collapsed morale, but producing and sustaining morale was a command, not a medical, problem. As the U.S. Army's inspector-general remarked about a like problem in his army: "The majority of [battle exhaustion] cases are not psychoneurotic conditions because medical officers wish to make patients out of them but because line officers have been unable to make soldiers out of them."[18]

It is necessary, then, to probe beyond the battlefield in exploring battlefield behavior. Explanations of soldiers' conduct connect the individual and his field unit to the entire complex process of transforming civilians into soldiers, a mob into a disciplined force. The army's manpower policies, enlistment practices, recruiting standards, training, leadership, and group cohesion all affected morale and, hence, the eventual outcome: whether or when, and in what circumstances, a soldier became psychologically ineffective. Some were in that state before joining up, others became so in training, more broke down early in combat, and yet others burned out after long exposure. All these stages offer fruitful research possibilities in neglected documentary, statistical, and anecdotal sources. A few themes suggest themselves.

MANPOWER POLICIES AND MILITARY EFFECTIVENESS

One theme is the ultimate effect on the battlefield of wide oscillations in Canadian wartime manning policies between indiscriminate recruiting and excessive personnel screening. The source of many of the army's early behavioral problems arguably lay in the chaotic scramble for bodies at the beginning of the war. When 57,000 men were enrolled in 1939 to form 1st and 2nd Infantry Divisions, the mere act of volunteering was assumed to be sufficient evidence of fitness for war. Medical instructions noted simply that "the recruit should have the appearance of being an intelligent and sober man and likely to become an efficient solder."[19] That premise proved deficient. Recruit motivations were bound to vary, especially in the social and economic aftermath of the Great Depression. The president of an Edmonton medical board, himself a World War I veteran, wrote about the men he saw. While some were "prompted by patriotism and ideals, willing to do anything they can and make any necessary sacrifice in defence of the cause," he thought many others were "prompted largely by a desire to wear a uniform, with pay and allowances [and] did not intend to do any real soldiering if they could get out of it. . . . [Moreover, a large number were] obviously mentally or physically unfit for the stress of front line warfare . . . and [there were] the unemployed, making a choice between two evils without seriously considering what is in store for them."[20] This was not unusual. Recruiting standards are invariably set by supply and demand. However, the army lacked a training organization that could systematically winnow out those either unable or unwilling to soldier. Instead, they were shipped untrained to Britain, where they formed a pool of persistent behavioral problems that severely taxed training and administrative resources.

Partially in response to the difficulties these soldiers created, the social sciences were mobilized. In the early 1940s, psychologists assumed that they were able to predict an individual's potential military effectiveness by evaluating his personality. They persuaded personnel administrators, in turn, that once neurotic, psychopathic, and other personality defects were excluded, few behavioral problems would remain. Consequently, the army formed a Personnel Selection Service and the manning pendulum swung rapidly from no winnowing at all to full-scale screening.[21]

Employing screening methods derived from dubious World War I and industrial models, personnel selection officers tested and interviewed thousands of recruits to assess their intelligence, aptitudes, functional capabilities, and personality profiles. The degree to which examiners were able to rationalize the use of available manpower talent by, for instance, identifying potential officers, NCOs, and skilled tradesmen, is problematic, but they probably helped. Less successful were their efforts to screen out personality defects according to a scheme of unproven presuppositions. No one knew what personality profile made a successful soldier, let alone an effective combat infantryman. Casual selective criteria like "good nervous stability[,] . . . interested in hunting and outdoor life generally[,] . . . likes the notion of commando training," were hardly helpful.[22]

While recruits were scrutinized in Canada, the overseas army was also intensively screened. The random initial recruiting process had scattered talent indiscriminately throughout units. Too many cooks were driving trucks and too many drivers were cooking. Hastily organized teams of examiners canvassed units to find round pegs for round establishment holes. The primary selection premise was that the war would be a mechanized one fought by specialists rather than infantrymen. Consequently, the examiners identified those with useful civilian skills and trades and those who might potentially acquire them, and posted them for specialist training. Infantry battalions were thus stripped of many of their best qualified men and left with the rest.

Several unfortunate results trailed the mass screening exercise. Unit commanders became understandably disturbed when "agents of a superior body, Canadian Military Headquarters[,] . . . [arrived] to spy out and remove some of their best men." Commanders' efforts to foster unit cohesion, which provided the external supports that individual soldiers needed in battle, were not helped by the disruptive turnover. In addition, excessive numbers of specialists were trained while infantry requirements were neglected. Further, large numbers of soldiers were jarred loose from their unit homes and sent for reallocation to those dismal repositories of the unwanted, Reinforcement Units. Some, unable to successfully complete training, settled into housekeeping jobs somewhere in the system until called on as reinforcements. Still others, detached from their familiar homes and lacking direction and leadership in Reinforcement Units, ended up in the Headly Detention Barracks and the Aldershop psychiatric outpatients' clinic.[23]

As manpower resources grew scarce, manning policy swung away from rigid selection. Large numbers of recruits were being rejected while shortages loomed. Critics charged that standards were too high when army recruiters were having difficulty in filling infantry ranks from a diminishing supply of volunteers. Consequently, standards were lowered and indifferently applied across the country. Filling a recruiting quota, however, did not necessarily mean obtaining more trainable men. One medical officer at an advanced training center that had to prepare these men for battle described his experience. Believing that

an ounce of exclusion is worth a pound of discharges, [he] interviewed each man on his arrival . . . [and] could hardly believe the number who were obviously misfits. . . . However, we could and did pamper, bully, and encourage most of them through their training and send them overseas. I have seen them either just out of hospital following investigation and with a diagnosis of 'No Appreciable Disease,' or just out of detention and labelled a "bad actor," bundled off with special precautions to see that they do not escape the troop train.[24]

Overseas psychiatrists agreed that it made little sense to send unprepared men to combat. It simply passed the disposal problem overseas, where several thousand combat noneffectives had already accumulated. One extreme example was of a man going directly from ship to psychiatric ward on arrival. Colonel Fred Van Nostrand, the army's chief psychiatric consultant, protested that

Regarding the effectiveness of the present method of screening recruits at intake and weeding out of the unfit, we are not in a position to express opinion, except to state that neither the rejection of recruits, nor the weeding during training have been too strict, since we are still getting as reinforcements a fair number of soldiers who give histories of former inadequacy or mental ill-health, and who break down under the stress of very short battle experience. The rate of psychoneurotic breakdown in both theatres of war has been higher in reinforcements than in soldiers serving with units to which they had been posted during the training period. . . . One soldier who stated that he enlisted in Canada on D-Day, was invalided from France in August with psychiatric disability. A fair number of other casualties admitted to [the psychiatric hospital] at this time had less than six months in the army.[25]

Similarly, a staff officer wrote of self-inflicted wound incidents that "in the normal case the soldier is young, 18 to 21, and in most cases has arrived in the UK from Canada in late Spring or early Summer of 1944, and is sent almost at once as a reinforcement to France."[26]

The gaps in the army's manning and training system beg to be explored further, because maintaining a dependable supply of trained and motivated men was vital to unit performance. Part of that process was ensuring that soldiers could be integrated into cohesive sections and platoons. Sustaining fighting groups was exceptionally difficult when a well-placed machine gun or an ill-timed mortar concentration could wipe out months of hard training in a few minutes. The Royal Winnipeg Rifles, for instance, lost a company on D day, the equivalent of two more on 8 June, and a like number a month later. A short time later the South Saskatchewan Regiment was maimed in the Foret de la Londe, after which it "reformed four rifle companies—23 men in A Company, 21 in B Company, 9 in C Company and 12 in D Company."[27] Reinforcements sent forward as individuals to shattered battalions like these, even if well trained, too often lacked an opportunity to form the self-supporting groups that were the key to combat effectiveness. The army was unable to take full advantage of its regimental system to sustain units overtaken by casualties. By the fall of 1944 it was engaged in an unseemly scramble for bodies to fill depleted combat ranks.

Reinforcement problems struck morale, and if there is a grain of truth to the truisms about the significance of morale in battle, it would be remarkable if diminished motivation did not affect operational performance. The most evident impact at the front was through the incremental drain of burnt-out leaders and reliable men who could not easily be replaced. A company commander in Italy described how, on moving forward to an attack,

before D Company had even reached the area of the guns 4 men had deserted. During the subsequent ten days of action the men were unreliable, partly owing to lack of good NCO's. Once was killed and four wounded out of D Company during the first attempt to cross the River Savio . . . because they had to go back, or expose themselves unduly so as to force their men to go with them. The company went into action 20 men under strength, and the men knew that few if any reinforcements would be coming up. . . . In mid-December, men who became lance corporals in October, were commanding platoons in action.[28]

Cumulative losses in companies meant that control, initiative, and effectiveness suffered throughout the chain of command. General Vokes described how heavy physical and psychiatric casualties at Ortona wore out his 1st Division. "It is most noticeable that the standard of minor tactics and unit tactics has deteriorated," he wrote, "and opposition which at one period would have been brushed aside in their stride, now causes untold delay and stickiness."[29] The staff of 7 Brigade in the Normandy bridgehead remarked similarly how losses slowed their capacity to react quickly. They wrote:

For set piece attacks, higher formations and brigades must leave units more time, firstly for outline planning and recce, and secondly between final orders and H hour. . . . Commanding Officers and sub unit commanders require more time for orders than formerly due to the large number of green reinforcement officers, NCO's and men. They must not only give orders in the normal way, but go into much greater detail as to the course to be followed by their officers, NCO's and men. Each time a battalion attacks is the first time in action for some officers and men, and they by no means know the correct action to be taken as a result of the approved concise verbal orders.[30]

Declining efficiency from accumulating losses was to be expected. However, by 1944 a badly flawed manning and reinforcement system that was unable to sustain infantry battalions effectively had become the army's most serious deficiency.

Neglected links between recruiting practices, training, personnel policies, unit integration, discipline, and battle exhaustion hold much research promise. Equally worthy is the interaction between morale and behavior on the one hand and operational doctrine on the other. It seems reasonable to suppose that doctrine, or the manner in which soldiers were deployed in combat, also affected morale and, consequently, battle worthiness.

OPERATIONAL DOCTRINE AND BATTLE PERFORMANCE

There is some suggestive evidence about that obscure seam in the detailed questionnaires that scores of combat officers completed on returning from Italy and Normandy.[31] One persistent thread in their responses to items concerning morale was their lack of opportunity to exercise initiative. This seems odd because the message runs counter to commonly received wisdom about Canadian soldiers. Nonetheless, their view from the bottom was of higher staffs issuing detailed, inflexible plans that they were expected to implement. When, often, battle procedures were foreshortened, they then had little time to brief their subordinates adequately. When leaders became casualties, their soldiers, knowing little of their unit's mission except to follow a moving artillery barrage toward an objective circled on a map, went to ground and forward movement stopped. A variation of this approach to battle was the curious habit of always attacking the enemy at his strongest point, with one exhausted battalion being committed after another decimated one.[32] As well as adversely affecting morale and performance, this style of war prompted skepticism of higher commanders. Morale was not enhanced when these same commanders habitually faulted their soldiers for not successfully implementing their "perfect" plans.

Was that the doctrinal chicken to the behavioral egg? There are World War I echoes in these fighters' complaints about higher commanders and their staffs. There are also doctrinal tactical links between the two wars that are worth exploring. Much has been written during the past decade about the origins of modern tactical doctrine, especially *auftragstatik* as practiced by the *Wehrmacht*, which accounted for its extraordinary battlefield flexibility. In *Stormtroop Tactics*, Bruce Gudmundsson traced the roots back to the decentralized pre–World War I German Army, which produced two quite different tactical responses to the open battlefield. Some commanders chose to retain traditional close-order ranks because they were unsure how their soldiers would react if dispersed. They feared that too many would find convenient holes to avoid battle. In contrast, other commanders accepted dispersion and loose control to gain flexibility. Much of the initiative to find ways of maneuvering on the battlefield came from below, from relatively junior officers in the trenches and, Gudmundsson remarked, "Despite the fears of some pre-war officers, battalions and companies advancing in open order did not degenerate into purposeless masses of individuals trying to avoid combat."[33] That doctrinal foundation was codified between the wars and practiced after 1939. One practitioner has observed that delegated responsibility throughout the chain of command leading by mission, was made possible only because German soldiers were made full shareholders in their operations.[34]

British/Canadian tactical doctrine evolved differently, with soldiers being handled more as unconsulted employees than shareholders. Tactical stalemate produced a highly centralized planning structure whose purpose was to eliminate, not exploit, the natural chaos of the battlefield. One observer remarked that as early as 1916, "a mechanistic theory of the conduct of war was being developed which bade fair to make cyphers of the individual and the unit. The foundation of a bureaucratic means of handling operations was well and truly laid during the winter lull."[35] The artillery barrage became the arbiter of tactical planning because staffs could control massed gunfire. Movement was less easily managed.[36] Staffs could not track infantrymen spread over an open battlefield as readily as they could impose a rectangular artillery grid over it. Even well-trained soldiers might not react predictably. Hence the Somme, where thousands of troops were herded toward fixed defences in packed ranks.

There were both doctrinal and behavioral reasons for this rigidity. Faith in organization, technology, and high explosives played a part. One British commander wrote that "nothing can exist at the conclusion of the bombardment in the area covered by [the barrage] and the infantry would only have to walk over and take possession." Lack of faith in soldiers also played a part. The New Armies were thought to be insufficiently trained or trustworthy or do other than follow a barrage. Tim Travers observed: "First, there was the underlying theme that sufficient 'weight' and 'energy' would always carry a position, and secondly . . . [a] 'social' feeling that it was more important to stress control and discipline of one's own troops than worry about the enemy. . . . In fact, Fourth Army sometimes seemed more worried by their own men than by the enemy."[37] As Bill Rawlings recently pointed out, the Canadian Corps reorganized its training after the Somme to emphasize platoon-level fire and movement drills which units implemented at Vimy Ridge.[38] However, at Vimy and elsewhere, artillery still dictated the limits of maneuver and tactical innovation remained largely concerned with rationalizing firepower.

The Somme was just the most disastrous example of systemic weakness. Whether this staff-driven management style evolved from a distinctive British/ Canadian mind-set or because of infantry inadequacies is arguable. The outcome was the same: a centralized bureaucratic structure that attempted to control the uncontrollable. That legacy, leading by command and not mission, persisted through World War II. With some notable exceptions, confining infantry movement to following a barrage remained the predictable tactical signature of Canadian operations, as the Germans frequently noted. The Canadian assaults on the Hitler Line in Italy in May 1944 or at Carpiquet airport in Normandy a month later, to cite just two of many examples, were mounted on a familiar World War I model.

The price paid for control and order in both wars was inflexibility. One German commander observed after the Somme that ''the individual English soldier is well trained and shows personal bravery. The majority of the officers, however, are not sufficiently trained. They are lacking in ability to exploit a success and follow it up quickly.''[39] In 1944 the British Army distributed a tactical paper that suggested a remarkable continuity. ''Our own tactical methods are thorough and methodical but slow and cumbersome,'' it concluded. ''In consequence our troops fight well in defence and our set-piece attacks are usually successful, but it is not unfair to say that through lack of enterprise in exploitation we seldom reap the full benefits of them.''[40] Rather than flowing freely, battlefield movement still resembled that of a child's slinky toy, confined to lurches within the range of the artillery's 25-pounder field piece. It is ironic that an authoritarian society produced a more flexible, decentralized approach to battle than its democratic enemy, but that seems to have been the case.

Again, it is unclear whether the British/Canadian approach derived from predilections for the technological efficacy of artillery or was a pragmatic command response to uncertain soldierly behavior and morale. The latter view surfaces in records of discussions at infantry training centers, where a proper battlefield balance between fire and movement was endlessly debated. Some thought that platoons should maneuver internally with their own mutually supporting sections. Most preferred the company as the smallest practicable movement unit, and then only behind an artillery shield. Brigadier Lorn Campbell, who won his Victoria Cross in North Africa, concluded that soldiers' actual battlefield behavior dictated reliance on massive artillery support. ''One of the most surprising differences between war as it is and war as one imagined it would be is the ease with which men break and run,'' he wrote.

Few troops, the enemy's or our own, will wait till it comes to real hand-to-hand fighting. In face of a determined attack the defenders withdraw or, if the attackers are too close, surrender; quite often they withdraw in face of fire alone. The attack which meets a stubborn defence halts short of the objective or fades back to where it started.[41]

In order to compensate for the infantry's reluctance to close, Campbell advised using massive artillery supporting fire:

a barrage or a line of concentrations from overwhelming artillery, which starts at a fixed time, moves ahead of the attackers at a pre-determined rate from start line to objective. . . . All the infantry has to do then is walk steadily behind the shells, keeping as close as possible, halting for nothing and turning neither to right or left. It is the simplest way of "getting from here to there and stopping there."[42]

This was virtually the same argument cited before the Somme debacle. Unfortunately, as before, artillery fire too often moved inexorably along at its own mechanical rate while the following infantry became machine gun targets. Failure to close that intellectual and physical gap between fire support and infantry movement in turn drove down morale and induced soldiers to avoid the stress of battle. The loop connecting doctrine and behavior was all encompassing.

The link between doctrine and behavior demands further exploration because one inevitably affects the other. In the meantime, a United States Marine Corps veteran of Vietnam has described the symbiotic relationship as well as anyone. "Faulty doctrine frustrates an intelligent and otherwise capable soldier and then exposes him to enemy fire," he wrote.

The soldier then feels the lack of trust, lack of information, the betrayal of unrealistic training and the shock of fire, all competing with his desire to act with and in support of his unit. When fear wins the competition, the individual sinks into anomie and fails to participate. When courage is frustrated by the impossible situation, there can be a nervous breakdown. Physical exhaustion hastens the process.[43]

Any exploration of soldiers' reactions to battle, or more properly to combat, in Roger Spiller's fine distinction, builds naturally on his insights, along with those of John Keegan, John Ellis, Denis Winter and a few others who have looked at old facts through new glasses. Their imaginative projections of ordinary human beings reacting to the extraordinary strains of combat touch anyone who follows. Several possibilities hold promise for illuminating further the murky realities of battlefield behavior. One is following the soldier's behavioral trail backwards from the battlefield to look closely at how he was enlisted, trained and motivated to withstand the extraordinary conditions of combat. A particularly important aspect of that theme concerns the handling of reinforcements. Training a formed unit beforehand is a much more straightforward matter than sustaining it effectively once it has become actively engaged in combat.

The sources of operational doctrine, and how they may have affected battlefield behavior, also beg further exploration. Presumably an army's collective soul, its style of war, will be shaped in some fashion by its country's norms, practices and civil institutions. In the Canadian case, military doctrine which emphasized bureaucratic centralization followed naturally the style of the country's business, commercial and other civil institutions. Rigid hierarchical control, limiting flexibility and discouraging initiative, will dampen morale in the trenches or the workplace. The state of a soldier's morale will affect his responses when leaderless and directionless. Cross-disciplinary research may illustrate elusive continuities between civil and military experience.

ACKNOWLEDGMENT

The author is grateful to the editors, Jack Granatstein and Desmond Morton, and to colleagues at the Canadian Forces College, including Col. Keith Eddy, LDSH, and Lt. Col. Michael Greene, USMC, and David Buchanan, RAR, for their stimulating advice, not all of which (possibly unwisely) found a way into the text.

NOTES

1. The correspondence on this case and on self-inflicted wound handling is in National Archives of Canada (NAC), RG 24, vol. 12, 726.

2. For more detailed discussion, see Terry Copp and Bill McAndrew, *Battle Exhaustion: Soldiers and Psychiatrists in the Canadian Army, 1939–1945* (Montreal: McGill-Queen's University Press, 1990).

3. Roger Spiller, "Isen's Run: Human Dimensions of Warfare in the 20th Century," *Military Review* 68 (May 1988) p. 31. See also Roger Spiller, "The Tenth Imperative," *Military Review* 69 (April 1989), pp. 2–13.

4. Donald Pearce, *Journal of a War* (Toronto: Macmillan 1965), p. 179.

5. Roger Spiller, "Shell Shock," *American Heritage* 41 May-June 1990, p. 78.

6. Lt. Gen. Charles Foulkes to Gen. H.D.G. Crerar, 7 December 1944, NAC, Crerar Papers, vol. 7; Steve E. Dietrich, "The Professional Reading of General George S. Patton, Jr.," *Journal of Military History* 53 (October 1989): 418.

7. Norman Craig, *The Broken Plume* (London: Imperial War Museum, 1982), p. 75.

8. David L. Thompson, "With Burnside at Antietam," *Battles and Leaders of the Civil War*, vol. 2 (New York, 1887), p. 662.

9. Tony Ashworth, *Trench Warfare, 1914–1918: The Live and Let Live System* (New York: Macmillan, 1980).

10. Copp and McAndrew, *Battle Exhaustion.* See also A. M. Doyle, "The History and Development of Canadian Neuropsychiatric Service in the CMF," and J. C. Richardson, "Neuropsychiatry with the Canadian Army in Western Europe," NAC, RG 24, vols. 12630 and 12631.

11. Copp and McAndrew, *Battle Exhaustion.*

12. On discipline, see Judge Advocate General, "Record of Trials by Court Martial during the Period 1 Sep 39 to 30 Sep 46," copy in author's possession. On Italy, see the "Stats Bible" and "Liaison Letters," in War Diary, No. 2 Echelon CMF, NAC, RG 24, vol. 10410. On Northwest Europe, see vols. 10734 and 10825.

13. A. M. Doyle, "Report of Survey of Canadian Soldiers under Sentence in the CMF," NAC, RG 24, vol. 12631.

14. A. E. Moll, "Psychosomatic Disease Due to Battle Stress," in Eric D. Wittkower and R. A. Cleghorn, eds., *Recent Developments in Psychosomatic Medicine* (Montreal: J. B. Lippincott, 1953), pp. 436–54; and case reports of No. 2 Canadian Exhaustion Unit, NAC, RG 24, vol. 12559.

15. For example, see Captain C. D. Taylor, "Resume of 223 cases at No 1 Canadian General Hospital," January 1943, NAC, RG 24, vol. 2089.

16. F. M. Richardson, *Fighting Spirit: Psychological Factors in War* (London: Leo Cooper, 1978), p. 4.

17. W. R. Feasby, *Official History of the Canadian Medical Services*, vol. II (Ottawa: Queen's Printer 1953), p. 77.

18. Quoted in A. J. Glass, ed., *Neuropsychiatry in World War II*, vol. 2 (Washington, DC: 1973), pp. 103–4.

19. Canadian Army Medical Instructions, 1939, copy in Directorate of History, National Defence Headquarters, Ottawa (D Hist).

20. H. H. Hepburn to J.P.S. Cathcart, 27 November 1939, NAC, RG 24, vol. 19466.

21. H.S.M. Carver, "Personnel Selection in the Canadian Army," Directorate of Personnel Selection, 1945, D. Hist.

22. Ibid.

23. Ibid. See also H.D.G. Crerar to A.G.L. McNaughton, 24 August 1943 and 25 September 1943, NAC, RG 24, vol. 10771; B. H. McNeel, "Report of Survey of Soldiers under Sentence at the Canadian Detention Barracks, November 1943 to April 1944," NAC, RG 24, vol. 12630; C.E.G. Gould, "Observations on 1000 Referred Neuropsychiatric Cases," NAC, RG 24, vol. 2089.

24. Captain R. A. Stanley, "Why Did the Psychiatrist Turn Him Down?" *Journal of the Canadian Medical Services* 1, no. 4 (May 1944), p. 334.

25. F. Van Nostrand to Brigadier W. P. Warner, 2 November 1944, NAC, RG 24, vol. 2089.

26. Major L. R. MacDonald, "Memo to File," 11 November 1944, NAC, RG 24, vol. 12726.

27. Quoted in D Hist., AHQ Report No 63, "Manpower Problems of the Canadian Army during the Second War."

28. "State of Morale in D Company" *PPCLI*, D. Hist. 145.2P7011 (D3). See also Captain T. J. Allen, "Summary of Operations," NAC, RG 24, vol. 10881.

29. C. Vokes to GOC 5 Corps, 3 January 1944, copy in D. Hist CMHQ Report No 165.

30. "Combat Lessons, 7 Brigade," copy in author's possession.

31. The questionnaires are in NAC, RG 24, vol. 10450.

32. The United States Army had similar practices and problems, see R. L. Brownlee and W. Mullen, *Changing an Army: An Oral History of General William E. Depuy* (Washington, DC: U.S. Military History Institute and U.S. Army Center of Military History, 1988).

33. Bruce I. Gudmundsson, *Stormtroop Tactics: Innovation in the German Army, 1914–1918* (New York: Praeger, 1989).

34. Oberst Hans Von Luck to author, 18 April 1985.

35. *The War the Infantry Knew* (London: Cardinal, 1987), p. 177.

36. The best account of the evolution of artillery is Shelford Bidwell and Dominick Graham, *Fire-Power: British Army Weapons and Theories of War, 1904–1945* (London: George Allen & Unwin, 1982).

37. Henry Rawlinson, quoted in Michael Howard, "Men against Fire: The Doctrine of the Offensive in 1914," in Peter Paret, ed., *Makers of Modern Strategy* (Princeton, NJ: Princeton University Press, 1986). Tim Travers, *The Killing Ground: The British*

Army, the Western Front and the Emergence of Modern Warfare, 1900–1918 (London: Allen Unwin, 1987), pp. 144–46.

38. William Rawling, "Tactics and Technics: Technology and the Canadian Corps, 1914–18" (Ph.D. thesis, University of Toronto, 1990).

39. Quoted in Travers, *Killing Ground*, p. 152.

40. "Notes from Theatres of War, No 20, Italy, 1943–44," D. Hist 82/ 267.

41. Minutes of Training Conferences, and Campbell, "Ideas about Battle, June 1944," D. Hist 171.009 (D160). General William E. DePuy, USA, observed, in a similar vein: "Well, I certainly came away with a feeling that only a small percentage of the soldiers did almost of the fighting. If you just left them alone then some all 10 percent of the soldiers were the ones who actually took the initiative, moved, fired their rifles, threw hand grenades, and so on. . . . I learned that you couldn't depend on them doing things simply because there was a plan to do it, or because of some generalized order to do it, and this included the junior officers. You had to say, "do this," "do that," "now fire there," "now do this," and "now move there," You would always end up with a good sergeant or a good officer and three or four men doing all the work. Brownlee and Mullen, *Changing an Army*, p. 45.

42. Ibid. Canadian doctrine was unavoidably influenced by an uncritical acceptance of General Montgomery's approach to battle which, Sir Michael Howard has recently observed, was "determined by his perception of the limited capacity of the troops under his command. Montgomery was concerned to keep everything simple by the greatest possible amount of preparation before the battle as he did not expect the units under his command to take any bold initiatives. . . . He was in fact a very good First World War general, and he did not regard his troops as capable of any higher performance." Richard H. Kohn, ed., "The Scholarship on World War II: Its Present Condition and Future Possibilities," *Journal of Military History* 55 (July 1991), p. 379. General William E. De Puy, USA, has remarked that: "I really believe based on my experience, that the combat power provided by the artillery, I'm sorry to say, probably represented 90 percent or more of the combat power actually applied against the enemy. That's why I say that getting a forward observer to a high piece of ground and protecting him was the most important function that the infantry performed in that war. That's not to degrade the infantry, it's just objective analysis." Brownlee and Mullen, *Changing an Army*, p. 91.

43. Lt. Col. Michael Greene USMC, a member of the Directing Staff of the Canadian Forces Command and Staff College, to author, 16 April 1991.

5

Naval History: The State of the Art

W.A.B. DOUGLAS

History, theory, and doctrine form a triumvirate that has had varying degrees of influence, not always benign, on naval affairs. In the British and American cases, and this is probably true of most other national examples, sailors have not placed the same emphasis on history as soldiers, but they have used history to further naval aims, particularly in competition with their army and airforce counterparts.

When it has suited their purposes, naval hierarchies have put history into commission with all the flair and energy of which the seafaring profession is capable; at other times they have put it aside, like the hulks they used to keep "in ordinary" before sail gave way to steam. This has not prevented historians from plying their trade, sometimes to the discomfort of the naval profession, nor has it prevented naval professionals from consulting the history books. The waxing and waning of support for history has, however, made historical research less important to naval doctrine and policy than, for instance, technological development, and it has affected the way in which historians approach the naval past.

Naval historians are more numerous now than they were a century ago, in 1890, when Alfred Thayer Mahan published *The Influence of Sea Power upon History*. Mahan's disciples continue to preach his gospel and the most powerful navy in the world continues to frame policy according to the tenets of his theology, but heresies abound and change is in the air. That is not to say that the relationship between history, theory, and doctrine has altered, but the scope and the methods of modern historical research are different than they were when Mahan set pen to paper.

Much of Mahan's work, and that of his contemporaries, meets the most rigorous demands of modern scholarship, but much is unacceptable because it is based on either too narrow a concept, too limited a selection of documents, or too great a tendency to select evidence according to preconceived notions. The purpose of this statement is not to hold up today's naval historians and theorists as paragons of scholarly virtue, because some of them patently are not. Nor is it to claim for today's naval historians a measure of innovative ability and influence greater than their nineteenth-century predecessors, because if anything, there has been a decline, if not in ability, then in influence.[1] Mahan's biographer had something to say about this:

Fastest pen in New York was A. T. Mahan. However, he was not for hire by William Randolph Hearst and other such purveyors of the sensational "yellow" journalism that Mahan so cordially detested—not even for the dollar per word that Hearst offered him in 1898. Mahan was adaptable, but only when the price was right and the general point of view of the magazine (or its editor) was compatible with his own. Hearst's imperialistic opinions suited Mahan. It was the poor taste in Hearst's columns that turned him off.[2]

Because Mahan was eager to spread his gospel and could dictate the terms on which it was spread, he built up a powerful constituency in the reading public, a public whose members were at once militant and convinced of the moral rectitude he ascribed to them. Consequently, to quote Donald Schurman's observation, "Everybody, it seems, must make reference or obeisance to Mahan, before going on to talk of other naval historical . . . or strategic concerns. I have just done so in this paragraph!"[3]

Schurman has done more than any other historian to pull Sir Julian Corbett, that other great naval historian and theorist who came to prominence at about the turn of the century, out of Mahan's shade. Schurman, indeed, was one of the first historians to seek a connection between historiography and naval policy,[4] something that has engaged the attention of several of the most innovative people working in the field since World War II, and something that also provides a useful starting point for any discussion on the state of the art in naval history.[5]

Mahan and Corbett focused on what Corbett called the great game of war. Both understood and used power to get their message across: Corbett did so through his connections in British political and naval circles, such as Lord Esher of the Committee of Imperial Defence and Admiral Sir John Fisher; Mahan worked through a complicated network of publishers, educators, and the small number of American naval officers who were sympathetic to him. This brought him into contact with important political figures on both sides of the Atlantic Ocean, none of whom was more important than Theodore Roosevelt. Roosevelt was himself a respectable historian whose *Naval War of 1812* has stood the test of time reasonably well.[6]

Mahan, Corbett, and Roosevelt, and others like the Colomb brothers, shared a belief in what have come to be known as blue water navies: navies with sufficient ships of sufficient firepower to destroy the fleet of any opponent.[7] They also had in common the need and desire to persuade people in parliamentary democracies that strategy had pride of place over liberal ideology. Bernard Semmel, who has analyzed naval thought in terms of nineteenth-century liberalism, made the interesting point that Clausewitz did not have this problem because he wrote within the framework of a society not yet affected by the industrial and democratic (which he equates with the industrial) revolutions. "Democratic electorates," wrote Semmel, "needed to be persuaded that a war morally justified the sacrifice of its sons and the expenditure of its subsidies."[8] Consequently, Mahan and Corbett needed to illustrate and explain naval history, theory, and doctrine to a wider audience.

In other matters there was a diversity of opinion among historians, theoreticians, and practitioners of the naval art that Schurman and Semmel have documented in detail. Schurman has demonstrated that Mahan and Corbett wrote in Jominian and Clausewitzian terms respectively, and that Corbett consequently not only wrote much more convincingly about the use of navies in trade war but also had a better grasp of navies as a means of projecting power in various ways, especially through limited wars and conjoint operations. Semmel argued, not entirely convincingly, that the navalism—that is to say, the advocacy of powerful naval forces—resulting from both historians' work was reflected in the battle between historical and materiel schools in the Royal Navy (RN).[9] Reactionaries of the historical school like Admiral Sir Reginald Custance, he suggested, supported an offensive strategy with smaller rather than larger ships, with small rather than large caliber guns providing a hail of fire rather than a steady rate of long-range gunnery, thus comparing the historical school with the French army's devotion to *l'offensive à l'outrance*. History suggested to the adherents of this school that the RN had prevailed in the past by using a larger number of smaller, less capable ships aggressively and with considerable skill.[10] In opposition to this, Jackie Fisher and the materiel school advocated what Semmel described as a Corbettian defensive strategy because Britain was a 'have' power, and "it is easier to keep money in our pocket than to take it from another man's."[11]

From this summary it would appear that Corbett had more influence on naval policy. After all, the Royal Navy built big ships and trusted in materiel until well after World War I. In fact, and this I believe underscores a certain weakness in Semmel's argument, "Mahanian certitudes" (the phrase is Hervé Coutau-Bégarie's) gave more comfort than Corbettian realities to both the British and American navies after World War I. Admiral Sir Herbert Richmond, who wrote history in the Corbettian more than the Mahanian would—he developed his argument from systematic analysis of the documents rather than setting out principles and subsequently demonstrating their validity—derived his theory and doctrine accordingly.[12] He was not popular among the men who wielded power in the RN. Barry Hunt has made a persuasive case for the argument that Richmond's advocacy of a flexible naval policy between the wars, with its emphasis on maintaining firm control of trade routes (a view of naval strategy vindicated by events in World War II), had minimal effect on Admiralty decisions.[13] In the United States, as William Braisted, David Trask, and others have documented, the naval establishment rejected Admiral William S. Sims's views (which could be described as Corbettian) in favor of the conventional Mahanian outlook of Admiral William S. Benson. The result, pointed out Coutau-Bégarie, was a limited choice of policies: the fortress fleet of an isolationist America or the rigid alliance of the wartime experience.[14]

Coutau-Bégarie performed a useful breakdown of naval thought as it has developed out of the study of history into chronological and cultural fields. Chronologically, 1918–1925 was a period of uncertainty, when, as a result of wartime experience in the North Sea, the role of the decisive battle came into question. It was followed by reaction between 1925 and 1939 when the idea of the decisive battle again came back into fashion, and then what Coutau-Bégarie perceived as a decline between 1940 and the present day, when naval thought descended to a general level of mediocrity. In this last period he saw exceptions to the rule: Herbert Rosinski and Bernard Brodie during and after World War II, and later in this period, Arthur Marder, Stephen Roskill, Donald Schurman, Gerald Graham and Brian Ranft. In the 1970s there were still more signs of renewal, with Kenneth Booth (who is not a historian), Robert Seager, Philippe Masson, Clark Reynolds and Paul Kennedy. For the 1980s he named Geoffrey Till.[15] In addition to distinct periods and important writers, Coutau-Bégarie also saw naval historical writing falling into quite distinct national or cultural groupings. The cultural groupings he identified are: American, German, British, French, and secondary (among whom he included Russian, Spanish, Japanese, and Chinese).

Coutau-Bégarie constantly seeks linkages between history and theory, and his assessment reflects the perceived importance of such a linkage. The fact is, ironically, that among these groupings and periods, apart from Mahan and Corbett one finds very little attempt by historians in the twentieth century to make the leap from history to theory. The British Admiral Sir Herbert Richmond and the Dewar brothers, the French Admiral Castex, and the German Vice Admiral Wolfgang Wegener did so, but they had to contend with navies that placed limited faith in their contributions. "Of all the bodies which Richmond had hoped to influence," wrote Barry Hunt, "the Admiralty was least affected." Richmond was an embarrassment to his service, and there is much to suggest that his early retirement was the direct result of a letter he wrote to the *Times* in 1929 that challenged Admiralty policy. One correspondent to that newspaper reached "the disquieting conclusion in connection to the loss to the Service of Admiral Richmond . . . that there is room in the Royal Navy only for those who hold no views, or who are echoes of the official views, or who carefully conceal their views."[16]

Historians have found themselves unpopular with naval establishments on far more occasions than this, of course. Wegener's career in the German Navy,[17] and Mahan's in the U.S. Navy,[18] are evidence of that. Sometimes the fault lay partly with the historians themselves—both Mahan and Richmond were difficult to get along with, but the naval profession, and the naval bureaucracy, have often refused to take history seriously when it conflicted with views held by senior personnel or the aims of the administration.

Perhaps one of the least known and most revealing examples of this tension between the revelations of historical inquiry and the prevailing interests of the service is that of Corbett and the Russo-Japanese War. Donald Schurman, in his *Julian S. Corbett, 1854–1922* (a book that deserves far more exposure than it has received), made some very wise observations about this episode. The Lords of the Admiralty wanted Corbett to write a naval history of the war because they wanted to record secret information provided by Britain's Japanese allies and the navy had no professional capable of doing the work. The British Army, which shared access to the intelligence, did not want Corbett to do it because he was a civilian and his views on strategy were believed to be unsound. "Whether the army thinkers were right or wrong is a question of judgement," writes Schurman, "but that most naval officers did not really grasp the nature of the anti-army case," that good scholars can, and do, have a solid grasp of military issues, "let alone press it home politically, it clear. That Corbett was able to maintain himself at the Admiralty . . . is a minor miracle in those circumstances." Schurman went on to observe, "Like most arrangements made with men of power concerning (in their eyes) non-vital work and involving a number of people, this one was not fruitful." For security reasons, only six copies of the first volume of the so-called Japanese confidential history were issued, which made it next to useless. Corbett also had to prevent the naval officer with whom he had been discussing the draft chapters from taking precedence over his name on the title page. The second volume appeared in 400 copies, just before the beginning of the First World War. Schurman sums up the results of writing this history:

The First Sea Lord, Prince Louis of Battenburg, an intelligent man, read it before the war began, but he was soon hounded from office by the Germanophobia that occurred during Britain's entry into the war. So it lay on the shelves of the Admiralty Library unheeded and forgotten by any but [Rear Admiral Edmond J.] Slade [Director of Naval Intelligence], Corbett, Prince Louis and perhaps a few others through two world wars. Corbett, who did not need the money, was some £1000 richer, if that meant anything.[19]

What Schurman has to say about the production of the official history of the Royal Navy in World War I is an important corollary to Corbett's earlier experience.

The heartless application of bureaucratic pressure and its resultant uncertainty were nothing more than one would expect from non-intellectual men with reputations to protect, with power to wield in secret corridors, men who had an inflated idea of their own intellectual powers. That their behaviour was vulgar in its application of the history ought to surprise no one. But it is useful to let the light of day shine on such processes from time to time.[20]

Official historians of any age or any country can probably identify with this scenario, and would wholeheartedly agree to the last sentence.

It is generally accepted that the World War I experience, which was mirrored by influences on Otto Groos, the German official historian, and in the production of official histories of the armies and air forces of most of the nations involved in that conflict, led to much better terms of reference for official historians of World War II.[21] Stephen Roskill and S. E. Morison certainly had more academic freedom than Corbett or Groos, and the German World War II history now being produced by the *Militärgeschichtliches Forschungsamt* promises to be an outstanding scholarly production.

That being said, there is still much to criticize about the use of history by navies. Admirals, suggested the British historian D. W. Waters in 1984, do not, as a rule, read books.[22] Thus, it was as a prisoner of war in Italy that he set to thinking about the use of history as a naval tool and allied himself with a physicist to transform some historical truths into mathematical statements, because senior naval officers never failed to be impressed by numbers, preferably in the form of complicated equations. He produced studies of convoy that found their way into the postwar Naval Staff History (the two-volume *The Defeat of the Enemy Attack on Shipping*, of which one volume is a valuable set of tables, charts, and graphs) and a series of articles called "The Science of Admiralty" and published in the *Naval Review*. This indefatigable advocate of convoy continues to toil in his vineyard, exposing what he considers to be the fallacies of the U.S. Maritime Strategy that derive in his view, from the misreading of history.[23]

Official British and American naval histories of World War II, as a discussion of postwar developments in naval history will show, provided much of the impetus for the work of subsequent years, but it is worth noting here that the Canadian naval historian did not fare as well as his British and American counterparts. Why this occurred merits attention. The cynic might argue that British and American naval authorities had important interservice rivalries to keep up and that they had learned how to use history to support their arguments. Canada had no previous experience of such requirements, and perhaps Canadian naval professionals felt that British and American official historians could tell them all the 'lessons of the past" necessary for the understanding of modern naval strategy and tactics. It is almost certain that they considered the modest naval forces that Canada raised in World War I had done nothing worth serious attention by students of naval doctrine, and the much larger naval effort of World War II had been part of an Anglo-American undertaking. They no doubt thought that British and American interpretations of the naval war would confer universal benefit. For them, the principal purpose of an official history seems to have been to protect the service from future crippling cutbacks like those that had prevailed between the wars.

There was only one naval historian of note in Canada before World War II, Gerald Graham. The navy did not call on him to serve as official historian, possibly because the naval establishment knew nothing about him (he does not appear to have volunteered for the position). In any case, he was a man of strongly independent views, and probably would not have tolerated the establishment gladly.[24] It was Gilbert Tucker (whose area of specialization was nineteenth-century Canadian commercial history) who became the Canadian naval historian for the duration of World War II. Working with a small and widely scattered team, he produced a volume on shore activities in 1952. He did not produce a volume on Canadian naval operations.

Tucker evidently felt unable to write such a book without access to German sources, which was reason enough not to attempt a serious scholarly history,[25] but it is also evident that the Canadian naval staff was not prepared to accept the judgment of mere historians on the wartime operational activities of the Royal Canadian Navy (RCN).[26] Captain Herbert Rayner, director of operations, commented on one preliminary manuscript that it should be based purely on what the official reports of the senior officers present had said. He added: "Presumably this is supposed to be narrative and not an analysis. Therefore the author's opinions are not required." It is not surprising that the modest, rather unwell, highly professional, and totally unmilitary Tucker went along with the solution of giving the operational history to someone else.[27]

The "official account" (not "official history") of operations eventually came from the fluent pen of a wartime public relations officer, Joseph Schull. Taking its title from Mahan, *The Far Distant Ships* was a superb popular book that captured the flavor of the wartime navy but was of little use as a basis of theory or doctrine for Canadian naval purposes.[28] Without a more substantial work, Canadian naval professionals have, in fact, until recently relied almost entirely on British and American accounts for their understanding of operations between 1939 and 1945.

"If there is never a scholarly and critical history of Canadian naval operations based on all the records, including the other side's," wrote the official historian of the Canadian army, C. P. Stacey, "blame it on Brooke Claxton [minister of national defence, 1947–1954]."[29] So be it; the Minister of the Crown should take the ultimate responsibility, but it is clear that both the navy and the naval historian must also take their share. Canadian sailors acted true to form: History served their purpose of apparently consolidating the position of the RCN in the popular imagination as an object of national affection. Given the circumstances of the case, it could hardly have been otherwise, although the navy's honeymoon with the nation was to be a short one.[30] (The postscript to this episode is that Canada's minister of national defence in 1989 approved the preparation of a three-volume scholarly history of the RCN, which will provide ample data of Canadian naval experience for any reference by future naval professions. Whether it will serve ulterior motives is another question.)

Theory and doctrine tend now to be the province of strategic analysts who borrow from historians and social scientists, and who sometimes undertake historical research themselves. Recent examples include Colin S. Gray and Norman Friedman, who exerted some influence on U.S. naval doctrine under the Reagan administration.[31] Friedman, although not trained as a historian, has published a number of first-class monographs on technical matters, several with important historical evidence.[32] Whether this talent translates into a new understanding of past naval doctrine is an open question. A possibly more fruitful development is the marriage of history and tactical doctrine by a naval officer, Captain Wayne Hughes, USN, who found himself writing far more about historical examples than he had anticipated would be necessary when he began writing his book.[33]

Hughes is by no means the first to do this, but he did so at a time when tactics have become increasingly wedded to computers and simulators. In the realm of both policy and operations, therefore, fully documented historical accounts are still important—perhaps even more important than they used to be—to ensure the provision of complete and accurate information to both practical and academic users who are not necessarily trained historians themselves.

Historians, in their turn, borrow much more than they used to from other disciplines. What Maurice Matloff has called the "ecological" school offers opportunities for reexamining the past, not only in the light of new knowledge— as, for instance, the need to bring out new studies of World War II operations with reference to previously inaccessible intelligence sources and the availability of newly released German, Japanese, and now Russian material—but also in the light of new methodology. Naval history has an ever-widening base.[34]

It is important to stress that the best naval historians have always begun from very strong and broadly based foundations. Mahan and Corbett brought to their work a catholic mélange of interests. Corbett was a lawyer and novelist before he became a historian; Mahan had deep religious beliefs, about which he wrote and published extensively, and a wide acquaintance with non-naval people and affairs. Both had superbly cultivated minds, which showed in what they wrote. Similar comments can be made about Admiral Sir Herbert Richmond. What is new and different about modern practitioners of the art is their formal academic training and the nature of their specialization. Most important historical scholarship since World War II has been the product of specialists in a given field of history who have consciously developed their area of expertise to illuminate naval problems. (Captain S. W. Roskill, who was somewhat in the tradition of Richmond, is an exception that proves the rule.) Historians, in other words were going a step further than the writers who, like Mahan and Corbett, had had to cater to a much wider audience than predecessors like Clausewitz, who had written for an essentially preindustrial, frequently princely, and mostly uniformed elite. Now academics were entering the field because it was a fruitful area of historical scholarship—good fodder for theses, books, and academic promotions. It was indeed cause for some astonishment that publications focusing on military problems seemed also to appeal to a wider public.

Samuel Eliot Morison was first off the starting block, largely by virtue of self-promotion. Having taught and published in the field of maritime history, he offered himself as a candidate for official historian of U.S. naval operations during World War II, and ultimately produced a fifteen-volume history that incorporates a wealth of scholarship by a team of exceptionally well qualified researchers, an example of what the naval establishment will do when concrete benefits for both publicity and indoctrination purposes are obvious.[35] Subse-

quently, Morison's other books of maritime history also made significant contributions to naval historiography.[36]

R. G. Albion, Morison's contemporary and the official historian of U.S. naval
policy, not only made even more significant contributions to naval historiography
(his doctoral thesis, published as *Forests and Seapower*, broke entirely new
ground), but also ran into the problem of service interference.[37] The U.S. Navy
never sponsored publication of his monograph, *Makers of Naval Policy, 1798–
1947*, a somewhat critical and controversial treatment of the subject which lan-
guished in manuscript and microform for more than thirty years before Rowena
Reed edited it for publication in 1980. In spite of this, Albion remained on the
best of terms with the navy, enjoyed unusual opportunities of sailing in USN
vessels, and continued to foster naval and maritime history for the rest of his
life.

World War II sparked an interest in postgraduate work, especially under Albion
and two other influential teachers, Arthur Marder and Theodore Ropp. Marder's
six-volume history of the Royal Navy from 1880 to the end of World War I
superseded anything that had gone before; his work in the field generally opened
up a whole new range of scholarship.[38] Ropp's seminal work on the French
Navy from 1871 to 1904 (his own doctoral thesis) remained hidden in obscurity
until 1987,[39] but his seminar in military history produced a steady stream of
graduates, among whom perhaps Clark Reynolds has been the most prolific in
the naval field.[40]

On the other side of the Atlantic, new academic stimuli for naval history also
had their effect. For example, Gerald Graham and Ian Christie, both at King's
College, London, ran lively graduate seminars. Graham, a Canadian who held
the Rhodes Chair of Imperial History, had broken new ground with his studies
of trade and sea power in eighteenth-century North America. Besides publishing
widely on the navy as an instrument of imperial policy,[41] he served as adviser
to Donald Schurman, who was then working on his doctorate at Cambridge, and
to a series of his own students.[42]

Ian Christie's seminar was oriented more to administrative than imperial history, and his graduate students have produced a series of valuable eighteenth-
century studies that add a new dimension to military and naval history.[43] As in
the case of broadly based historical studies, it is important to emphasize that the
administrative history of navies is not new, but the techniques of research and
writing are. This is particularly evident if you compare the writings of Michael
Oppenheim and Sir Oswald Murray with those of Daniel Baugh and James
Pritchard.[44] The former are highly informative but based on a more limited range
of material than the latter. Daniel Baugh, for instance, read virtually all the
Captains' letters for the period, and discovered the importance of institutions
that earlier historians had ignored or taken for granted. James Pritchard has
achieved similar results by combing the French naval archives, not only in Paris
but also at Brest, Rochefort, and Toulon.

In other words, some of the trends in modern scholarship have their roots in the late nineteenth century, but today's historians are more concerned that their predecessors in the field with relating their work to the mainstream of national or thematic historiography. This is almost certainly why social and technological naval studies have been another postwar development, encouraged no doubt by increasing emphasis on these fields in the universities of Europe and North America. Among social histories, Michael Lewis has written useful books about the Royal Navy in the eighteenth and nineteenth centuries, while Nicholas Rodger published an outstanding account of the Georgian Navy. The Canadian Julian Gwyn wrote the first analysis of an eighteenth-century naval officer's prize fortune. The American writer Eugene L. Rasor has produced the best treatment of nineteenth-century reform in the Royal Navy, while Frederick Harrod has dealt with that all-too-neglected subject, the lower deck in the first half of the twentieth century. Peter Karsten has produced a scathing analysis of the U.S. naval officer corps in the nineteenth and early twentieth centuries.[45] We have yet to see comparable histories of more recent periods, but the subject cries out for attention, and it seems likely that historians will soon fill the gap.

Technological history, by contrast, is a crowded field. Theodore Ropp's study of the French Navy is a model to emulate. Under Ropp's supervision, Alex Roland produced his superb history of the submarine in the age of sail. Jon Sumida's studies of A. H. Pollen, and—as a forerunner in this aspect of naval studies—Elting Morrison on his father-in-law, William S. Sims, are among other outstanding contributions.[46]

These examples of new and important scholarship are perhaps sufficient to make the point that there is a growing body of literature that allows historians to construct, with increasing confidence, a framework for new interpretations of naval history. The best-known example is Paul Kennedy's *The Rise and Fall of British Naval Mastery* (published in 1976 and reprinted in 1982), which served as a foretaste to his even better known *The Rise and Fall of the Great Powers* (published in 1987).[47] Kennedy entered the field of naval history through his diplomatic studies of late-nineteenth-century Europe and has synthesized a huge body of literature in order to place his own work in some sort of universal context. By extending the sweep of his study over a longer period than Mahan, he felt he could obtain a more satisfactory perspective for analyzing the nature of sea power. His linkage of global economic mastery with naval mastery, and the increased importance of continental as opposed to oceanic factors as elements of international influence, led to a pessimistic assessment of Britain's position in the world, which is comparable to that of Spain in the middle of the eighteenth century. Indeed, the thesis that Britain, which was no longer a world naval power, is crippled by "strategic overextension," provided a theme for Kennedy's next major book.

Kennedy arrived at his conclusions from an examination of "the established data of the past," but there is so much going on in the field that new interpretations are turning up to question that data with greater frequency than they did when Mahan and Corbett wrote. One may doubt the conclusions of George Modelski and William Thompson, who considered sea power in terms of cyclical periods in history and arrived at a rather different view of the role of navies than did Kennedy. They seem deliberately to have rejected many of the inconstant factors historians take into account.[48] However, recent work on the eighteenth century, on the Battle of the Atlantic in the twentieth century, and many other topics, both modify existing views and show the need for more research.

The preindustrial age, about which there has been a large literature in the last twenty years, is one of considerable importance because it was a period of change on which historians are not at all agreed.[49] Clearly, during the 18th century there were major shifts in terms of how British public opinion saw the navy, how Britain came to deal with the problems of transatlantic warfare, how British and French navies learned to deal with the needs of naval construction, training, manning, and finance. On the strengths of these changes the case can be made for a military revolution in both the British and the French navies during the century leading up to the end of the Napoleonic Wars. When this is considered in tandem with the financial capabilities of Britain and France, improved naval efficiency—as much, perhaps, as the global economic dominance demonstrated by Paul Kennedy—can be said to lie behind the role of the Royal Navy in establishing, by 1815, the political domination of Britain in the Western World, whatever the reverses suffered in North America between 1765 and 1783.[50]

New research on the Battle of the Atlantic, about which there was so much certainty in the years after World War II, is turning up some interesting variations on a theme. Moreover, as the Western alliance came to see conventional weapons as a crucial part of deterrence and essential to maintaining the nuclear threshold of an east-west conflict, the importance of the Second World War experience to modern navies increased in the 1970s and 1980s. History was relevant, even if controversial. When, in 1980, Jürgen Rohwer was preparing his analysis of some convoy battles, he remarked that, with the revelation of intelligence data, it was clear that there was more significance to determining how confrontation was avoided than how it was resolved.[51] He had calculated in a 1972 study that, in the last six months of 1941, the Submarine Tracking Room of the Admiralty had saved between 1.5 and 2 million registered tons of shipping (about 300 ships) by evasive routing of convoys based on Enigma intelligence.[52] Studies of convoys in subsequent years reinforced that conclusion. As Marc Milner put it, "The principle means of *defending* shipping in the Second World War was avoidance of the enemy."[53]

The role of the air weapon in this phase of the war is still a matter of discussion. More has been claimed for the Biscay offensives than the statistics suggest should be claimed, and the role of auxiliary aircraft carriers in the RN seems to have been more diverse than intended under the Lend-Lease agreement.[54] Milner doubted that the Battle of the Atlantic had the decisive effect on the invasion of Europe that some have argued, especially those who regard Allied intelligence superiority as a war-winning asset. He argued that naval construction had outstripped sinkings before the battle reached its climax in May 1943; that the decisive defeat of the German attack on shipping that year advanced the invasion date by a month at the most. At the same time, failure to react efficiently to the U-boat could have given the Germans a decisive victory.[55]

What will come out of these debates, which lead to the necessity of still more research, is still a matter of speculation. Those who have advocated the American Maritime Strategy suggest that the antisubmarine experience of the two world wars is less instructive than the Royal Navy's late-nineteenth-century plans for naval construction. If technological considerations were all that mattered, the argument would have considerable force, but it is surely dangerous to adopt such a one-dimensional approach to the data on which naval doctrine is to be formulated. It could indeed be argued that this line of thought demonstrates what one naval officer described in a doctoral dissertation as the "Negative Influence of Mahan on the Protection of Shipping in Wartime."[56]

Whether debating the issues leads to a modification of naval doctrine by one navy or another, or whether these issues permit a successful challenge to Paul Kennedy's principal thesis, they indicate that naval history is in a healthy state of flux, constantly seeking to explain change. In a period of radical change like the present, that should interest the naval profession, and in some cases there is evidence that it does. Each year the German Navy conducts a day of historical discussion in which serving officers prepare historical studies of naval issues. Guided by professional historians and informed by participants in some of the past events they discuss, these naval professionals are forced to come to grips with historical evidence themselves. In 1990 the Canadian Navy mounted a similar exercise. At the same time the output of naval historical writing in Canada has reached unprecedented levels. One popular history of the RCN has even found its way to the best-seller list.[57] It will be instructive to see how naval people react to this unaccustomed attention and to what degree they will accept the guidance of professional historians in the use of this asset. History can serve naval ends, but not simply because it can confirm a belief or serve as a public relations device. The true litmus test is how far sailors will go to use history as one of the vital sources of knowledge from which doctrine and policy can be derived.

NOTES

1. John B. Hattendorf and Lynn C. Hattendorf, *A Bibliography of the Works of Alfred Thayer Mahan* (Newport, RI: Naval War College Press, 1986) demonstrates the enormous range of Mahan's publications.

2. Robert Seager II, *Alfred Thayer Mahan: The Man and his Letters* (Annapolis, Md: Naval Institute Press, 1977), pp. 329–30.

3. D. M. Schurman, "Historical Strategy in Large and Small Navies, in W.A.B. Douglas, ed., *The RCN in Transition, 1910–1985* (Vancouver: University of British Columbia Press, 1988), p. 51.

4. D. M. Schurman, *The Education of a Navy: The Development of British Naval Strategic Thought* (London: Cassell, 1965); D. M. Schurman, *Julian S. Corbett, 1854–*

1922: Historian of British Maritime Policy from Drake to Jellicoe (London: Royal Historical Society, 1981); D. M. Schurman, "Mahan Revisited," in *Sätryck ur Kungt Kriegsvetenkapsakademiens Bihäfte-Militärhistorisk Tidskrift 1982*, pp. 29–43. With reference to the first of these titles, the publishers insisted on the title *Education of a Navy* in preference to Schurman's suggested "The Pens behind the Fleet," which might better have described the role of history in forming strategic thought.

5. For example, Hervé Coutau-Bégarie, *La puissance maritime: Castex et la stratégie navale* ([Paris?]: Fayard, 1985); Paul Kennedy, *The Rise and Fall of British Naval Mastery* (London: Allen Lane, 1976); Carl-Axel Gemzell, *Organisation, Conflict, and Innovation: A Study of German Naval Planning, 1888–1940*, (Lindt, Sweden: Benlingska Boktryckereit, 1973); Barry Hunt, *Sailor-Scholar: Admiral Sir Herbert Richmond, 1871–1946* (Waterloo, Ontario: Wilfrid Laurier University Press, 1982); Arthur Marder, *Portrait of an Admiral: The Life and Papers of Admiral Sir Herbert Richmond* (London: Cape, 1952); Theodore Ropp, *The Development of a Modern Navy: French Naval Policy 1871–1904*, ed. Stephen S. Roberts (Annapolis, MD: U.S. Naval Institute Press, 1987); Seager, *Mahan*; Bernard Semmel, *Liberalism and Naval Strategy: Ideology, Interest and Seapower during the Pax Britannica* (London: Allen and Unwin, 1986); Herbert S. Rosinski, "German Theories of Sea Warfare," in *Brassey's Naval Annual* (1940), pp. 88–101.

6. Theodore Roosevelt, *The Naval War of 1812* (New York, 1882; Review of Reviews ed., 2 vols., New York, 1910).

7. The Colomb brothers were Vice-Admiral Philip Howard Colomb and Captain Sir John Charles Colomb.

8. Semmel, *Liberalism*, p. 11.

9. Semmel made a sharp distinction between Clausewitzian and Annihilation schools of military thought, without reference to the derivation in the German military tradition of the dogma of the battle of annihilation from a distortion of Clausewitz that masqueraded under a Clausewitzian label. Jehuda L. Wallach, "Misperceptions of Clausewitz' *On War* by the German Military" in Michael A. Handel, ed., *Clausewitz and Modern Strategy* (London: Frank Cass, 1986), pp. 213–39.

10. Mahan, putting forward the same argument in 1906, came up against Admiral William Sims, who successfully challenged the historian in the U.S. Naval Institute *Proceedings*. Seager, *Mahan*, pp. 525–33.

11. *Nineteenth Century and After* 61, no. 360 (February 1907): 202–4, cited by Semmel, *Liberalism*, p. 141.

12. See, for example, *The Navy in the War of 1739–48*, 3 vols., (Cambridge: Cambridge University Press, 1920); *The Navy in India, 1763–1783* (London: E. Benn, 1931); *Imperial Defence and Capture at Sea in War* (London: Hutchinson, 1932); *Sea Power in the Modern World* (London: Bell, 1934); and *The Naval Role in Modern Warfare*, (London, 1940).

13. Hunt, *Sailor-Scholar*, pp. 218–22, and Richmond's article cited by Hunt, "The Case against the Big Battleship," *Nineteenth Century*, CXVI, (August 1934), pp. 186–93.

14. David Trask and Mary Klashko, *Admiral William Shepherd Benson: First Chief of Naval Operations* (Annapolis, MD: Naval Institute Press, 1987); William Braisted, "On the American Red and Red-Orange Plans, 1919–1939," in Gerald Jordan, ed., *Naval Warfare in the Twentieth Century, 1900–1945: Essays in Honour of Arthur Marder* (London: Croom Helm, 1977), pp. 167–85; Ronald Spector, *Professors of War: The Naval War College and the Development of the Naval Profession* (Newport, Rhode Island:

Naval War College Press, 1977), p. 150; Michael Vlahos, *The Blue Sword: The Naval War College and the American Mission, 1919–1941*, (Newport, RI: Naval War College Press, 1980), pp. 97–130; Coutau-Bégarie, *Castex*, p. 52.

15. There are some interesting omissions in this list, as will become apparent.

16. Hunt, *Sailor-Scholar*, pp. 202, 206.

17. Vice Admiral Wolfgang Wegener, *The Naval Strategy of the World War*, trans. and with an introduction by Holger H. Herwig, Classics of Sea Power Series (Annapolis, MD: Naval Institute Press, 1989). Herwig's introduction is a brilliant summary of Wegener's career.

18. See Seager, *Mahan*, who among many other instances quoted the following from a letter Mahan wrote to a friend in 1893: "I am . . . debarred from doing what I have shown particular capacity for. It is not a pleasant feeling—especially when accompanied by the knowledge that the headstrong folly of my youth started me in a profession, which, to say the least, was not the one for which I have the best endowments" (p. 262).

19. *Corbett* pp. 131–51. The quotations are on pages 141, 142 and 144 respectively.

20. Ibid., p. 176.

21. Wegener, *Naval Strategy*, Introduction.

22. D. W. Waters, "The Science of Admiralty," parts 1–5, *Naval Review* 51 and 52 (October 1963–July 1964).

23. Those who heard D. W. Waters speak at the Naval History Symposium at Annapolis in 1989 will recall his scornful reference to modern strategic jargon:

> I must go down to the seas again, to the lonely sea and the sky,
> And all I ask is a tall 'Sea Line of Communication' and a star to steer her by.

24. Graham did serve in both the Canadian army and naval historical sections for short periods during World War II, but he appears to have produced nothing of note. C. P. Stacey, in conversations with his colleagues, used to recall his association with Graham in a markedly offhand manner.

25. C. P. Stacey, *A Date with History* (Ottawa, Deneau, 1983), p. 196.

26. W.A.B. Douglas, "Filling Gaps in the Military Past: Recent Developments in Canadian Official History," *Journal of Canadian Studies* 19, no. 3 (Autumn 1984): 112–24.

27. Ibid.

28. Joseph Schull, *The Far Distant Ships: An Official Account of Canadian Naval Operations in the Second World War*, 2nd ed., (Ottawa: King's Printer, 1961). This should not be taken as a comment on Schull's competence: He wrote several highly regarded books on Canadian history after the war. A reprint of the book was authorized in 1988. Unaccountably, Stoddart, the publishing house that undertook this reprint, used the unrevised first edition, which contains a number of errors, so that the second edition remains the most valuable.

29. Stacey, *Date with History*, p. 196.

30. In 1949 three mutinies in the RCN led to the creation of a commission of enquiry, the so-called Mainguy Commission, which revealed a number of weaknesses in the navy's personnel policies and confirmed a popular, if not necessarily accurate, stereotype of the service as a pale imitation of the Royal Navy. Rear Admiral E. R. Mainguy, RCN, L. C. Audette, and Leonard Brockington, *Report on certain Incidents which occurred on board HMC Ships ATHABASKAN, CRESCENT, and MAGNIFICENT and on other matters concerning the Royal Canadian Navy* (Ottawa: King's Printer, 1949). See also, for

example, James Eayrs, *In Defence of Canada*, vol. 3, *Peacemaking and Deterrence* (Toronto: University of Toronto Press, 1972), citing Jean François Pouliot: "Even if it is done that way in England, why should we follow that example here in Canada? . . . Is there anything more foolish than that they should wear a black tie to mourn the death of Lord Nelson?" (p. 124).

31. Colin S. Gray, *Maritime Strategy, Geopolitics, and the Defense of the West* (New York: National Strategy Information Center, 1986). See also his *Canadian Defence Priorities: A Question of Relevance*, (Toronto: Clarke, Irwin, 1977).

32. See his "U.S. Maritime Strategy," *International Defense Review* 18, no. 7 (1985): 1071–75; and for the best example of his contributions to naval history, *British Carrier Aviation: The Evolution of the Ships and Their Aircraft* (London: Conway Maritime Press, 1988).

33. Wayne P. Hughes, *Fleet Tactics: Theory and Practice* (Annapolis, MD: Naval Institute Press, 1986).

34. Maurice Matloff, "The Nature of History," in John E. Jessup and Robert W. Coakley, eds., *A Guide to the Study and Use of Military History*, (Washington: Center of Military History, U.S. Army, 1979).

35. S. E. Morison, *The Maritime History of Massachusetts, 1783–1860* (Boston: Houghton Mifflin, 1921); *Portuguese Voyages to America* (Boston: Little, Brown, 1940); and *Admiral of the Ocean Sea: A Life of Christopher Columbus* (Boston: Little, Brown, 1942).

36. S. E. Morison, *History of the U.S. Naval Operations in World War II*, 15 vols. (Washington, DC: Government Printing Office, 1947–1962); *The Ropemakers of Plymouth: A History of the Plymouth Cordage Company, 1824–1949* (Boston: Little, Brown, 1950); *Strategy and Compromise* (Boston: Little, Brown, 1958); *John Paul Jones: A Sailor's Biography* (Boston: Little, Brown, 1959); *"Old Bruin," Commodore Matthew C. Perry, 1794–1838* (Boston: Little, Brown, 1967); and *The European Discovery of America* 2 vols. (New York: Oxford University Press, 1971–1974).

37. R. G. Albion, *Forests and Seapower, the Timber Problem of the Royal Navy, 1623–1852* (Cambridge, MA: Harvard University Press, 1926); *Square Riggers on Schedule: The New York Sailing Packets to England, France and the Cotton Ports* (Princeton, NJ: Princeton University Press, 1938); *The Rise of New York Port* (Hamden, CT: Archon Books, 1939); *Sea Lanes in Wartime: The American Experience, 1775–1945*, 2d ed. (Hamden, CT: Archon, 1968); *The Development of the Naval Districts, 1903–1945* (Hamden, CT: Archon, 1945); *Seaports South of Sahara: The Achievements of an American Steamship Service* (New York: Appleton-Century Crofts, 1959); and *Makers of Naval Policy, 1798–1947* (Annapolis, MD: Naval Institute Press, 1980).

38. A. J. Marder, *The Anatomy of Sea Power: A History of British Naval Policy in the Pre-Dreadnought Era, 1880–1905* (Hamden, CT: Archon, 1940); A. J. Marder, *From the Dreadnought to Scapa Flow*, 5 vols. (London: Oxford University Press, 1961–1970); A. J. Marder, *Fear God and Dread Nought: The Correspondence of Admiral of the Fleet Lord Fisher of Kilverstone* 3 vols. (London: Cape, 1952–1959).

39. Theodore Ropp, *The Development of a Modern Navy: French Naval Policy, 1871–1904* (Annapolis, MD: Naval Institute Press, 1987).

40. For example, C. G. Reynolds, *The Fast Carriers: The Forging of an Air Navy* (Huntington, NY: Krieger, 1968); and C. G. Reynolds, *Command of the Sea* (New York: William Morrow, 1974).

41. G. S. Graham, *British Policy and Canada, 1774–1791: A Study in 18th Century*

Trade Policy (London: Longmans Green, 1930); *Sea Power and British North America, 1783–1820: A Study in British Colonial Policy* (Cambridge, MA: Harvard University Press, 1941); *Empire of the North Atlantic: The Maritime Struggle for North America* (Toronto: University of Toronto Press, 1950); *The Politics of Naval Supremacy* (Cambridge: Cambridge University Press, 1965); *Britain in the Indian Ocean: A Study of Maritime Enterprise 1810–1850* (Oxford: Clarendon Press, 1967); and *Tides of Empire* (Montreal: McGill-Queens University Press, 1972).

42. See, for example, Barry Gough, *The Royal Navy on the Northwest Coast of North America, 1810–1914* (Vancouver: University of British Columbia Press, 1971).

43. See, for example, David Syrett, *Shipping and the American War, 1775–83: A Study of British Transport Organization*, University of London Historical Series, no. 27 (London: Athlone Press, 1970); Norman Baker, *Government and Contractors: The British Treasury and War Supplies, 1775–1783*, University of London Historical Series, no. 30 (London: Athlone Press, 1971); and Richard Middleton, *The Bells of Victory* (Cambridge: Cambridge University Press, 1985).

44. Michael Oppenheim, *A History of the Administration of the Royal Navy and of Merchant Shipping in Relation to the Navy (1509–1660)* (London: J. Lane, 1896); O.A.R. Murray, ''The Admiralty,'' *Mariner's Mirror* 33–35 (1937–1939); Daniel Baugh, *British Naval Administration in the Age of Walpole* (Princeton, NJ: Princeton University Press, 1965); James Pritchard, *Louis XV's Navy, 1748–1762: A Study of Organization and Administration* (Kingston, Canada: McGill-Queens University Press, 1987).

45. Michael Lewis, *The Social History of the Royal Navy, 1793–1815* (London: Allen and Unwin, 1960); Michael Lewis, *The Navy in Transition, 1815–1864: A Social History* (London: Hodder and Stoughton, 1965); N.A.M. Rodger, *The Wooden World: An Anatomy of the Georgian Navy* (London: Collins, 1986); Julian Gwyn, *The Enterprising Admiral: The Personal Fortune of Admiral Sir Peter Warren*, (Kingston, Canada: McGill-Queen's University Press, 1974); Eugene L. Rasor, *Reform in the Royal Navy: A Social History of the Lower Deck, 1850–1880* (Hamden, CT: Archon Books, 1976); Frederick S. Harrod, *Manning the New Navy: The Development of a Modern Naval Enlisted Force, 1899–1904* (Westport, CT: Greenwood Press, 1978); Peter Karsten, *The Naval Aristocracy: The Golden Age of Annapolis and the Emergence of Modern American Navalism* (London: Collier-Macmillan and Free Press, 1972).

46. Ropp, *Development of a Modern Navy*; Alex Roland, *Underwater Warfare in the Age of Sail* (Bloomington: Indiana University Press, 1978); Jon Sumida, *In Defence of Naval Supremacy: Finance, Technology and British Naval Policy, 1889–1914* (London: Unwin Hyman, 1989); Elting Morison, *Admiral Sims and the Modern American Navy* (Boston: Houghton Mifflin, 1942). See also his *Men, Machines and Modern Times* (Cambridge, MA: Massachusetts Institute of Technology, 1966).

47. Paul M. Kennedy, *The Rise and Fall of British Naval Mastery* (London: Allen Lane, 1976, repr. 1982), and *The Rise and Fall of the Great Powers*, (New York: Random House, 1987).

48. George Modelski and William R. Thompson, *Seapower in Global Politics, 1494–1993* (Seattle: University of Washington Press, 1988).

49. Jeremy Black and Philip Woodfine, ed., *The British Navy and the Use of Naval Power in the Eighteenth Century* (Atlantic Highlands, NJ: Humanities Press International, 1989); Stephen Fisher, ed., *Studies in British Privateering, Trading Enterprise and Seamen's Welfare, 1779–1900*, Exeter Papers in Economic History no. 17 (Exeter, England: University of Exeter Press, 1987); Stephen Gradish, *The Manning of the British*

Navy during the Seven Years War (London: Royal Historical Society, 1980); H.S.K. Kent, *War and Trade in Northern Seas: Anglo-Scandinavian Economic Relations in the Mid-Eighteenth Century*, (Cambridge: Cambridge University Press, 1973); R. McNeill, *Atlantic Empires of France and Spain: Louisbourg and Havana, 1700–1763* (Chapel Hill: University of North Carolina Press, 1986); Pritchard, *Louis XV's Navy*; Rodger, *Wooden World*; Nicholas Tracy, *Navies, Deterrence and American Independence: Britain and Sea Power in the 1760's and 1770's* (Vancouver: University of British Columbia Press, 1988).

50. This accords with the finding of Geoffrey Parker, *The Military Revolution: Military Innovation and the Rise of the West, 1500–1800* (Cambridge: Cambridge University Press, 1988), that naval gunnery played an important part in the development of European society.

51. Jürgen Rohwer and W.A.B. Douglas, " 'The Most Thankless Task' Revisited: Convoys, Escorts and Radio Intelligence in the Western Atlantic, 1941–1943," in J. A. Boutilier, ed., *The RCN in Transition* (Vancouver: University of British Columbia Press, 1982), pp. 187–234.

52. Jürgen Rohwer, "Die Einfluss der allierten Funkaufklärung auf den Verlauf des Zweiten Krieges," *Vierteljahrschafte für Zeitgeschichte* 27, no. 3 (1972): 325–69.

53. Marc Milner, "The Battle of the Atlantic," *Journal of Strategic Studies* (Special Issue: *Decisive Campaigns of the Second World War*, ed. John Gooch, 13, no. 1 (March 1990): 45–66.

54. Norman Friedman, *British Carrier Aviation: The Evolution of the Ships and Their Aircraft* (London: Conway Maritime Press, 1988), p. 188; W.A.B. Douglas and David Syrett, "Die Wende in der Schlacht in Atlantik: Die Schliessung des 'Grönland-Luftloche,' 1942–43," Trans. Jürgen Rohwer, *Marine Rundschau* 83, nos. 1–3 (1986); W.A.B. Douglas, "Anti-Submarine Warfare: Operational Concepts and Missions" (Paper delivered at a conference on "The Underwater Dimensions of Maritime Strategy," Halifax, Nova Scotia, June 1989); John Terraine, *Business in Great Waters: The U-boat Wars, 1916–1945* (London: Leo Cooper, 1989).

55. Milner, "Battle of the Atlantic."

56. R. A. Bowling, Captain, USN (Retired) "The Negative Influence of Mahan on the Protection of Shipping in Wartime: The Convoy Controversy in the Twentieth Century" (Ph.D. dissertation, University of Maine, 1980).

57. Tony German, *The Sea Is at Our Gates: The History of the Canadian Navy* (Toronto: McClellan and Stewart, 1990). Since preparing this paper, *Reflections on the Royal Australian Navy* (Sydney: Kangaroo Press, 1991), the proceedings of a conference on Australian naval history, which included some British, New Zealander, and Canadian comparative contributions, indicates that other Commonwealth navies are pursuing a similar route.

6

Air War History:
The State of the Art

ROBIN HIGHAM

It is not easy to recommend professional reading to a flying officer. In the past few years some thoughtful books have appeared in the air historical field, but the most distinguished, with the exception of Mark Clodfelter's *The Limits of Airpower: The American Bombing of North Vietnam* (1989), have been concerned with the massive protracted operations of World War II, the likes of which we may never see again. At the other extreme are many readable works that have concentrated on either a single operation or memoirs that may or may not be of the line-shooting, bragging variety.

A legitimate question about the literature of air warfare is, "Why has aviation history been so slow to move from the hands of the buffs to those of the professional historian?"

The short answer is that the first serious efforts at aviation history did not sell, though they became classics; moreover, the market was too small and the subject too antiquarian.[1] In addition, there were avid readers of the memoirs and tales of the aces and the supposed glamor of air fighting above the trenches in 1914–1918, though these were largely distorted stories, as Denis Winter has shown in *The First of the Few* (1982). Moreover, except for the official histories, which dribbled out and were in some cases not finished before World War II began, the archives—the repositories of the official historical records—were closed.

What started to change all this was World War II which, in its six years, produced a great number of survivors as well as an air-conscious world based on nuclear weapons, tactical airpower, and the civil airlines. From this wartime experience came a much higher class of official works culminating in the present history of the Royal Canadian Air Force.[2] At the same time, official air historians have gradually evolved into qualified professionals, who are often active and contributing members of scholarly bodies. However, that only began in the 1960s.

Universities in the past have been extremely slow to recognize aviation history as a legitimate field for theses and dissertations, and scholars have not been anxious to enter the field. They have been intimidated by the terminology and the technology, just as politicians have been. Thus, as scholars gradually came along who were former World War II pilots, the field began to open up. *Sputnik* in 1957 provided a boost in funding in the United States, and the Society for the History of Technology began to make that general field acceptable. Abroad, thanks in part to official historical offices, young historians became more serious.

THE WRITING OF AIR WAR HISTORY

The history of air war must be seen in relation to the development of history in general in this century. Airmen started out young and cocky, believing that aviation had no history. In part this was because the air arm internationally was not only a very junior service, it also suffered a high attrition rate among its very young officer corps. Moreover, immediately after World War I, the first major air war, those airmen who remained in the air service were either generally too busy fighting for military survival (rank) or too young and disinterested— one is tempted to say, too shallow—to care much about history. Indeed, the RAF, for example, drew no lessons from World War I, and by 1933, the chief of the Air Staff could lament that there was hardly anyone left in the service who could recall the "Great War" only fifteen years earlier.[3]

The overall development of military history in the twentieth century after World War I shows a pattern in the massive British and German series of official works concentrating on campaigns and battles and characterized by a narrow view and a lack of objectivity. Moreover, as in the British work, *The War in the Air*, the outlook was almost exclusively that of one service. Although that set was finished just before World War II, the German volumes were not, and the American histories were never written. No sooner, however, had the new conflict begun than change was felt in the historical air.[4]

This was certainly true in both the British and American historical services, not to mention the German and Soviet. The British led the way with the establishment of the Cabinet Office in control and the agreement early on that most campaign histories would be written from a tri-service viewpoint with a multiplicity of final authors, as well as those who compiled the basic narratives. One result was that about a decade after the cessation of hostilities, Denis Richards and Hilary St. George Saunders followed Saunders's 1944 account of World War I on the British side with an overall popular coverage of the RAF in the 1939–1945 struggle.[5] In between this and the 1961 blockbuster *The Strategic Air Offensive against Germany* (four volumes) by Charles Webster and Noble Frankland, Squadron Leader S. C. Rexford-Welch's useful three volumes appeared (*The Royal Air Force Medical Services*), a source of much information not found elsewhere.[6] The rest of the official history of the RAF in World War II has to be dug out of the various campaign volumes and from F. H. Hinsley's multi-volume series on British intelligence, which was only published at the end of the 1970s.[7]

If this were the whole picture, the professional reader would not have such a bad time of it. However, others followed suit. The British Commonwealth air forces each wrote their own histories. The slowest to appear, but in many ways the best, is the new history of the Royal Canadian Air Force (RCAF). The Canadian team has the advantage that the archives are open, the research team is composed of professionally trained historians, and time has distanced peoples' judgments. In many ways, too, the new service histories have the advantage over individual authors not only in terms of time available and group criticism, but also in funds provided.

In a different sector of air history, privately and commercially published works have fallen into four categories over the century: memoirs, biographies, popular works, and technical histories. Memoirs have been relatively small in numbers because fliers have not been great writers. It has not been because they have not lived long nor had interesting lives. They may have had to travel light, been less inclined to be authors, and have had back luck with their agents and publishers. Many, too, have had only the instant fame of a combat report. Biographies were, until recently, equally rare, due to the scarcity of personnel papers, restrictions at the archives, and a dearth of authors with the necessary technical expertise. Popular histories have been abundant, with many simply retelling heroic incidents or battles on a predictable publishing cycle. Last, there has been the group of books that range from Bruce Robertson's *Aviation Archaeology* (1983) to life stories of particular aircraft types or even individual machines. Some are instructive on the making of technical history or on the constants and changes in tactics, but selectivity must be practiced. Aviation technology has a wondrous uplifting fascination! There *are* now a small number of scholars who specialize in the field, at the least in the West.

The history of aviation cannot really be considered without seeing it against the pattern of world events. This has served both to its advantage and to its loss. The very early days of flight, which used to be safely in the hands of the antiquarians, are being rewritten in a broader context in relation to the society that produced it. World War I and the age of the biplane (which really extended to about 1934 and which many of us thought of as an unimportant dogfighting era), has undergone a stimulating reexamination by Winter in *The First of the Few* and by Syd Wise in the first volume of the RCAF history.

However, it is the four revolutions that began in the last half century that have really made aviation history come alive. The radicalization of aviation came in the form of the technological, the electronic, the jet, and the airfield revolutions, all of which occurred between 1935 and 1945. These revolutions coincided with World War II, which was in itself a radical socializing influence. Not only did the revolutions introduce whole new methods of flying aircraft in enclosed cockpits—at night and in cloud cover on electronic instruments, eventually cruising at speeds that had been world records only twenty years earlier—but also, the war sent the new host of aircrew drawn from all social classes on sorties all over the world. Wherever their aircraft landed, they were supplied with fuel, oil, food, and the necessities of life, not to mention navigation and medical facilities.

This radicalization violently altered the problem of writing history and the output of private works as well. Instead of service on either the Western Front or in the Mediterranean as in 1914–1918, the choices could now include India, China, the Southwest Pacific, and Australia, as well as in the independent grand strategic air offensives against Germany and Japan, with perhaps a landing in the Soviet Union (and that is only the view from the Allied side).

One peculiar hazard that only airmen faced was that they might leave home and family after lunch and have supper, if any, in an enemy prison cell. Out of that shocking experience came a new facet to an old literature, the stories of prisoners of war and their attempts to escape. These inspirational works show military commitment, ingenuity, and heroism under stress in the worst possible conditions.[8] At the same time, as a result of increasingly better training in World War II, casualties amongst aircrew dropped from the roughly 50 percent in the Royal Flying Corps (RFC) in 1914–1918 to the more manageable, yet still hefty, percentages of the 1939–1945 conflict.

The significance of all this has been much larger numbers of survivors from the vastly larger air arms of World War II. However, survivors of the "Great War" who might have written their memoirs in the declining years did not outlast World War II or came to feel that what they had to say was no longer relevant. This is part of a discernible cycle in which immediately after a conflict the heroes tell their stories, followed by a lull until the group starts to have reunions around age forty. From there it rises on into retirement, when the grandfathers tell their tales for the youngest generation. Much that these veterans or ex-servicemen have to say is technically invalid in the modern world, though it is useful and revealing to historians. In terms of institutional and human tales, much can be gleaned from the perusal of their stories, whether daring-do combat line-shoots or serious recounting of the joys and perils of piloting an airliner.

The future seems (in 1990) unlikely to consist again of massive air campaigns of the World War II sort dragging out over many years, which shifts the serving officer or airman's interest to works about peacekeeping, such as Air Marshal Sir David Lee's *Never Stop the Engine When It's Hot* (1983) and General William W. Momyer's *Air Power in Three Wars* (1979). There would be less reinvention of the wheel if those involved had a knowledge of what had passed before.

Since 1945, there have been a host of small—and some limited larger—wars, all of which have involved airpower. Not all, however, have had their proper histories, nor have they been set in a wider perspective. They each provide some light on the command level, but are still properly detached and guarded. For professional reading, however, much can be said for the memoirs of Colonel Jack Broughton, *Thud Ridge* (1969); Richard S. Drury, *My Secret War* (1979); and Robert Mason, *Chickenhawk* (1983), each of which supply insights into the Vietnam War and its morale problems. At the other end of the scale, General

Ezer Weizman's *On Eagle's Wings* (1976) provides acute insights into the absolute necessity for the Israeli Air Force to be the world's best because it must win a war in a few days or never fight another one.

Air history is the study of technological services, but only recently has attention really begun to be paid to the sinews on which airpower relies. Sir Stanley Hooker's *Not Much of an Engineer* (1984) and Rosario Rausa's biography of Ed Heinemann (1980) are glimpses into the lives and minds of two of those behind the scenes, and Gerhard Neumann's autobiographical *Herman the German* provides yet a third perspective. Unfortunately, we have precious few of such works.

What is most disappointing of all is the lack of solid, single-volume studies of most of the world's air forces, the infrastructures that support them, and their relationships to the societies they guard. Much the same is, of course, true for the older services. Not untypically, we know more about past enemies than we do about ourselves and our allies. One reason for this dearth is that there are not yet the secondary works on which such single volumes can be built.

The literature of air power is in part controlled by the fact that air powers have been few. In some areas, such as in Latin America, there have been writings, but in languages not read by most Anglo-Saxon writers. They will at least have help when the forthcoming bibliography of Latin American military history by David LaFrance and Errol Jones appears. Moreover, countries producing aircraft and their ancillary equipment have been limited in number and so, unless there has been an unusual air war (such as between India and Pakistan or Britain and Argentina), the literature has largely been confined to producing powers and their exploits and activities.

The history of aircraft manufacturing is a new field, as is business history itself. Moreover, it is not easy to get access to the documents and "company records." Few writers have the skills to write a work such as Charles D. Bright's *The Jetmakers* (1978) or Emmanuel Chadeau's *Latécoère*. Hayward's *The British Aircraft Industry* (1989) provides a short overview for undergraduates but concentrates on economics and employment more than on technology. Moreover, the products of these industries have been comparable in war and peace as, in many cases, opposing organizations have operated the same types. The past and the future are both affected by the fact that English has long been the language of aviation and that countries other than the United States have insisted on multilingual education. The other trend has been a keenness for aviation translated from railway days into registration rather than number spotting. As a result, individuals such as ex-test pilot Bill Gunston have made a nice living writing popular air history. Gunston is kind enough to acknowledge that he owes a debt to the scholars who have published some of the background information he uses. He is read especially by those who find airplanes the exciting images of power that an older generation found steam engines to be. Too, aviation has been largely a middle-class enthusiasm, tolerated and sometimes abetted by families, if not always by society in general. In the so-called classless societies of nations as diverse as Australia, the United States, and the Soviet Union, aviation had a special status because it meant contact with the modern outside world.

War literature of a different sort is found in the history of airlines, for they are "at war" every day. They operate the same equipment, make long-range plans, develop strategies, observe the world, and react to crisis. Moreover, they are run by people with a mix of skills. Three recent works on diverse airlines are John Gunn, *Challenging Horizons: Qantas, 1939–1954* (1987), Philip Smith, *It Seems Like Only Yesterday: Air Canada—The First Fifty Years* (1986), and W. David Lewis and Wesley Phillips Newton, *Delta: The History of an Airline* (1979).

One of the very serious recent problems for aviation history has been the decline of journals that provide ongoing and up-to-date coverage of books in the field. *Aerospace*, published by the Royal Aeronautical Society in London, is one of the few that provides some reviews and a list of books received as well as library acquisitions. Accession lists of the Ministry of Defence Library, London, also provide monthly access to significant articles and books mainly produced in Britain or the United States. Catalogues of certain specialized bookstores and publishers are also useful.

Bibliographies help, but are rare in the field. Richard Hallion updated the USAF Office of Air Force History's work in 1984. In the same genre, but much larger are the works in the Garland series: on French aviation by the late General Charles Christienne, Patrick Facon, Patrice Buffotot, and Lee Kennett,[9] and on German aviation by Edward L. Homze.[10] The RAF is covered in Stephen Harris's chapter in *British Military History*, edited by Gerald S. Jordon (1988), while the U.S. military air services are covered in general in Robin Higham and Donald J. Mrozek, *A Guide to the Sources of U.S. Military History* (1975) and supplements (1981, 1986, and 1991). The story of the official historical offices and lists of their publications can be found in Higham's 1970 *Official Histories* (which has a supplement in process).

The air historical offices have had varied careers. The German office had not finished its history of World War I when it was diverted by the Hitler regime and overtaken by World War II, in which many records were destroyed. Like I. B. Holley's 1964 *Buying Aircraft* for the U.S. Army Air Force (USAAF), the Luftwaffe's story appeared in an army series that ran through 1944. From 1945 to 1990, the historical sections of the two Germanies produced a number of volumes on different aspects of their air history. From the East German side there was Olaf Groehler's *Geschichte des Luftkriegs* (1975), an ambitious overall look at the history of aviation, and on the West German (now the surviving historical office), Horst Boorg's *Die deutsche Luftwaffenführing, 1935–1945* (1982).

The French *Service Historique de l'Armée de l'Air* did not come into being until 1945 and, as late as 1970, was only required to collect, and not to write or disseminate information unless requested to do so by the chief of staff or theater commanders. The service was galvanized into action in the 1980s with a series of air colloquia whose proceedings are now being published (1985, 1988, 1991). Because it was the largest air service in the world in 1918, the lack of publications (except for some scattered articles in *La Revue historiques des Armées*), is much to be lamented. This is partly made up for by the superb, well-illustrated magazine *Icare*, which is published by the French Air Line Pilots' Association; it consists of special issues devoted to both military and civil subjects.

The British air effort in the twentieth century has been largely and variously covered with an abundance of works and even with collateral work in the official series. The core of this work on World War I was the official *The War in the Air* (1922–1937), which has been condensed and updated in the first volume of the RCAF series by Syd Wise. A collateral imperial piece is F. M. Cutlack's *The Australian Flying Corps in the Western and Eastern Theatres of War, 1914–1918* (1923; 1984). It is a period piece which has to be used in conjunction with the photographic and medical volumes. Cutlack's tome benefited from being part of a whole series conceived and guided by C.E.W. Bean, and the same philosophy carried over into World War II under Gavin Long, a disciple. New Zealand which, like Australia, produced separate air volumes for World War II and later conflicts, did not do so for World War I.

In the 1939–1945 conflict, both the British and the Australians early on established the concept of a series under the aegis of the highest authorities, including production, medical, and welfare volumes. What is now needed is a single tome on the Commonwealth air forces at war, including politics, grand strategy, strategy and tactics, training, and logistics.

The British studied their enemy carefully and as a result, in 1948 published *The Rise and Fall of the German Air Force* (1948; 1983). This may be contrasted with Williamson Murray's official U.S. study, *Strategy for Defeat* (1983), which was reissued privately as *Luftwaffe* (1985).

The Soviets undertook a massive study of the "Great Patriotic War of 1941–1945," of which a version appeared in English in 1973 (edited by Ray Wagner) as *The Soviet Air Force in World War II: The Official History*. This may be contrasted with Von Hardesty's 1982 *Red Phoenix: the rise of the Soviet air power, 1941–45* and Robin Higham and Jacob W. Kipp's *Soviet Aviation and Air Power* (1977). What is currently happening in Russian air historiography will be interesting to observe in the post–Cold War era.

The Japanese were also late getting into the World War II history business for a variety of reasons, though they had led in the early twentieth century with their accounts of the Russo-Japanese War of 1904–1905. Various studies of Nipponese air power in the war in China and in the Pacific have been completed which tell of both the army and navy's efforts, but so far none has been translated into English. The best available works are P. S. Dull's *Battle History of the Imperial Japanese Navy* (1978) and John B. Lundstrom's excellent *The First Team* (1984), which compares the background, training, and early operations of the Imperial Japanese Navy (IJN) and U.S. Navy (USN) aviators.

Finally, there are the official histories produced in the United States. For World War I, neither the navy, which had little flying experience, nor the army, which only collected documents, published a history. The result was that the story of the U.S. Air Service had to await James J. Hudson's *The Hostile Skies* (1968). The World War I documentation was only published by the Office of Air Force history in 1978–1979. The USN has neither published a history (only a chronology) of naval aviation nor a study of air power in World War II, the nearest being Clark Reynold's commercial work *The Fast Carriers* (1968) and Norman Friedman's design history *U.S. Aircraft-Carriers* (1983). The basic story lies entwined in Samuel Eliot Morison's fifteen-volume semi-official *United States Naval Operations in World War II* (1948–1962). Its USAAF equivalent is the seven-volume set edited by Wesley F. Craven and James L. Cate (1948–1955), while the Marine Corps has a separate book on its exploits by Robert E. Sherrod (1952; 1984). Perry McCoy Smith's *The Air Force's Plans for Peace* (1970) expressed the view that the real war was irrelevant and victory would only come when the USAAF became an independent service.

THE STATE OF THE ART

Having described the historiography of air power, what works should be recommended to the reader? One place to start is Robin Higham's *Air Power: A Concise History* (1988), which itself contains a large bibliography. Then the reader can pick among the following works presented in chronological order. Harry Combs with Martin Caidin, *Kill Devil Hill* (1978) sets the Wright brothers in a modern historical perspective. Winter's *The First of the Few* dispels the more romantic myths about World War I fighter pilots in the several air forces, while Raymond H. Fredette's *The Sky on Fire: The First Battle of Britain* (1966; 1991) and Douglas H. Robinson, *The Zeppelin in Combat* (1962) evaluate the first grand strategic air offensive and make clear the oscillation between the offense and the defense in which science and technology were matched against human understanding. For the interwar years, there is Maurer Maurer, *Aviation in the U.S. Army, 1919–1939* (1987) and DeWitt Copp's *A Few Great Captains* (1980), as well as R. F. Futrell's massive two-volume study, *Ideas, Concepts, Doctrine: Basic Thinking in the USAF, 1907–1984* (1989); David E. Omissi, *Air Power and Colonial Control: The Royal Air Force, 1919–1939* (1990); Malcolm Smith, *British Air Strategy between the Wars* (1984); and the appropriate section in Charles Christienne and Pierre Lissarague, *A History of French Aviation* (1986). The story of the USN in the interwar years needs to be updated. Some of this may be found in E. B. Potter's biography of Halsey (1985) and more in the volumes mentioned above by Reynolds and Friedman as well as in the writings of Barrett Tillman, all of which, along with Charles M. Melhorn's *Two Block Fox* (1974), give some feeling for the development of the carrier strike forces. There is little on the Soviets other than in Higham and Kipp, *Soviet Aviation*, even though they were the premier air force in the world in 1934.

Moreover, as no German air force existed legally from 1919 to 1934, the prewar story is mainly contained in the works on the 1934–1945 period, with the exception of Raymond Proctor's *Hitler's Luftwaffe in the Spanish Civil War* (1983).

Now that we are heading into a long period of peace between the major powers, it seems, nineteenth-century peacekeeping operations may well be worth reexamining with due attention to the different milieu in which they will now have to be conducted. At the very end of that period, the Italians became involved in the first air war in Libya in 1911. Furthermore, in the interwar years their exploits were legion, not only in the promotion of air power, but also in the Ethiopian War of 1935–1936, for all of which there is literature in Italian but little in English. Richard McKenna's novel *The Sand Pebbles* (1962) made some of these peacekeeping dilemmas very plain, while *Civil Wars in the Twentieth Century*, edited by Robin Higham (1972), suggests other considerations, as does Anthony Clayton in *Great Britain as a Super Power* (1988).

By the end of the interwar years, more sinister developments were taking place, even in the democratic nations. To protect the secrecy of scientific developments, long-range scientific-technological decisions affecting the ultimate fate of a country were taken by a few men around a hidden table. One such decision was described by the novelist/scientist/bureaucrat C. P. Snow in his revised *Science and Government* (1962), which tells the behind-the-scenes history of the development of radar in Britain. An overview is in R. V. Jones's *The Wizard War* (1978). A comparable postwar story is that of the Avro jet fighter cancelation in Canada told by Murray Peden in *The Fall of an Arrow* (1987). A different story that has yet to be told, is that of the Saab Viggen, which was thirty years in production in a country with a limited industry.

Equally important for the balance of views is F. J. Adkin's *From the Ground Up: A history of RAF Ground Crew* (1983) and Jerold E. Brown's *Where Eagles Land: Planning and Development of U.S. Army Airfields, 1910–1941* (1990), almost the only work on the subject. Another novelist with something to tell readers of aeronautical history is Nevil Shute (Norway) whose autobiographical *Slide Rule* (1955) and fictional *No Highway* (1948) are revealing.

A number of top airmen of World War II have written, collaborated with an author, or had their memoirs ghosted. Probably the most controversial remains Marshal of the RAF Sir Arthur Harris's *Bomber Offensive* (1947; 1990) which is now balanced with biographies by Group Captain Dudley Saward of his staff (1984) and by Charles Messenger in the same year.[11] "Hap" Arnold, the USAAF leader, ghosted his memoirs, *Global Mission* (1984), whereas the controversial General Curtis E. LeMay was the coauthor of his own *Mission with LeMay* (1965). General Ira Eaker's life was written by his longtime aide, James Parton, as *"Air Force Spoken Here"* (1986). Marshall of the RAF Lord Tedder, deputy to Gen. Dwight Eisenhower in the latter part of World War II, very much wrote his own story with prejudice (1967). The man whom Winston Churchill regarded as the best of the chiefs of staff, Air Chief Marshal Sir Charles Portal, has only a weak biography by Denis Richards (1977). Nonetheless, these lives deserve to be read by those interested in what Air Vice Marshal E. J. Kingston-McCloughry called the "direction of war" (1955). Marshal of the RAF Sir John Slessor's *The Central Blue* (1956) provides many insights into the leadership, as do the newer biographies by Vincent Orange of Air Vice Marshal Keith Park, the famed commander in the Battle of Britain (1984), and of the great tactical leader, "Maori" or "Mary" Coningham (1991). Also deserving of attention is Martha Bird's *Chennault* (1987), the story of America's maverick general in China. Parallel to that is Robert Wright's revisionist study of Lord Dowding, *The Man Who Won the Battle of Britain* (1969). That the politics of the air marshals is only now beginning to surface as history proves that there is a history of air power and that it follows the patterns in other fields. On the German side there are a number of older memoirs, of which the work by Feldmarschall Kesselring (repr. 1988) is perhaps the most important, as well as the often-reissued *The First and the Last* (1955) by the fighter general Adolf Galland. David Irving, whose specialty is German aviation, has provided biographies of Erhard Milch (*The Rise and Fall of the Luftwaffe*, 1973) and Herman Göring (1989).

The overall history of RAF operations in Europe appeared from the pen of the noted World War I author, John Terraine, in 1987 in Britain as *The Right of the Line* and in the United States as *A Time of Courage*. This revisionist account was based both on the archives and on a rereading of the Air Historical Branch's basic narratives written immediately after the war. Combined with the new RCAF volumes and with Hinsley, they all three have the advantage of being written in the post–Ultra revelations era.

For the Pacific, Gordon Prange's volumes on Pearl Harbor, *At Dawn We Slept* (1981) and *Pearl Harbor: The Verdict of History* (1986), as well as his *Midway* (1982), are supplemented by the works of H. P. Willmott on the Pacific War (*Empire in the Balance*, 1982, and *the Barrier and the Javelin*, 1983) and John B. Lundstrom's *The First Team: Pacific naval air combat from Pearl Harbor to Midway* (1984). On flying various types of World War II aircraft, read Captain Eric "Winkle" Brown's *Wings of the Navy* (1980).

The grand strategic air offensive against Germany was much more deadly than the earlier attacks on Great Britain, but nothing as effective as the Persian Gulf War of 1991. The debate over the success of the bomber campaign has been waged both between service writers and among scholars. The first bombshell came with Webster and Frankland's official history, *The Strategic Air Offensive against Germany* (1961), which revealed the ineffectiveness of much of the offensive, just a year after the appearance of Martin Caidin's glorified account, *The Night Hamburg Died*. Two decades later came Max Hasting's *Bomber Command* (1979), Martin Middlebrook's *The Berlin Raids* (1988), and John Sweetman's *Operation Chastise* (1982). For an overall look at the air war, 1939–1945, see the book of the same title by R. J. Overy (1980).

Since the British archives were opened in 1972, more authors have been venturing into the official records and have begun increasingly to be skeptical of some of the original official stories, memoirs, and standard secondary sources. In some cases, the skepticism has been well justified, while in others, new versions of history are emerging from generational change and different world perspectives. The British and Americans both produced strategic bombing surveys that are mines of information. They were supplemented by the special studies of the Luftwaffe commissioned by the USAF Historical Research Center at the Air University, Maxwell Air Force Base. To these must be added now three studies that reflect the new scholarly detachment: Lee Kennett's *A History of Strategic Bombing* (1982); Ronald Schaffer's *Wings of Judgment* (1985), on the moral dimension of bombing; and Michael Sherry, *The Rise of American Air Power: The Creation of Armageddon* (1987). The latter two books both deal with human and technical errors that are likely to be repeated unless carefully watched.

At the next lower level of operational analysis, there have been fewer studies, though the rate is increasing now that we are in the middle of the reunion movement and those who have retired have the time and inclination to write and to get their memoirs of unit histories published. Below the level of Roger Freeman's *The Mighty Eighth* (1978) have been such works as Michael J. F. Bowyer's *No. 2 Group, RAF* (1974) and Ron Yoshino's *Lightning Strikes* (1988). The magazine *After the Battle* has taken great care to get the then-and-now picture in its books on *Airfields of the Eighth* (1978), *The Battle of Britain* (1978 and later), and *The Blitz* (1987 and 1988), to which can be added Francis K. Mason's *Battle over Britain* (1969), a detailed, day-by-day operational account. Brian Johnson and Terry Heffernan, in *Boscombe Down: A Most Secret Place* (1982), provides insights into wartime testing.

On the individual level there are a host of works that can be located in the bibliographies mentioned earlier. These show that weapons may change, but the principles of war do not. Furthermore, as the rebel Squadron Leader H. R. "Dizzy" Allen showed in *Who Won the Battle of Britain?* (1974), management and training are vital. Those who were badly trained or unlucky got shot down. They then might face *The Interrogator* as depicted by Raymond Tolliver (1978).

World War II had scarcely been demobilized when peacekeeping broke out. The general account of these wars and the aircraft employed in them is in Victor Flintham, *Air Wars and Aircraft . . . 1945 to the Present* (1990). The air war over Korea has been covered by R. F. Futrell officially, and from the naval side by Admiral Malcolm W. Cagle and Frank A. Manson in *The Sea War in Korea* (1957) and, more recently, Richard Hallion in *The Naval Air War in Korea* (1987).[12] "The highly interesting limited Arab-Israeli wars have been covered by many authors, but only Stanley Ulanoff and David Eshel give an overall air perspective in *The Fighting Israeli Air Force* (1985). However, the subject is rife with the strategic and tactical implications of technological developments and their interrelationship with a grand strategy that has foresworn attacks on urban areas.

It seems strange that twenty years have passed since the end in Vietnam, yet solid overall volumes on that conflict as air operations are still lacking. We do have excellent detailed studies such as Jack S. Ballard's official *Fixed-Wing Gunships, 1962–1972* (1982), Ray L. Bowers's *Tactical Airlift* (1983), and a U.S. Marine Corps (USMC) historical Division study of USMC helicopters (1976; 1978). There is no official naval history, but there is John B. Nichols and Barrett Tillman, *On Yankee Station: The Naval Air War over Vietnam* (1987) and the Stephen Coonts novel, *The Flight of the Intruder* (1986).

The last are not strictly books about the air war, but they are provocative: Alexander Dallin, *Black Box: KAL/007 and the Superpowers* (1985), on the Soviet destruction of a Korean airliner which had strayed off the assigned route, and *Destination Disaster*, by the *Financial Times* of London (1976), on the loss of a DC–10 aircraft near Paris, and Robert W. Drewes, *The Great Engine War* (1987), on the struggle to power advanced U.S. fighters.

CONCLUSION

Published aviation history has now become respectable and a substantial number of works are being printed each year. The archives are open except for the last thirty years. It is thus now possible to judge aviation history by the regular canons of the profession. The challenge is to get historians not only to be technical experts, but to see as well the wide range of adjacent subjects that must be addressed in order to place their works on the highest possible plane, while at the same time making them readable, and thus, salable. The challenge now is to get the manufacturing companies and the airlines not only to open their archives, but also to support legitimate writers so that everyone will benefit from the still hidden truths of the past.

The story of flying and of aviation is not only exciting to read, it is also enjoyable to research and write. However, it has been plagued in the past with an overwillingness on the part of publishers to keep retailing the same old tales, glorifying incidents and heroes without telling anything new. Whether the new history is based on oral accounts by people who recall Charles Lindbergh's significant solo flight across the Atlantic or on exhuming the records, there is much exciting work to be done and read.

NOTES

1. For examples of such classics, see C. F. Snowden Gamble, *The Story of a North Sea Air Station* (London: Oxford University Press, 1929); and R. Dallas Brett, *The History of British Aviation* (London: John Hamilton, 1933).

2. To date, the first two volumes of *The Official History of the Royal Canadian Air Force* have been produced: vol. 1, S. F. Wise, *Canadian Airmen and the First World War* (Toronto: University of Toronto Press, 1980); and vol. 2, W.A.B. Douglas, *The Creation of a National Air Force* (Toronto: University of Toronto Press, 1986).

3. P.R.O./AIR 10/1524 (*S.D.80*).

4. Much of what is noted here on official military histories comes from my *Official*

Histories (Manhattan: Kansas State University Library, 1970, now from Sunflower University Press) and from materials being gathered for a successor volume.

5. Hilary St. George Saunders, *Per Ardua* (London: Oxford University Press, 1944); Hilary St. George Saunders and Denis Richards, *The Royal Air Force 1939–1945*, 3 vols. (London: HMSO, 1953–1954).

6. 4 vols. (London: HMSO, 1961), and 3 vols. (London: HMSO, 1954–1958).

7. *British Intelligence in the Second World War*, vols. 1–3 (London: Cambridge University Press and HMSO, 1979–1988).

8. For example, see Arthur A. Durand, *Stalag Luft III: The Secret Story* (Baton Rouge: Louisiana State University Press, 1988).

9. *French Military Aviation: A Bibliographical Guide* (New York: Garland, 1989).

10. *German Military Aviation: A Guide to the Literature* (New York: Garland, 1984).

11. Dudley Saward, *"Bomber" Harris* (London: Cassell, 1984); Charles Messenger, *Bomber Harris and the Strategic Bombing Offensive, 1939–1945* (London: Arms and Armour Press, 1984).

12. R. F. Futrell, *The United States Air Force in Korea, 1950–1955* (New York: Duell, Sloan and Pearce, 1961).

7

Intelligence and Military History: A British Perspective

KEITH JEFFERY

Over the past fifteen years, academic intelligence studies (and not just from a historical perspective) have proven to be a growth industry. In the mid-1970s English-language revelations about the extent of signals intelligence (SIGINT) in World War II—the so-called "Ultra" secret—showed that during the war British and American signals intelligence agencies had been breaking German and Japanese codes and ciphers with a very significant degree of success.[1] The extent to which all accounts of World War II have been affected by these revelations is still the subject of much debate, but assisted by the release of some intelligence material into the public archives, historians have begun to reevaluate the history of World War II, taking into account the sometimes central role of intelligence.[2] This development has also influenced the way historians have looked at World War I and other twentieth-century conflicts, as well as the peacetime history of international relations, where the inclusion of intelligence matters—what has been described as "the missing dimension"—can powerfully illuminate at least some aspects of diplomatic history.[3]

FACTORS INFLUENCING THE GROWTH OF INTELLIGENCE HISTORY

The first observation one must make is that "intelligence history" per se, or work on the intelligence side of military history, did not suddenly spring fully armed in 1974 from the head of Group-Captain F. W. Winterbotham. Intelligence, or to put it more prosaically, information, about the enemy has been recognized as a crucial component in military strategy and operations from earliest times as even a cursory reading of the Old Testament or Sun Tzu's *Art of War* will confirm.[4] As the British Director of Military Intelligence observed in 1921, "there can be no successful operations without sound Intelligence."[5] Nevertheless, in modern times there has been both a qualitative and a quantitative change in the treatment of intelligence matters which has been prompted by a combination of factors.

In the first place there has been a qualitative change in the nature of the intelligence function itself; it has become more salient in military affairs. This development has been especially marked in the twentieth century. The British Army and the Royal Navy did not establish permanent specialist intelligence departments until 1873 and 1883, respectively.[6] In the United States the Navy's Office of Intelligence was established in 1882 and the Military Intelligence Division of the War Department in 1885.[7] Much of the work of these departments was comparable low-grade, drawing information from various open sources, collating attaché reports, and, perhaps most important of all preparing maps. The British Secret Intelligence Service MIG (later SIS), was not established until 1909, and even then it was a tiny department and starved of resources, a condition that continued in peacetime until after World War II.

Within the army itself, "intelligence" was not very highly regarded, a point illuminated in both fact and fiction. One of Aldous Huxley's characters (the son of a Military Intelligence general) in *Point Counter Point* (1928) remarks that in the *Encyclopaedia Britannica* "intelligence" is classified under three heads: Intelligence, Human; Intelligence, Animal; and Intelligence, Military.[8] One historian of British military intelligence, himself a former director of the Intelligence Corps, actually began his account of the topic before 1914 with a curious and rather sad statement regarding the low status of his expertise:

The British Army has never liked or wanted professional intelligence officers. It has continually been held that the best man to help a commander assess the capabilities of enemy infantry is an infantryman, the best man to judge the potential threat of cavalry is a cavalryman. To have an officer devote his military career to Intelligence was, in most Generals' opinion, a short sighted policy which would lead to the officer having a specialized and narrow outlook to problems which require a wide and practical background of military experience.[9]

Referring to the interwar period, the official historian of British intelligence during World War II, Sir Harry Hinsley, has also remarked on the fact that, with some notable exceptions, "the higher ranks of the armed forces showed some antipathy to the intelligence authorities, or at least a lack of interest in their work." These sentiments, moreover, produced a vicious circle in which

on the one hand, intelligence work was thought of as a professional backwater, suitable only for officers with a knowledge of foreign languages and for those not wanted for command. On the other hand, the activities of the many men of average or less than average professional competence who were thus detailed for intelligence confirmed the low estimate that had already been made of the value of intelligence work.[10]

Ralph Bennett who, like Hinsley, worked at Bletchley Park (the British SIGINT Center) during the war, has bluntly confirmed this conclusion. "Prominent among the shortcomings of the British Army in 1939," he wrote, "was its almost complete disregard of the value of intelligence, apart from the merely tactical information derivable from patrolling a static front line, and the consequent almost complete lack of intelligence officers in its ranks."[11]

Although no doubt, vestiges of this kind of attitude remain within the armed forces, the experiences of World War II, and subsequent conflicts, has clearly enhanced the contribution that a properly organized intelligence service can make to successful military operations. The improved status of intelligence was expressed in the British Army by the establishment of a regular Intelligence Corps in 1957. In the United States Army it was marked by the formation of a consolidated U.S. Army Intelligence Corps in 1961, and in the following year, the creation of an Army Intelligence and Security Branch in the regular army.[12]

The emergence of permanent specialized military intelligence formations reflects both the increasing demands placed on intelligence units and also the increasing capabilities of these units. In the former case it is clear that in peacetime, the intelligence function is boosted when any state perceives a serious military challenge. Thus, the expansion of the British intelligence community— military and diplomatic—in the years immediately before 1914 occurred at a time of rising Great Power rivalry, especially the challenge from Germany. After 1918, military intelligence establishments were rapidly reduced or disbanded. However, this pattern was not repeated after 1945, when the challenge of the Soviet Union and the Cold War clearly contributed to the retention of both civilian and military intelligence services in peacetime. Nevertheless, the increasingly specialized and technically sophisticated nature of military intelligence itself was, if anything, an even more powerful stimulus. The experience of both world wars clearly indicated the problems that accompanied the ad hoc establishment of intelligence agencies after war had broken out. For military intelligence, each war seemed to involve "reinventing the wheel," whether in terms of establishing networks of agents, processing and interrogating prisoners of war, collecting SIGINT, organizing photographic intelligence (PHOTINT), or in drawing up reliable intelligence assessments based on all these different sources.

To a very great extent, technological change has produced a need for specialized military intelligence units. The best illustration of this perhaps lies in the field of signals technology, where twentieth-century technical developments have stimulated what John Ferris described as a "revolution in the art of war." The "rise of radio," he wrote, has led to "a new system of relationships . . . between command, control, communications, signals intelligence and signals security."[13] Moreover, the demands of military intelligence in attempting to intercept or even just monitor enemy communications and counter intelligence (particularly signals security) required the help of specialists. The specialist agencies that emerged have, in turn, become objects of legitimate historical concern, both in themselves and regarding their influence on military decision making.

The second factor concerning the writings of intelligence history is the availability of evidence. Secret intelligence is a subject of such sensitivity that governments are prepared to go to extraordinary, and even absurd, lengths to prevent disclosures from occurring (as illustrated by the *Spycatcher* affair).[14] While military intelligence has not itself suffered quite the same degree of obsessive official secrecy, some aspects of its workings, particularly details about the sources and methods of acquiring intelligence, have remained classified. A further problem lies in the extent to which military intelligence, secret intelligence organizations, and covert operations agencies—about which governments are also often understandably reticent—overlap. In these circumstances the simplest line for a government to take is to deny all access to intelligence records and also to impose a vow of silence on present and former intelligence officers. Historically this was the attitude adopted by the British government and maintained, with only a few exceptions, until the mid–1970s.[15]

The story of how the signals intelligence side of World War II was progressively revealed is comparatively familiar. The publication in 1974 of Winterbotham's *The Ultra Secret* marked, in the words of one commentator, "the major turning-point in our understanding of the nature of the secret war."[16] However, it also signified an important shift in British official attitudes to the discussion of intelligence matters, at least from a historical point of view. Although Winterbotham was by no means the first person to reveal the "Ultra Secret," his book, which had been officially sanctioned, was the first work in the English language solely devoted to the subject.[17] Winterbotham, having broken the vow of silence imposed on everyone associated with Bletchley Park and the wartime code-breaking effort, was followed into print by others with specialist wartime intelligence knowledge, initially in reviews of *The Ultra Secret* and subsequently in books and articles of their own.[18]

On its own most of this memoir material was only of limited use to the academic historian; its importance lay simply in the fact that the "secret" was out. However, at about the same time the government reviewed its public records policy and began to release World War II intelligence–related archives. At the end of 1975 Naval Operational Intelligence Centre records, including Admiralty Ultra intercepts, began to arrive at the Public Record Office.[19] It was not until the autumn of 1977, however, that the first batch of the main body of Ultra material was released.[20] The government also commissioned an official history of the influence of British intelligence on strategy and operations during World War II, of which the first volume was published in 1979 and the fifth (and last) in 1990.[21] That the government still regarded the subject matter as sensitive is demonstrated by the delay in publishing the final two volumes of the official history. Although the texts of both were completed in 1980, they were not released to the public for ten years. The authors of the official history, led by Sir Harry Hinsley, were granted unrestricted access to the archives of the whole British intelligence community, including material that is never likely to be released to the public domain, notably the "domestic files of the intelligence-collecting bodies'' and papers not yet released, including various categories of high-grade decrypts.[22]

From the mid-1970s on the British government also began to open World War I intelligence files. Some papers relating to Room 40, the Admiralty code-breaking operation, were opened in 1976, and since 1980 a very substantial additional quantity of naval intelligence files has been released.[23] Much British intelligence material, however, remains closed. Although a considerable number of papers from the service intelligence branches is available, as already noted, the internal files of the secret intelligence agencies are closed and the British government continues to take a very restrictive line on any intelligence material generated in peacetime, whether before 1914, between 1918 and 1939, or after 1945.[24] Outside the public archives, intelligence documents have also survived in private collections that have escaped the attentions of the official weeders.[25]

In the United States, also from about the mid-1970s on, there was an expansion of intelligence studies and a release of documents into the National Archives.[26] Although the Ultra revelations undoubtedly stimulated American historical interest, the growth of scholarly concern in this area owed much to political worries (arising from the Vietnam War and the Watergate affair) about the growth of an apparently unaccountable intelligence community.[27] The resulting literature, in contrast to the historical focus of the so-called British school has been characterized by a political science approach and a concentration on contemporary intelligence matters.[28] The Freedom of Information Act and large-scale departmental declassification programs, which reflect a much more permissive attitude towards official records than that in the United Kingdom, provided the means whereby intelligence-related public archives could be opened.[29] British schools, too, have taken advantage of this legislation to secure in the United States records that are still unavailable in the United Kingdom.[30] The relaxation of official attitudes towards intelligence matters has also permitted the release of in-house studies, such as Bruce W. Bidwell's account of the Military Intelligence Division and Arthur Darling's history of the first five years of the Central Intelligence Agency (CIA).[31] By the early 1980s, therefore, the combination of memoirs, the availability of some documents in public archives, and official histories of various sorts had begun to provide a reasonable resource base for intelligence history.

The third factor is one of technical ignorance. In the absence of much reliable information about the organization of the intelligence community, departmental working methods, or intelligence-gathering techniques, the people best qualified to write intelligence history were those with some intelligence experience themselves. Until Winterbotham broke ranks, however, in Britain these people were unlikely to do anything of the sort. Nevertheless, since the mid-1970s some of the very best work has been written by scholars with inside experience. However, the opening up of the ''missing dimension'' and the cumulative impact of veterans' reminiscences, together with pioneering studies such as Christopher Andrew's *Secret Service*, have provided lay historians with the tools necessary not merely to research intelligence history but even to recognize the existence of a secret intelligence dimension at all.

A good example of this lies in the field of signals intelligence. In correspondence between Field Marshal Sir Henry Wilson, then chief of the Imperial General Staff, and his deputy, Sir Philip Chetwode, during 1921 there are references to information derived from the Director of Military Intelligence (DMI) *particulars* and from BJs.[32] Both these terms actually refer to signals intercepts, a fact that may not always be apparent from the context. *BJ* is short for *Black Jumbo*, which was, literally, a nonsense term for intercepts, coined in India and adopted for security reasons. The usage was confirmed, and apparently became quite widespread in the Foreign Office after 1929, when a new filing system was introduced which placed intercepts into blue folders. *BJ* henceforth came to be understood as meaning *Blue Jacket*.[33] This sort of information may seem trivial in itself, but it can help the historian understand the documentary sources (where reference to intelligence material are rarely themselves *en clair*) and to build up a picture of the range of intelligence available at any one time so that we can begin to estimate its contributions to the decision-making process.

Much of the scholarly work on intelligence that was written in the late 1970s and early 1980s is understandably narrative and descriptive. Indeed, the first priority for students of this hitherto obscure topic was simply to establish the historical framework of intelligence work. Only then could properly analytical studies be attempted. However, the emergence of a substantial volume of academic periodical literature in the second half of the 1980s illustrates how quickly the subject has advanced. The journal *Intelligence and National Security* published its first issue at the beginning of 1986. In this issue, the editors felt it necessary to stress that the journal's subject matter was "a proper field for scholarly research." Although the "past history of intelligence work" was only a part of the journal's original scope, in practice, more space has been devoted to historical articles than any other type.[34] Perhaps a more conclusive indicator of the rise of intelligence history has been the acceptance of articles by mainstream historical journals. Under the editorship of Christopher Andrew the *Historical Journal* published articles on the topic starting in the late 1970s.[35] In the mid–1980s when the editors of the *Journal of Contemporary History* conducted a trawl for a special issue on intelligence, the result was so successful that they devoted two issues to the topic.[36] Finally, in 1986, even the very traditional *English Historical Review* published an article on intelligence.[37]

CURRENT DEVELOPMENTS IN MILITARY HISTORY

The greatest volume of recent work investigating intelligence and military operations has been devoted to World War II.[38] Sir Harry Hinsley perceptively observed that the British gained intelligence from four sources:

1. physical contact in the form of captured documents, the censorship of mail, and the interrogation of prisoners;

2. espionage;

3. aerial reconnaissance, particularly aerial photographic reconnaissance (PR); and

4. signals intelligence

However, the lion's share of this work has been devoted solely to the last of these, and especially to Ultra. Of course, Hinsley himself affirmed that the general superiority of British intelligence during the conflict stemmed from SIGINT successes, which also enabled it to maximize the efficiency of the other intelligence sources.[39]

As noted earlier, the extent to which the history of World War II needs to be reassessed in the light of what is now known about intelligence is still a debatable question. In terms of general accounts, it is interesting to compare the two editions of one of the best single-volume treatments: *Total War* by Peter Calvocoressi and Guy Wint (with John Pritchard for the second edition).[40] Calvocoressi himself had worked at Bletchley Park and so was well informed about Ultra; indeed, he wrote a short book on the subject in 1980.[41] However, when he was writing the original edition of *Total War*, which was published in 1972, his requests to be allowed to mention Ultra were rebuffed. As a result, he wrote his history "in the full knowledge of certain things which I might neither mention nor explain."[42] This led him into making the occasional firm but unilluminated statement. Referring, for example, to General Bernard Montgomery's advantageous position in North Africa in the autumn of 1942, he simply remarked, "Last but not least,' British Intelligence was giving British field commanders unparalleled assistance."[43] (In the second edition, published in 1989, "British Intelligence" has been altered to "Ultra.")[44] Calvocoressi's account of the Battle of the Atlantic in the first edition is similarly discreet. He refers to signals intelligence twice: the first time to say that the Germans were able to read British naval ciphers up to mid–1943 and the second to observe mysteriously that at about the same time, "there was also a dramatic and decisive turn in the war of codes and ciphers."[45] In the later edition the role of Ultra is specifically covered.[46]

The addition of Ultra material to Calvocoressi's book, however, did not dramatically change his account of the conflict; the Germans still lost the war. However, it explains that outcome more completely. Intelligence itself did not win the war and, as F. H. Hinsley has observed, even the number of operations "on which intelligence exercised an absolutely decisive effect . . . was by no means as large as is widely believed." However, the intelligence advantage held by the Allies certainly shortened the war. Hinsley has hazarded some calculations suggesting that without it, the conflict would have been prolonged by at least three years.[47]

Hinsley's own official history is now an essential part of the literature on World War II. The work, however, is predominantly an account of strategic policy and the impact of intelligence in Whitehall. Although the series is subtitled "Its Impact on Strategy and Operations," the authors did not attempt to estimate the extent to which "intelligence influenced the individual decisions of the operational commands." Apart from indicating what intelligence commands had at their disposal, Hinsley and his colleagues deliberately left this matter to the attention of other scholars.[48] Had the Ultra secret been revealed in time, this aspect might have been addressed in other parts of the official war history series. As it was, intelligence matters were either passed over in silence or falsified, as by Stephen Roskill in *The War at Sea* (1954). Roskill was well aware of Ultra's role yet, like Calvocoressi, he was unable to refer to it. In his first volume, for example, he stressed the importance of "wireless intelligence" against U-boats but asserted that it was used only for direction finding.[49] The final three parts of the land operations series dealing with the Mediterranean and Middle East were published in the 1980s, but they study the role of intelligence only at field level where, for security reasons, the role of Ultra was necessarily limited. Otherwise, the reader is referred to Hinsley's volumes for material on intelligence.[50]

As has already been noted, some of the very best work on the influence of signals intelligence has been produced by former SIGINT specialists themselves. On the military side, Ralph Bennett is preeminent in the field. Bennett combines his experience from Bletchley Park, working with Germany Army Ultra, with a professional training as a medieval historian. This is not at all an unsuitable preparation for the student of twentieth-century British intelligence which, like the medieval world, is frequently characterized by a lack of documentary sources. Bennett's books and articles are models of lucid historical scholarship and are properly supported by full source references, an especially important feature in as difficult a subject as intelligence history.[51] One of Bennett's main concerns is the actual impact of Ultra on military operations, a theme examined in a usefully comparative context by Harold Deutsch. In contrast to some of the wilder claims made for SIGINT in World War II, Deutsch concluded that much precious Ultra material was ignored by British and American commanding generals.[52] The interest that the "Ultra secret" has stimulated in signals intelligence generally has begun to have an impact in studies of SIGINT at a lower level, especially regarding field intelligence. Mesmerized, perhaps, by the astounding successes achieved against the German Enigma machines, historians have not always recognized the very considerable achievements of other Allied (and, indeed, enemy) SIGINT formations. However, the very first issue of *Intelligence and National Security* contained a memoir by Christopher Morris who had worked at Bletchley Park on German naval hand ciphers.[53] The following year the journal published a similar piece by Noel Currer-Briggs, who had worked on German military, Schutzstaffel and police hand ciphers both at Bletchley Park and in the Mediterranean.[54] More recently a very comprehensive, though very poorly referenced, account of the *Y Service*—the military units that actually intercepted enemy signals—has been published.[55] John Ferris, one of the leading scholars specializing in the more technical aspects of signals intelligence, has published two admirable articles on the subject: one deals with signals and security in North Africa in 1940–1942, while the other is a ground-breaking examination of British cipher security from 1906 to 1946.[56] The relative lack of information we have on British aspects of signals security prompts the general reflection that in intelligence history we usually know more about intelligence failures than successes. While the Ultra story is one of Allied intelligence success, it is also that of a catastrophic German intelligence failure, and the reason we know more about Enigma than "Type-X," the equivalent British cipher machine, is precisely because the latter was more successful than the former.

In a review of historical research on the British intelligence community published in 1988, Christopher Andrew identified World War I as "perhaps the most fruitful field at present for detailed research on the operational role of British intelligence in the twentieth century . . . principally because official censorship is less rigid for wartime than for peacetime records."[57] However, the existing literature on World War I also illustrates one of the points already made about the historically low status of intelligence. Despite the fact that Sir James Edmonds himself worked in military intelligence before 1914 (though he proved to be a notably gullible counterintelligence officer), the British official histories of military operations in France and Belgium, which he compiled, provide no *specific* treatment of intelligence.[58] By contrast, the subject is covered, though not extensively, in some of the "sideshow" volumes.[59]

Serious work on World War I intelligence dates from about the mid–1980s. In 1984 David French published an article on the intelligence service of the British Expeditionary Force in 1914–1915.[60] Christopher Andrew's *Secret Service*, of which a substantial portion deals with the "Great War" period, came out the following year. One of the many merits of this book is that, despite the tremendous wealth of very good stories, it succeeds admirably in demythologizing the history of intelligence. During World War I, *Humint* (human intelligence), far from being the preserve of glamorous secret agents of the Bulldog Drummond type, was more the realm of the French and Belgian train watchers whose monotonous and painstaking work behind German lines produced much valuable information. The successes of Room 40 in decrypting German diplomatic cables, such as the Zimmerman telegram, were already well known,[61] but the indefatigable John Ferris has also revealed the great significance of army signals intelligence in the field.[62] His planned volume for the Army Records Society on the topic will constitute an important documentary source. Unexpectedly, intelligence in the Middle Eastern campaigns has attracted more scholarly attention than the Western Front, with two studies of Mesopotamia in 1914–1916 and one about Allenby in Palestine in 1917–1918.[63]

However, work on World War I intelligence is also subject to sensationalization. It is a pity that while useful, sober, and well-researched work is being produced, scholars can still be tempted to sensationalize their books, presumably encouraged by publishers questing after station (or airport) bookstall sales. An example of this is Michael Occleshaw's *Armour against Fate*, published in 1989, with the subtitle *British Military Intelligence in the First World War and the Secret Rescue from Russia of the Grand Duchess Tatiana*. At the core of this book is an industriously informative account of British military intelligence that is based on Occleshaw's doctoral dissertation.[64] While uncovering much interesting information in the official archives, Occleshaw has also depended quite heavily on a handful of private papers, including those of Richard Meinertzhagen whose diaries form a valuable source for military intelligence work in East Africa and the Middle East. They also, however, are the basis for Occleshaw's sensational narrative of an improbable attempt to rescue the Russian imperial family from Ekaterinburg in the summer of 1918. The story ("A Riddle No More") is presented as "a fine example of the courage and ingenuity of the officers of British Military Intelligence."[65] It also, sadly, demonstrates that even a volume with copious footnotes and source references can give intelligence history a bad name.

A final sphere of military intelligence activity concerns the counterinsurgency operations.[66]

Charles Townshend's definitive work on the British campaign in Ireland in 1919–1921,[67] which provides a limited amount of information about intelligence, has been excellently supplemented by Eunan O'Halpin.[68] Although the intelligence aspects of other interwar colonial campaigns await examination, the postwar conflicts are quite well covered. David Charters's monograph on Palestine in 1945–1947 is very informative on intelligence matters,[69] as is Anthony Short's monograph on Malaya, which was commissioned as an official history (though later repudiated by the Malayan government). Supposedly, Short was given "full access" to secret records.[70] Of more recent conflicts, Randall Heather has written an account of intelligence during the Mau Mau emergency in Kenya in the 1950s,[71] and an American anthropologist, Dale F. Eickelman, has produced an intensely interesting study of intelligence in Oman, where British military intelligence officers played a major role in counterinsurgency campaigning during the late 1950s and 1960s.[72] There is scope for further work on Cyprus, Borneo, and South Arabia, as the records become available. As the Northern Ireland conflict is ongoing, there is little "hard" documentary evidence available, and thus, the few existing scholarly accounts tend to be incomplete.[73] Nonetheless, as Stuart Farson has pointed out, these and other works on the British counterinsurgency experience are valuable for the light they shed on relations between the intelligence services and the military and police intelligence branches.[74]

It is clear that over the past fifteen years, much very good work on military intelligence has been published that has altered and deepened our understanding of the influence of intelligence on military decision-making. However, there are dangers that an exclusive concentration on "intelligence" can distort the historical picture and that "born-again" intelligence historians might themselves fall under the spell of the subject matter in precisely the same way as the popular authors they so like to ridicule. Perhaps by concentrating on specialist intelligence work, this essay may have done the subject a disservice, for the real impact of the "intelligence revolution" will not necessarily be in specialist texts, but in general accounts. If there has been such a revolution, it should mean that no general military history, and certainly no treatment of military operations, can now ignore the intelligence dimension. However, I am not actually sure that this is yet the case.

NOTES

1. The publication of F. W. Winterbotham's *The Ultra Secret* (New York: Harper and Row, 1974) is usually taken as the starting point of these revelations.

2. See, for example, Ronald Lewin, *Ultra Goes to War* (New York: McGraw-Hill, 1978); and Jurgen Rohwer, "The Operational Use of ULTRA in the Battle of the Atlantic," in Christopher Andrew and Jeremy Noakes, eds., *Intelligence and International Relations 1900–1945* (Exeter, UK: University of Exeter, 1987), pp. 275–92.

3. The phrase "the missing dimension" was coined by Sir Alexander Cadogan. See editorial introduction, p. 1, in Christopher Andrew and David Dilks, eds., *The Missing Dimension: Governments and Intelligence Communities in the 20th Century* (London: Macmillan, 1984).

4. See, for example, the epigraphs by Sun Tzu quoted in Michael I. Handel, ed., *Intelligence and Military Operations* (special issue of *Intelligence and National Security*, henceforwards *INS*) 5, no. 2 (April 1990).

5. Quoted in W.R.V. Isaac, "A History of the Development of the Directorate of Military Intelligence in the War Office, 1855–1939" (1957: typescript preserved in Ministry of Defence Whitehall Library), p. 1.

6. Christopher Andrew, *Secret Service: The Making of the British Intelligence Community* (London: Heinemann, 1985), pp. 11, 13.

7. Bruce W. Bidwell, *History of the Military Intelligence Division, Department of the Army General Staff: 1775–1941* (Frederick, MD: University Publications of America, 1986), p. 51.

8. Huxley was almost correct. The actual categories in the encyclopaedia were "Intelligence, or Understanding"; "Intelligence, Military"; and 'Intelligence in Animals."

9. B.A.H. Parritt, *The Intelligencers: The History of British Military Intelligence up to 1914*, 2d ed. (Ashford, Kent, UK: Intelligence Corps Association, 1983), p. 1.

10. F. H. Hinsley et al., *British Intelligence in the Second World War*, vol. 1 (London: HMSO, 1979), p. 10.

11. Ralph Bennett, "Intelligence and Strategy: Some Observations on the War in the Mediterranean, 1941–45," *INS* 5, no. 2 (April 1990): 450.

12. The Army Intelligence and Security Branch was redesignated the Military Intelligence Branch in 1967. John Patrick Finnegan, *Military Intelligence: A Picture History* (Arlington, VA: U.S. Army Intelligence and Security Command, 1985), p. 144.

13. John Ferris, "The British Army, Signals and Security in the Desert Campaign, 1940–42," *INS* 5, no. 2 (April 1990): 256.

14. The British government tried and failed—after a lengthy and embarrassing court battle—to prevent former MI5 Officer Peter Wright from publishing his memoir *Spy-*

catcher (Toronto: Stoddart, 1987). After all the fuss and publicity, Wright's revelations proved to be quite modest.

15. For example, a retired head of MI5 published his (anodyne) memoirs: Sir Percy Sillitoe, *Cloak without Dagger* (London: Cassell, 1955).

16. David Syrett, "The Secret War and the Historians," *Armed Forces and Society* 9, no. 2 (Winter 1983): 298.

17. Jean Stengers noted seven (albeit relatively minor) English-language leaks concerning the secret before 1974, as well as Gustave Bertrand, *Enigma ou la plus grande enigme de la guerre 1939–1945* (Paris: Plore, 1973). Jean Stengers, "Enigma, the French, the Poles and the British, 1931–1940," in Andrew and Dilks, *Missing Dimension*, pp. 127, 133, 272 n. 48.

18. For example, Peter Calvocoressi, David Hunt, Hugh Trevor-Roper, and Ralph Bennett. For details, see Syrett, "Secret War."

19. These are filed in class ADM 233. See Patrick Beesly, *Very Special Intelligence: The Story of the Admiralty's Operational Intelligence Centre, 1939–1945* (London: Hamish Hamilton, 1977), p. 261.

20. These are filed in class DEFE 3. See Ralph Bennett, *Ultra in the West: The Normandy Campaign of 1944–45* (London: Hutchinson, 1979), p. 248.

21. F. H. Hinsley et al., *British Intelligence in the Second World War*, vols. 1–3: *Its Influence on Strategy and Operations* (1979–88); vol. 4: *Security and Counter-Intelligence* (1990); vol. 5 (by Michael Howard): *Strategic Deception* (1990).

22. Hinsley, *British Intelligence*, vol. 1, pp. vii–viii.

23. Patrick Beesly, *Room 40: British Naval Intelligence 1914–1918* (Oxford: Oxford University Press, 1984), p. 321.

24. For the service intelligence branches, some historians particularly recommend the AIR files in the Public Record Office on the grounds that the departmental weeders, acutely conscious of the Air Ministry and RAF's lack of history, have taken very little out of the archive before releasing it.

25. Such collections include the Lloyd George Papers (House of Lords Record Office), the Curzon Papers (India Office Records), and various collections at the Churchill College Cambridge Archives Centre, including the Hall, Denniston, Clarke, and Christie papers.

26. See Edward J. Drea, "Ultra and the American War against Japan: A note on sources," *INS* 3, no. 1 (January 1988): 195–204.

27. See, for example, Victor Marchetti and John D. Marks, *The CIA and the Cult of Intelligence* (New York: Dell, 1974); and Loch K. Johnson, *America's Secret Power: The CIA in a Democratic Society* (Oxford: Oxford University Press, 1989).

28. Identified by D. Cameron Watt, "Intelligence Studies: The Emergence of the British School," *INS* 3, no. 2 (April 1988): 338–41.

29. Private commercial efforts include the Declassified Document Reference System and the National Security Archive, which in 1990 produced a large microfiche collection on the U.S. Intelligence Community, 1947–1989.

30. Some examples are given in Christopher Andrew, "Historical Research on the British Intelligence Community," in Roy Godson, ed., *Comparing Foreign Intelligence: The U.S., the USSR, the U.K. and the Third World* (London: Pergamon-Brassey's, 1988), pp. 50–51, nn. 17–19.

31. Bidwell's study was completed in 1954 and published in 1986; see note 5 above; see also Arthur B. Darling, *The Central Intelligence Agency: An Instrument of Government to 1950* (University Park, PA: Penn State University Press, 1990).

32. See the letters in the Wilson Papers (Imperial War Museum), HHW 2/58A/9, 23, 39, 53.

33. Andrew, *Secret Service*, p. 352.

34. The other aims of the journal regarding intelligence work were "the analysis of its contemporary functions and problems, and . . . the assessment of its influence on foreign policy and national security" (*INS* 1, no. 1 [January 1986]: iii).

35. Including his own pioneering "The British Secret Service and Anglo-Soviet Relations in the 1920s. Part I," *Historical Journal* 20, no. 3 (September 1977): 673–706.

36. "Intelligence Services during the Second World War," parts 1 and 2, *Journal of Contemporary History* 22, nos. 2 and 4 (April and October 1987).

37. Nicholas Hiley, "Counter-Espionage and Security in Great Britain during the First World War," *English Historical Review* 101, no. 3 (1986): 635–70.

38. The following remarks are supplementary to the bibliographical essays by David Syrett (note 13 above); Stuart Farson, "Schools of Thought: National Perceptions of Intelligence," *Conflict Quarterly* 9, no. 2 (Spring 1989): 52–104; and Wesley Wark, "Intelligence Since 1900" in Gerald Jordan, ed., *British Military History: Supplement to Robin Higham's Guide* (New York: Garland, 1988), pp. 501–23.

39. F. H. Hinsley, "British Intelligence in the Second World War," in Christopher Andrew and Jeremy Noakes, eds., *Intelligence and International Relations 1900–1945* (Exeter, UK: Exeter University Press, 1987), pp. 209–10.

40. Peter Calvocoressi and Guy Wint, *Total War* (Harmondsworth, UK: Penguin Books, 1974); Peter Calvocoressi, Guy Wint, and John Pritchard, *Total War*, 2nd ed., 2 vols. (Harmondsworth, UK: Penguin Books, 1989).

41. Peter Calvocoressi, *Top Secret Ultra* (London: 1980).

42. 2nd ed., vol. 1, p. xvii.

43. 1st ed., p. 362.

44. 2nd ed., vol. 1, p. 382.

45. 1st ed., pp. 444, 447.

46. 2nd ed., vol. 1, p. 468. Other general accounts of World War II issued to capitalize on the fiftieth anniversary of its outbreak have covered Ultra, for example, Martin Gilbert, *Second World War* (London: Weidenfeld and Nicolson, 1989); R.A.C. Parker, *Struggle for Survival: The History of the Second World War* (Oxford: Oxford University Press, 1989); and Philip Warner, *World War II: The Untold Story* (London: Bodley Head, 1988), a popular work with an inaccurate title that describes itself as "the first history since the publication of the Official History of Intelligence." Another "market-led" volume with a specific intelligence chapter is John Campbell, ed., *The Experience of World War II* (London: Harrap, 1989).

47. Hinsley, "British Intelligence," pp. 215, 218.

48. Hinsley, et al., *British Intelligence*, vol. 1, p. x.

49. *War at Sea*, vol. 1 (London: HMSO, 1954), pp. 356, 469.

50. See, for example, C.J.C. Molony, *The Mediterranean and Middle East*, vol. 6, part 1 (London: HMSO, 1984), p. ix.

51. Apart from the works cited at notes 11 and 20 above, Bennett published "Intelligence and Strategy in World War II" in K. G. Robertson, ed., *British and American Approaches to Intelligence* (London: Macmillan, 1987), pp. 130–52; "Army Ultra in the Mediterranean Theatre: Darkness and Light," in Andrew and Noakes, *Intelligence and International Relations*, pp. 235–52; "Knight's Move at Drvar: Ultra and the Attempt on Tito's Life, 25 May 1944," *Journal of Contemporary History* 22, no. 2 (April 1987):

195–208; and "Fortitude, Ultra and the 'Need to Know'," *INS* 4, no. 3 (July 1989): 482–502.

52. Harold C. Deutsch, "Commanding Generals and the Uses of Intelligence," *INS* 2, no. 2 (April 1987): 274–90.

53. Christopher Morris, "Ultra's Poor Relations," *INS* 1, no. 1 (January 1986): 111–22.

54. Noel Currer-Briggs, "Some of Ultra's Poor Relations in Algeria, Tunisia, Sicily and Italy," *INS* 2, no. 2 (April 1987): 274–90.

55. Hugh Skillen, *Spies of the Airwaves* (Pinner, Middlesex, UK: Published by the author, 1989). One index of the increasing sophistication of the literature is the degree to which we are no longer prepared to treat unsourced accounts as very valuable.

56. John Ferris, "The British Army, Signals and Security," *INS* 5, no. 2 (April 1990); and "The British 'Enigma': Britain, Signals Security and Cipher Machines, 1906–46," *Defence Analysis* 3, no. 2 (May 1987): 153–163.

57. Andrew, "Historical Research," p. 53.

58. See Andrew, *Secret Service*, pp. 45, 49–57.

59. For example, the volumes on Macedonia, Egypt, and Palestine.

60. David French, "Sir John French's Secret Service on the Western Front, 1914–15," *Journal of Strategic Studies* 7, no. 4 (December 1984): 423–40.

61. See, for example, Beesly, *Room 40*, pp. 204–24.

62. "The British Army and Signals Intelligence in the Field during the First World War," *INS* 3, no. 4 (October 1988): 23–48.

63. Peter Morris, "Intelligence and Its Interpretation: Mesopotamia 1914–1916," in Andrew and Noakes, eds., *Intelligence and International Relations*, pp. 77–102; and Richard Popplewell, "British Intelligence in Mesopotamia, 1914–16," *INS* 5, no. 2 (April 1990): 139–72; Yigal Sheffy, "Institutionalized Deception and Perception Reinforcement: Allenby's Campaigns in Palestine, 1917–18," *INS* 5, no. 2 (April 1990): 173–236.

64. "British Military Intelligence during the First World War," (Ph.D. dissertation, University of Keele, Staffs, U.K., 1984).

65. *Armour against Fate* (London: Columbus Books, 1989), p. 287. For a more convincingly critical view of Meinertzhagen, see Mark Cocker, *Richard Meinertzhagen: Soldier, Scientist and Spy* (London: Secker, 1989).

66. There is outline coverage of this topic in Charles Townshend, *Britain's Civil Wars* (London: Faber and Faber, 1986); and Keith Jeffery, "Intelligence and Counter-Insurgency Operations: Some Reflections on the British Experience," *INS* 2, no. 1 (January 1987): 118–49. See also Thomas R. Mockaitis, *British Counterinsurgency, 1919–1960* (London: Macmillan, 1990); and David A. Charters, "From Palestine to Northern Ireland: British Adaptation to Low Intensity Operations," in David A. Charters and Maurice Tugwell, eds., *Armies in Low-Intensity Conflict: A Comparative Analysis* (London: Brasseys, 1989), especially the section on intelligence, pp. 215–23.

67. *The British Campaign in Ireland* (London: Oxford University Press, 1975).

68. "British Intelligence in Ireland, 1914–21," in Andrew and Dilks, *Missing Dimension*, pp. 69–77. There is also some material on the subject in Keith Jeffery, "British Military Intelligence following the First World War," in Robertson, *British and American Approaches*, pp. 55–84.

69. David A. Charters, *The British Army and Jewish Insurgency in Palestine, 1945–47* (London: Macmillan, 1989). He treated intelligence in a more thorough and detailed

manner in "British Intelligence in the Palestine Campaign," *INS* 6, no. 1 (1991): 115–40.

70. *The Communist Insurrection in Malaya, 1948–60* (London: Muller, 1975). I understand that a revised edition is in preparation.

71. Randall W. Heather, "Intelligence and Counter-Insurgency in Kenya, 1952–56," *INS* 5, no. 3 (July 1990): 57–83.

72. "Intelligence in an Arab Gulf state," in Godson, *Comparing Foreign Intelligence*, pp. 89–114.

73. Keith Maguire, "The Intelligence War in Northern Ireland," *International Journal of Intelligence and Counter Intelligence* 4, no. 2 (1991): 145–65; see also the remarks in Keith Jeffery, "Security Policy in Northern Ireland: Some Reflections on the Management of Violent Conflict," *Terrorism and Political Violence* 2, no. 1 (Spring 1990): 21–34.

74. Stuart Farson, "Schools of Thought: National Perceptions of Intelligence," *Conflict Quarterly* 9, no. 2 (Spring 1989): 62–64.

8

Low-Intensity Conflict: Its Place in the Study of War

IAN BECKETT

In 1896 one of the adherents of what has been characterized as the "British Imperial" school of military thought, T. Miller Maguire, commented thus on what he regarded as the obsession of a rival "continentalist" school:

While looking at the stars, we may tumble in a ditch, and while lost in wonder at how to move effectively from Strasbourg, Mayence and Metz towards Paris with many divisions of cavalry and armies consisting each of from three to eight corps, we may forget how to handle a few battalions in the passes of the Suleiman Range or in the deserts of Upper Egypt.[1]

In many respects that conveys the essence of the problem of the status of low-intensity conflict in the study of warfare. While low-intensity conflict has most frequently been the actual practical soldiering experience of Western soldiers in the nineteenth and twentieth centuries, it is the dream of what French soldiers knew as *la grande guerre* that has commanded the attention of theorists and of historians in turn. There are, therefore, two aspects to the question of the status of low-intensity conflict: the place that it has enjoyed in the study of war and the place that, it might be argued, it actually should enjoy.

To consider first the place that low-intensity conflict can be said to have occupied hitherto in the study of war and the reasons for it, a good starting point may be the two editions of the well-known *Makers of Modern Strategy*. The first, edited by Edward Mead Earle in 1943, comprised 547 pages of main text and had twenty separate chapters on the development of military theory from Niccolò Machiavelli to Adolf Hitler. Just one chapter of 25 pages—that by Jean Gottman on the French Marshals Thomas A. Bugeaud, Joseph Simon Gallieni and Louis H. G. Lyautey—could be said to be directly concerned with any form of low-intensity conflict.[2] The second edition, which was edited by Peter Paret in 1986, specifically claimed to take a "broader view" than the original; its 871 pages of main text now had two out of twenty-eight chapters devoted to matters of relevance to low-intensity conflict. The chapter on Bugeaud, Gallieni, and Lyautey was completely rewritten by Douglas Porch and expanded to 31 pages. An entirely new chapter of 47 pages on revolutionary war was contributed by John Shy and T. W. Collier, on the grounds that what had "not existed" in 1943 had become a significant, though conceivably short-lived, factor through the decline of European colonial power and of war between nation states. However, while Porch rightly pointed to the general neglect of colonial warfare, no other chapters were devoted to non-French theorists, although Russell Weigley's chapter on "American Strategy" had approximately 1 page out of 35 on low-intensity experience in the nineteenth and twentieth centuries. Similarly, Shy and Collier devoted only three paragraphs (embracing a brief reference to Charles Callwell) to what they referred to as the colonial response to insurgency; four paragraphs to the French concept of *guerre revolutionnaire*; one uninformative paragraph on the British experience, which failed to mention either Sir Robert Thompson or Frank Kitson; and five paragraphs to American counterinsurgency efforts, the whole amounting to just approximately six pages. The bibliographical note accompanying the chapter, then had a seemingly disparaging reference to Roger Trinquier and Thompson as "experts" on counterinsurgency.[3]

It would appear, therefore, that little has changed over forty-three years in the perception of low-intensity warfare as a legitimate subject for study. Most other standard histories of warfare or of military thought are equally dismissive of the claims for inclusion of colonial warfare and its theorists prior to 1945 and of the experience and exponents of counterinsurgency since. No reference at all will be found in the first four editions of *Men in Arms* by Preston, Wise, and Werner; or in such works as *The Conduct of War* by J.F.C. Fuller, *War in the Modern World* by Theodore Ropp, or *War in European History*, by Michael Howard. By contrast, the 723 pages of *The Art of War in the Western World* by Archer Jones has a number of references to "means of defence and offence" against guerrillas under the general heading of "raiding strategy," but these include Romans, Byzantines, and Vikings. Only some two pages are devoted to nineteenth-century colonial warfare, with Bugeaud the only real exponent of low-intensity warfare given adequate coverage.[4]

Even those general works specifically devoted to modern warfare since 1945, while invariably covering theorists of revolutionary and guerrilla warfare, barely mention theorists of low-intensity warfare or counterinsurgency. Among such works could be numbered those by successive professors of war studies at King's College, London; *Arms and Strategy* by Laurence Martin with 2 pages out of 313 on counterinsurgency; and *Atlas of Global Strategy* by Lawrence Freedman, which has three references in 187 pages. The standard student text, *Contemporary Strategy* by Baylis, Booth, Garnett, and Williams, had 19 pages in 312 devoted to revolutionary warfare in its original 1975 edition, including approximately 2 1/2 pages on counterinsurgency. The much extended two-volume edition in 1987 was not much better at 23 pages on revolutionary warfare out of 518 (of larger print) with the section on counterinsurgency extended to some 4 pages, principally by a discussion of the Soviet intervention in Afghanistan. The West Point Military History series, which presumably reflects what is taught at the United States Military Academy, has but one of its ten current volumes on post–1945 conflict: *Selected Readings in Warfare since 1945*. Its case studies are the Arab-Israeli, Korean, and Chinese civil wars, of which only the last could be described as low-intensity. However, a Vietnam volume is apparently under preparation.[5]

There are, of course, some exceptions. Perhaps surprisingly, as long ago as 1961, *The Art of War* by Cyril Falls had an eleven-page chapter on "small wars" which actually mentioned Callwell, but also concluded that those that the author chose to describe as "partisans" had exerted less influence on history than is "commonly asserted." More recently, Hew Strachan's *European Armies and the Conduct of War* devoted a full chapter to colonial warfare in its survey of the development of warfare between 1700 and 1945, though one owing much to Callwell. The essays by diverse hands in *Warfare in the Twentieth Century: Theory and Practice*, edited by Colin McInnes and Gary Sheffield, also include both one on colonial warfare between 1900 and 1939 and another on insurgency and counterinsurgency since 1945.[6] Nonetheless, there is little doubt that attention is not customarily given to low-intensity conflict in most studies of warfare.

The reason for this, as indicated by my opening remarks, is, of course, that armies perceive themselves to exist primarily to wage conventional war, whatever their actual experience. The United States Army affords a particularly good example. Between 1866 and 1890, American soldiers fought over 1,000 separate engagements with hostile Indians, but there was a continuing tendency to regard the army's only fixed mission of policing the moving frontier as an irrelevance, with each campaign a tiresome distraction from the study of "real war" in Europe.[7] In fact, the army fought the Indians as if they were conventional opponents. Despite, or rather because of, the frustrating experience of countering insurgency in the Philippines between 1900 and 1902, the army was evidently relieved to be able to turn to the study of the more professionally rewarding fields of St. Mihiel and the Argonne after the "Great War." Less than 1 percent of successive editions of field service regulations in the 1940s dealt with counter-guerrilla operations. The army's special forces had to struggle for recognition within the military establishment long after their creation in the 1950s. Similarly, the United States Marine Corps, which had gained considerable experience of low-intensity conflict in the interwar period, resulting in the production of the *Small Wars Manual* of 1935, had become so immersed in its World War II amphibious role that the manual apparently had been totally forgotten by 1960. Marine performance in counterinsurgency was arguably superior to that of the army in Vietnam, but the Marines also conducted at least sixty amphibious beach assaults, in the hope that the enemy would oblige by opposing them.[8]

Indeed, as has been shown by the fine studies of American low-intensity doctrine by such scholars as Douglas Blaufarb, Larry Cable, Andrew Krepinevich, and D. M. Shafer, the thrust behind the new counterinsurgency doctrine of the early 1960s was from civilians such as Walt Rostow and Roger Hilsman and especially from John F. Kennedy as president.[9] Presidential identification of communist-inspired insurgency as the predominant threat to the interests of the United States was not shared by an army, as Cable puts it, "configured, equipped and trained according to a doctrine suitable for conventional warfare, or for warfare in the nuclear battlefield of Europe." As Krepinevich argued equally persuasively, that doctrine—the "army concept"—was that of Bradley's 12th Army Group and the road from St. Lo to the Elbe. Thus, institutional resistance to counterinsurgency was pronounced, and if there was one quotation to be graven on the heart of the American military after Vietnam, it was perhaps that celebrated remark by a general officer: "I'll be damned if I permit the United States Army, its institutions, its doctrine and its traditions, to be destroyed just to win this lousy war."[10]

In the immediate aftermath of Vietnam there were still those such as Harry Summers who were prepared to argue that there had been too much rather than too little emphasis on counterinsurgency. Moreover, while American military interest in low-intensity conflict revived in the mid- to late 1980s, there was clearly still significant resistance to the concept as a whole, and distaste for counterinsurgency (or foreign internal defense, as it now appears to be called) in particular.[11] Indeed, Rod Paschall's *LIC 2010* has recently suggested that, in the future, the counterinsurgency role could even be contracted out to commercial security organizations, so destructive is it of what he regards as military "norms."[12]

It is not, however, just a matter of institutional conservatism and a preconceived notion of the nature of "real" war, which Victor Davis Hanson, for one, would date back to classical Greece. Low-intensity conflict is no shortcut to the triumphant ride through Persepolis. In reality, it is distinctly unglamorous. Results will not be obtained quickly and, in any case, success cannot often be measured in conventional military terms of decisive battles won. Careers may not be enhanced even by such success as can be demonstrated. Above all, what General John Galvin has called "uncomfortable wars" confront soldiers with both political and societal pressures to a far greater extent than most other forms of conflict.[13]

While the American military has so far been singled out in this chapter, such considerations apply equally to other forces. Indeed, in the case of both the French and the British armies, which tended to take low-intensity conflict seriously in the nineteenth century and at least for the first half of the twentieth, there was always something of a division. In the case of the French army, of course, it was the supposed influence of "Africans" unfamiliar with European conditions that was blamed for defeat against the supreme continentalists of the Prussian and other German armies in 1870. In fact, the French high command contained fewer soldiers with colonial experience in 1870 than in either the Crimean or the Franco-Austrian wars, when it might be argued that they had succeeded. For all its wide colonial experience, the French Army still clung to the vision, in the words of Paddy Griffith, of "the golden days of Austerlitz and the Boulogne camp."[14]

Much British military thought in the nineteenth century was merely a slavish imitation of the continental, and of Jominian theory in particular. While imperial requirements were a dominating factor at all stages of the army's development, it was only in the 1880s that what Peter Burroughs has described as a "compelling doctrine" of the imperial role was fully articulated by those associated with the "Wolseley ring," such as Henry Brackenbury and Frederick Maurice, who now rejected a reliance on Prussian or other continental theory.[15] Since the army fought no less than seventy-four campaigns during Victoria's reign, of which only the Crimea and the first phase of the South African War could be regarded as major conventional conflicts, this was only a recognition of reality. Indeed, with the possible exception of the early pioneers of armored warfare such as Fuller, it could be argued that the concept of small wars that emerged from the late Victorian army is the only truly distinctive contribution of the British to military theory. There is a clear line of succession that can be traced from Callwell's *Small Wars* through Sir Charles Gwynn's *Imperial Policing* in 1934 and H. J. Simson's *British Rule, and Rebellion* in 1937 and then to Thompson and Kitson after World War II even if, in practice, experience was transmitted informally and not as an officially established doctrine.[16]

Nonetheless, the exponents of small wars were not without their critics in the late Victorian army, as that rejoinder of Maguire's quoted at the very beginning of this chapter indicates. One long serving lecturer at the Staff College, Colonel Lonsdale Hale, dismissed small wars as "the play of children" in 1876. Fuller and others were equally critical of what they regarded as the failure of the army to learn from the "Great War." Particular scorn has often been reserved for that celebrated declaration by the chief of the Imperial General Staff in 1926, Sir George Milne, that the Great War had been "abnormal" although, in fact, the apocryphal "real soldiering" on the frontiers of empire to which regulars were supposedly eager to return in 1918 did actually represent the collective experience of the interwar army.[17]

Low-intensity conflict of one form or another has been no less the principal fare of the British Army since 1945. One calculation is that only fourteen out of ninety-four separate operational commitments between 1945 and 1982 were not in the form of low-intensity conflict. The only significant conventional experience comprised thirty-five months of British participation in the Korean War involving only sixteen battalions, of which no more than five were present at any one time, ten days at Suez in 1956 and twenty-five days of the land campaign in the Falklands in 1982. Since then, of course, there has been 100 hours of land operations in the Persian Gulf. However, there is an element of truth in J. Bowyer Bell's otherwise unconvincing analysis of British experience when he argues that the British were almost always taken by surprise by the outbreak of each successive emergency, and much more in David Charters's perceptive critique of the absence of an institutional memory, since echoed by Tom Mock-aitis's fine account of the army's "historical amnesia."[18]

In many respects, the latter problem has been addressed in recent years, but the new doctrinal emphasis is slanted heavily toward conventional operations. Richard Clutterbuck, of course, has pointed to the penchant for "nostalgic" World War II–style large-scale sweeps during the Malayan Emergency, and it is significant that the new "core campaign" to be studied by all officers at various points in their professional careers is Northwest Europe in 1944–1945. At the Royal Military Academy, Sandhurst counterinsurgency accounts for just two academic periods in fifteen on the Standard Graduate Course, two in twenty-eight on the Standard Military Course, and two in seventy on the Junior Command and Staff Course. The first publication to emerge in 1989 from studies undertaken on the new Higher Command and Staff Course at the Staff College concerned the "operational level of war" in possible future operations in Europe.[19]

It can be seen, therefore, that even in those armies that have enjoyed arguably the most success in low-intensity warfare, the lure of "real" war still holds sway. It is small wonder that low-intensity conflict figures so little in accounts of the development of the art of war. However, turning to the place that it should occupy in the study of war, it is important to emphasize that the experience of the major Western armies in the nineteenth and twentieth centuries was over-whelmingly in low-intensity conflict. All commentators, whether they are kindly disposed toward this form of military activity or otherwise, not only acknowledge that it has been the most prevalent form of conflict in the modern world, but also that it will continue to be so for the foreseeable future. In that regard, Milne was quite correct: for all their profound impact on global development, the two total wars of the twentieth century are wholly abnormal in the context of the overall pattern of military activity over the last two centuries.

Given that "real" war is something few soldiers will actually experience in the modern world, then the inclusion of low-intensity conflict within the full pantheon of military studies is profoundly necessary. It is not just Bugeaud, Gallieni, and Lyautey who would then be studied but other Frenchmen, such as Suchet and Roguet; Englishmen like Callwell and Gwynn; Americans like Harold Utley; Soviets such as Soviet Marshal Mikhail Tukhachevsky, who is now only generally regarded as a theorist of armored warfare; and all the other neglected theorists of counterinsurgency as well. Then, too, proper recognition could be afforded Henrique de Paiva Couceiro, the Portuguese soldier who has been compared to Gallieni and Lyautey; to Captain K. van der Maaten, whose two-volume study of counterinsurgency in the Dutch East Indies, published in 1896, has been compared with that of Callwell in the same year; or even to the Spanish nobleman the Marques de Santa Cruz, whom Christopher Duffy has characterized as having put into effect in the early eighteenth century the kind of theories advanced by Thompson, Kitson, and Roger Trinquier in the twentieth.[20] More-over, the crucial role of air policing in the colonies in the development of strategic bombing theory might also be more widely recognized. *Makers of Modern*

Strategy devoted a single paragraph to the subject, which is now attracting considerable scholarly interest.[21]

Fortunately, scholars are devoting greater attention to low-intensity warfare in general, and to counterinsurgency in particular. There are increasing numbers of individual campaign studies and syntheses of at least twentieth-century military experience as well as a growing number of academic journals.[22] Military doctrine may be a lost cause; Larry Cable perceptively remarked that its creation "is an exercise in highly selective historical interpretation." However, bearing in mind John F. Kennedy's declaration in National Security Action Memorandum (NSAM) 124 of 18 January 1962 "that subversive insurgency . . . is a major form of politico-military conflict equal in importance to conventional warfare," historians themselves should be capable of persuading their peers of the importance of low-intensity conflict in the study of war.[23] Perhaps a third edition of *Makers of Modern Strategy* in another forty years would then be rather different, and the confines of Miller Maguire's starlit ditch no longer such a temptation, even to soldiers.

NOTES

1. Quoted in Howard Bailes, "Patterns of Thought in the Late Victorian Army," *Journal of Strategic Studies* 4 (1981): 31.

2. Jean Gottman, "Bugeaud, Gallieni, Lyautey: The Development of French Colonial Warfare," in E. M. Earle, ed., *Makers of Modern Strategy* (Princeton, NJ: Princeton University Press, 1943), pp. 234–59.

3. Douglas Porch, "Bugeaud, Gallieni, Lyautey: The Development of French Colonial Warfare," in Peter Paret, ed., *Makers of Modern Strategy from Machiavelli to the Nuclear Age* (Princeton, NJ: Princeton University Press, 1986), pp. 376–407; John Shy and T. W. Collier, "Revolutionary War," in Paret, *Makers of Modern Strategy*, pp. 815–62, 931–32.

4. R. A. Preston, S. F. Wise, and H. Warner, *Men in Arms* (London: Atlantic Press, 1956); J.F.C. Fuller, *The Conduct of War*, 2d ed., (London: Methuen, 1972); T. Ropp, *War in the Modern World* (New York: Collier, 1973); Michael Howard, *War in European History* (Oxford: Oxford University Press, 1976); Archer Jones, *The Art of War in the Western World* (London: Harrap, 1988). The fifth edition of *Men in Arms*, edited by Preston, Wise, and Alex Roland (1991) includes one chapter (out of twenty-two) and 32 pages of text (out of 392) on low-intensity conflict. It shares some of the flaws of the chapter by Shy and Collier in Paret's *Makers of Modern Strategy*. It is almost devoid of historical context, most of the chapter being devoted to relatively recent events. The British experience in Malaya and elsewhere is not mentioned. Curiously, the Algerian war, Vietnam, and Afghanistan (which gets only one paragraph) are discussed in the previous chapter on *conventional war*. Bibliographic references under "The World since 1945" include none of the standard, classic works on insurgency or counterinsurgency (except for Mao Tse-tung) and only one (a chronology) on terrorism.

5. L. Martin, *Arms and Strategy* (London: Weidenfeld and Nicolson, 1973); L. Freedman *Atlas of Global Strategy* (London: Macmillan, 1985); J. Baylis, K. Booth, J. Garnett, and P. Williams, *Contemporary Strategy* (London: Croom Helm, 1975; 1987);

T. E. Griess, ed., *The West Point Military History Series* (Wayne, NJ: Avery Publishing, 1984–).

6. C. Falls, *The Art of War* (Oxford: Oxford University Press, 1961), p. 95; Hew Strachan, *European Armies and the Conduct of War* (London: Allen and Unwin, 1983), pp. 76–89; Keith Jeffery, "Colonial Warfare, 1900–1939," in Colin McInnes and G. D. Sheffield, eds., *Warfare in the Twentieth Century* (London: Unwin Hyman, 1988), pp. 24–50; Ian F. W. Beckett, "Guerrilla Warfare: Insurgency and Counterinsurgency since 1945," in McInnes and Sheffield, *Warfare in the Twentieth Century*, pp. 194–212.

7. R. M. Utley, *Frontier Regulars*, (2nd ed., (Bloomington, Ind.: Indiana University Press, 1977), pp. 44–58, 410; R. M. Utley, "The Contribution of the Frontier to the American Military Tradition," in J. P. Tate, ed., *The American Military on the Frontier* (Washington, D.C.: Office of Air Force History, 1978), pp. 3–24; J. M. Gates, "Indians and Insurrections," *Parameters* 13, no. 1 (1983): 59–68.

8. R. Paschall, "LIC Doctrine: Who Needs It?" *Parameters* 15, no. 3 (1985): 33–45; R. Schaffer, "The 1940 Small Wars Manual and the Lessons of History," *Military Affairs* 35 (1972): 46–51; Paddy Griffith, *Forward into Battle*, 2nd ed., (Swindon, UK: Crowood, 1990), p. 8.

9. D. S. Blaufarb, *The Counterinsurgency Era* (New York: Free Press, 1977); L. E. Cable, *Conflict of Myths* (New York: New York University Press, 1986); A. F. Krepinevich, *The Army and Vietnam* (Baltimore, MD: Johns Hopkins University Press, 1986); D. M. Shafer, *Deadly Paradigms* (Leicester, UK: Leicester University Press, 1990).

10. Cable, *Conflict of Myths*, p. 282; Krepinevich, *Army and Vietnam*, p. xi; Brian Jenkins, *The Unchangeable War* (Santa Monica, CA: RAND Corporation, 1972), p. 3. The quote may be found in Ward Just, *Military Men* (New York: Avon, 1970), p. 189.

11. Harry Summers, *On Strategy* (Novato, CA: Presidio Press, 1983), pp. 71–80. For opposing views on the desirability of the new interest in low-intensity conflict, compare the generally hostile essays in M. T. Klare and P. Kornbluh, eds., *Low Intensity Warfare* (New York: Pantheon, 1988) with the sympathetic contributions to Max Manwaring, ed., *Uncomfortable Wars* (Boulder, CO: Westview, 1991).

12. R. Paschall, *LIC 2010* (New York: Brassey's, 1990), p. 125–26.

13. Victor Davis Hanson, *The Western Way of War* (New York: Oxford University Press, 1990); E. Evans, *Wars without Splendour* (Westport, CT: Greenwood, 1987), pp. 31–32; General J. R. Galvin, "Uncomfortable Wars," in Manwaring, *Uncomfortable Wars*, pp. 9–18.

14. Richard Holmes, *The Road to Sedan* (London: Royal Historical Society, 1984), p. 51; Paddy Griffith, *Military Thought in the French Army, 1815–51* (Manchester, UK: Manchester University Press, 1989), pp. 114–18.

15. Peter Burroughs, "Imperial Defence and the Victorian Army," *Journal of Imperial and Commonwealth History* 15, no. 1 (1986): 55–72; Bailes, "Patterns of Thought," pp. 29–45.

16. Brian Bond, ed., *Victorian Military Campaigns* (London: Hutchinson, 1967), p. 309; Ian F. W. Beckett, "The Study of Counterinsurgency: A British Perspective," *Small Wars and Insurgencies* 1, no. 1 (1990): 47–53; Tom Mockaitis, *British Counterinsurgency, 1919–60* (London: Macmillan, 1990), pp. 180–91.

17. Bailes, "Patterns of Thought," pp. 29–45; Brian Bond, *British Military Policy between the Two World Wars* (London: Oxford University Press, 1980), p. 36.

18. David Charters, "From Palestine to Northern Ireland: British Adaptation to Low-Intensity Operations," in David Charters and Maurice Tugwell, eds., *Armies in Low-*

Intensity Conflict (London: Brassey's, 1989), pp. 169–214; J. Bowyer Bell, "Revolts against the Crown: The British Response to Imperial Insurgency," *Parameters* 4, no. 1 (1974): 31–46 (reprinted in R. Weigley, ed., *New Dimensions in Military History*, San Rafael, Presidio Press, 1975, pp. 359–84); Mockaitis, *British Counterinsurgency*, pp. 180–91.

19. R. Clutterbuck, *The Long Long War* (London: Cassell, 1966), p. 51; Chief of the General Staff, *Design for Military Operations: The British Military Doctrine* (Chief of the General Staff, 1989); J.J.G. Mackenzie and Brian Holden Reid, eds., *The British Army and the Operational Level of War* (London: Tri-Service Press, 1989).

20. Jeffery, "Colonial Warfare," p. 40; J. A. de Moor, "Colonial Warfare Theory and Practice: The Dutch Experience in Indonesia, 1816–1949" (Paper presented to the Dutch-Japanese Symposium on the History of Dutch and Japanese Expansion, Tokyo and Kyoto, 9–14 October 1989); C. J. Duffy, *The Military Experience in the Age of Reason* (London: Routledge and Kegan Paul, 1987), p. 308.

21. J. L. Cox, "A Splendid Training Ground: The Importance to the RAF of Iraq, 1913–32," *Journal of Imperial and Commonwealth History* 13, no. 2 (1985): 157–84; D. J. Dean, "Air Power in Small Wars: The British Air Control Experience," *Air University Review* 34, no. 5 (1983): 24–31; D. J. Killingray, "A Swift Agent of Government: Air Power in British Colonial Africa, 1916–39," *Journal of African History* 25, no. 4 (1984): 429–44; C. Townshend, "Civilisation and Frightfulness: Air Control in the Middle East between the Wars," in C. Wrigley, ed., *Warfare, Diplomacy and Politics* (London: Hamish Hamilton, 1986), pp. 142–62; D. Omissi, *Air Power and Colonial Control* (Manchester, UK: Manchester University Press, 1990); P. Towle, *Pilots and Rebels* (London: Pergamon, 1989): Paret, *Makers of Modern Strategy*, p. 633.

22. See, for example, the bibliographies of the individual chapters in Ian F. W. Beckett, ed., *The Roots of Counter-Insurgency: Armies and Guerrilla Warfare, 1900–1945* (London: Blandford, 1988), and Ian F. W. Beckett and John Pimlott, eds., *Armed Forces and Modern Counter-insurgency* (London: Croom Helm, 1985). Two journals largely devoted to low-intensity conflict are *Conflict Quarterly* and *Small Wars and Insurgencies*.

23. Cable, *Conflict of Myths*, p. 13; Klare and Kornbluh, *Low Intensity Warfare*, p. 11.

9

The New Military History: Its Practitioners and Their Practices

DON HIGGINBOTHAM

IN SEARCH OF THE NEW MILITARY HISTORIAN

This essay looks at the people who are military historians, broadly defined, and then examines the history they are writing. It is framed by a crude form of quantification, analyzing data from approximately ninety-two applicants for a position in military history at the University of North Carolina at Chapel Hill, a search that was conducted during the academic year 1989–1990 and was chaired by the author, with the able assistance of three colleagues. Although our committee probably could not have agreed on a definition of the "new military history," we were sure that we did not want to recruit a "drum-and-bugle" type. There was a consensus on this point, in spite of considerable evidence that there is a strong predisposition for that kind of history on the part of our athletes and "Greeks" who throng into our two-semester American military survey course and whose presence explains why its numbers have not infrequently reached 250 to 300. Our advertisement stated that we particularly welcomed applications from scholars trained in social, intellectual, and technological topics, as well as those informed on the rise and character of the national security state. We were also quite open-minded about geographic considerations. Our military historian would have to teach the above-mentioned survey course, but a scholar who met that specification could certainly be more of a Europeanist, for example, than an Americanist in his or her orientation.

Now we should add a word about such a sampling approach. Obviously, many military specialists did not apply, but we had twice or more the number of applications to consider than confronted any of the other three departmental search committees that year. It is also worth noting that the American Historical Association's publication *Perspectives* listed only three advertisements for military historians from academic institutions. Since this was not a good year for military historians in the marketplace, we can assume that our numbers represented a substantial slice of the field. For that matter, there has hardly been a halcyon year for fledglings in the profession in the last half of the 1980s. There were three advertised openings in 1986, a highwater mark of eight in 1987, and four in 1988.

Where our sample would at first glance appear especially vulnerable is with regard to applicants at the very senior levels—full professors and chaired professors, for we were not authorized to make an appointment at those heights. However, several full professors applied, people who were willing to take a reduction in rank, in the short run at least; moreover, we had candidates from the armed forces and governmental agencies who surely had the credentials for full professorships at major universities. Last, it may be argued in defense of my approach that there are not that many full professors teaching at research-oriented schools because academic military history is a relatively new field. In fact, when this author entered the profession in the 1950s one could probably name all the senior people in the field on two hands: Theodore Ropp, Louis Morton, T. Harry Williams, Bell Wiley, and a few more.

What about the institutional backgrounds and current affiliations of our candidates? They had received their highest graduate degrees from fifty different universities in the United States, three in the United Kingdom, and two in Canada. Needless to say, there are not that many universities with doctoral programs in military history. Many of our candidates were trained in other fields such as U.S., British, Modern European, and Russian history. Even so, most of them could be taken seriously because of the quality of their work on a military topic and because most were consciously trying to become military experts. Therefore, our committee hardly held it against them if they had not been trained by an eminent authority such as Theodore Ropp at Duke, Peter Paret at Stanford, Edward M. Coffman at Wisconsin, John Shy at Michigan, Russell Weigley at Temple, or Allan Millett at Ohio State. Most of these six distinguished historians had themselves obtained the doctorate under mentors who focused on other areas of American history. Which schools contributed the most applicants? There were six each from Temple and Ohio State, five from Duke, five from Chicago, and four from Michigan. It could be that several other schools with strong military programs would have had more entries except that they did not wish to see several of their students competing against each other for the same position.

As for the whereabouts of our candidates in the spring of 1990, the findings were rather grim. Indeed, it was yet another reminder (as if any were needed) that a dramatic upturn in the academic job market has scarcely occurred; this is a truism for the military history field as well as other specialties in our discipline. More than 40 percent (38 in all) were either unemployed or in non-tenure track slots. Twenty-six seemed relatively secure in their academic bailiwicks (although not necessarily happy, for about two-thirds of them were teaching at institutions where they had limited time for research and teaching their field). Nineteen of our total would have considered leaving their current positions with the armed forces—at schools, records centers, and various agencies. The remainder ran the gamut of professions—one was even a missionary. Obviously, white males predominated. To our knowledge, no blacks appeared on the list; but five females did apply, and all were highly qualified for an appointment at the rank of instructor or assistance professor. Therefore, women appear to be advancing on this front, but few would appear to have reached mid-range or senior levels.

The figures given thus far from the North Carolina search are more meaningful when they are examined in the context of the aggregate of history departments that do and do not offer courses in military history. Accordingly, the author turned to the AHA's *Guide to Departments of History, 1989–1990: Colleges, Universities, and Research Institutions in the United States and Canada*. The guide had its limits for my purposes; for example, two-year colleges were not included, and a host of four-year schools regularly elect not to appear in the publication. Even so, 554 institutions in the United States were affiliated, of which 164 listed at least one person with a teaching responsibility in military history.[1] We also learned that 2 percent of all historians were military historians, or it may be more accurate to say that, in some cases, military history was one of two or more teaching specialties listed. Four percent of these military history teachers were women, a statistic very close to what we found with regard to female applicants for the North Carolina opening.

There is room for encouragement about the military field in all the above, but it needs to be tempered. Twenty percent of our total of 278 historians taught at the three principal service academies in the United States. West Point and the Air Force Academy have virtually all professional officer faculties, and roughly half of the Naval Academy's history department is a uniformed one. Some Canadian comparisons are also instructive and sobering to American scholars. Fifty-one percent of the Canadian history departments supplying information had at least one person offering military studies, and 4 percent of the total number of Canadian historians stipulated a military specialty, although none were women.

Another way to view the academic status of military history in the United States is to compare it with other so-called "new" histories, the most fashionable and popular being social history and women's history. The guide revealed that 337 departments had a social history category and 310 departments had a women's history designation. In other words, both subject areas outpaced military history by a factor of about two-to-one.

Clearly, military history still has a way to go. Even among those who teach it, there may be a lurking sensitivity concerning how our colleagues view the pursuit of Mars. It probably was revealed in the fact that 70 percent of those history departments listed in the guide did not have a military history teacher or specialist. It is also reflected, I suspect, in the way some of the scholars in the military history schools refer to their designations: for example, naval and maritime, military and security, war and revolution, war and social structure, art of war, armaments expansion, civil-military relations, military social, and comparative military systems.

Still another factor limiting opportunities for young specialists in the field is the fact that countless historians who teach military history were not trained in that area and do so only as a service to their departments. This is not to say they do a poor job of undergraduate teaching, but it probably does indicate that some do not keep up with the literature as do most of the applicants for the position at North Carolina. The largest number of military history teachers to earn the doctorate in any of the last three decades is ninety-two, and they did so in the 1960s, when few graduate programs in war studies were in place. In fact, the lowest number in the last three decades is the sixty-seven who received the Ph.D. in the 1980s (and thirty-six of those taught at the service academies; that, of course, means that most are not civilian historians).

There are many people teaching military history because someone has to offer it to satisfy the requirements of ROTC programs, which call for one or more courses in military or naval history. Since the 1960s the U.S. Army has tried to address the need in a systematic way. For some years specified officers destined for ROTC schools spent six weeks at West Point, where they received a whirlwind course in American military history. Then, in the late 1970s, General Donn A. Starry was appointed commander of the army's Training and Doctrine Command, where he became concerned about inadequately trained officers teaching history and the general lack of historical instruction in the components of the army under his jurisdiction. He was especially sensitive to the performance of officers in the classrooms of civilian institutions in the aftermath of the campus backlash against the Vietnam War. General Starry was perceptive in recognizing that perhaps for a variety of reasons, it was desirable for civilian professors to teach the military history course for ROTC students. Indeed, at some institutions (certainly the University of North Caolina was one) the faculty mandated that military history as well as some other ROTC courses be offered by the traditional academic departments and be opened to non-ROTC students as well.

There was a problem, however. Few civilian historians were trained to teach about battles and campaigns and the other aspects of war. The result was that in 1981 the army's six-weeks summer minicourse in military history became a program for civilian academics, who would afterward return to enlighten undergraduates about the American military experience. During the decade the new program has run, several hundred academic historians have imbibed of Alexander, Frederick, Napoleon, Grant, and other great captains. It would be difficult to locate all of them today and determine their classroom offerings, but we do know that there are just over 400 army ROTC units, of which two-thirds or more now have civilians teaching military history on their campuses. If, then, there are perhaps slightly more than 250 West Point–trained civilian professors teaching military history, some are at the schools recorded in the AHA directory, but most probably are at less prestigious schools that do not even list their history departments with the AHA.

What is the likelihood that these and other institutions will in the near future turn to scholars who really specialize in military history and who, as our North

Carolina search revealed, are often seeking an academic fortress? Although better-trained people are available in growing numbers, Roger W. Spiller, of the Combat Studies Institute at Fort Leavenworth, which has monitored the army's summer program, is not optimistic. In a memorandum designed to survey trends since the appearance of the 1971 *Report of the Ad Hoc Committee on the Army Need for the Study of Military History*, he expressed the opinion that many civilian academics, products of the era of Vietnam War protests, still are unwilling to give military history a high priority and indeed are often strongly opposed to full-time appointments in that field. "The chance for change in such attitudes is rather slight," he declared.

I have not found such attitudes among graduate students in general or among younger faculty members. I do not expect student interest in military history to wane; if anything, the effect of our military expeditions will create more demand for military history courses. But, in sum, I do not think military history will ever be regarded in academic circles as anything other than a marginal field of study, quite without regard to the quality of work done in it. Perhaps indifference is the most we should dare hope for.[2]

IN SEARCH OF THE NEW MILITARY HISTORY

From the practitioners, the essay now turns to their practices—to the kind of history they are writing. If one can offer no more than guarded optimism for the future of military history in the halls of ivy, it is possible to speak with greater confidence about the quality and diversity of the new military history itself.[3] Owing perhaps to the indifference of which Spiller spoke, the new military history has not come under assault from certain heavy guns in the profession as have the other new histories. The onslaught is not against the attention devoted to previously neglected members of society—blacks, women, and indigenous peoples being the groups most readily identified. Rather, it is that specialists in these other new fields tend to be deconstructionists, splintering and fragmenting the past so that we learn more and more about less and less. Their investigations are not adequately related to larger historical questions. The result has hardly been inspiring; devoid of narrative treatment and often dehumanized, people are dealt with as statistics without individual names and profiles.[4] Critics also see— or fear—a lessening appreciation for statecraft in all its dimensions, an apprehension that was the theme of William E. Leuchtenburg's presidential address before the Organization of American Historians a few years ago.[5]

What, then, is the new military history? When did it first appear? What is its approach, and how does it differ from the old genre? Military historians themselves do not agree on the answers. Richard A. Preston has suggested that Canadians were laboring in this vineyard in the decade after World War II, combining "a professional military internalist approach and a civilian contextual method." Canadians have taken a lead, he said, because they "long lacked a professional army" and "also because any Canadian military problems bore very heavily on Canada's social and political development . . . George Stanley's classic *Canada's Soldiers* is a case in point."[6]

Part of the problem of dating and defining is that some historians have always had a variety of topical interests. Where, for example, does one position Martin Van Creveld, who pursues strategy, command, logistics, technology, and so-called "lessons learned," all vintage subjects, but in his hands often given unique twists and comparative contexts?[7] To some degree he is a preacher, as were the old-fashioned military writers, but at times a sermon is what we need. Who would disagree with his homily that logistics constitute 90 percent of the business of soldiers, but the topic of wartime supply comprises only 1 percent of our military literature?

However we pigeonhole Van Creveld, there is perhaps a consensus that more good military history is being written. If the old military history lavished loving attention on battles, military organizations, and leadership, with some attention to technology, the new military history includes all the above and more: Armies are now viewed in a societal context; their ranks elicit our scrutiny from the vantage points of the soldiers' backgrounds, their group dynamics, and their psychological experience in battle; and they are analyzed in the context of the geopolitical and economic resources of the state, including the state's large-scale technological potential. Somewhere, probably inextricably enmeshed in all of these categories, is a sensitivity to what war and things military do to the lives and minds of both civilians and soldiers.

These categories and definitions, to be sure, were found in the doctoral dissertation topics, articles, and monographs of the candidates for the position at North Carolina. There unquestionably was some of the old, but there was more of the new. The old is pretty respectable history, for that matter, and free of bombast, it is a reminder that well-written and well-researched scholarship will always have a place, whether it be Bruce Catton's stirring Civil War battle-and-campaign narratives, Douglas S. Freeman's biographical studies of R. E. Lee and George Washington (both great captains), or Forrest Pogue's magisterial life of George Marshall, a preeminent soldier-statesman. The old historical tapestry, if properly fashioned, evokes the drama of the past, the crucial place of personalities and human factors generally in history, the unpredictable and the unforeseen—in short, the dangers of deterministic explanations. Probably no one ever said it better than Carl von Clausewitz in his classic *On War*: "From the very start there is an interplay of possibilities, probabilities, good luck and bad, that weaves its way throughout the length and breadth of the tapestry. In the whole range of human activities, war most closely resembles a game of cards."[8]

Our applicants produced studies of American ideas about war and war making, the impact of wartime conditions on civilians, military thought, technology and weaponry, insurgency and counterinsurgency, postwar adjustments, presidential and uniformed leadership, intelligence operations, the military-industrial complex, soldiers in combat, and national security issues. In all, it was a rich and varied fare, testimony to the fact that the new military history is not always as new as has been claimed and that, new or not, it offers too much to face the charge of narrowness or parochialism.[9] Moreover, our search committee found little in the dissertations and monographs of professional soldiers that was didactic and self-serving as was so much of the military history written by soldiers between the day of Emory Upton in the Gilded Age and William A. Ganoe and Oliver L. Spaulding between the world wars.[10]

Today's seminar-trained officers are as capable as civilian authorities of critically probing war and war-makers. Let me take just two examples, both from Air Force officers with Ph.Ds. First James W. Titus's *The Old Dominion at War: Society, Politics and Warfare in Late Colonial Virginia* (1991) is a sophisticated history of the French and Indian War in Virginia, which Titus describes as one of the first unpopular conflicts in American history, one in which the poor were asked to fight in a conflict that benefited the upper echelons (shades of Vietnam). The second is Mark Clodfelter's *The Limits of Airpower: The American Bombing of North Vietnam* (1989), which sharply challenges the orthodoxy within his own service concerning what aerial attacks can accomplish in a war restricted by various political and technological considerations, to say nothing of the environment of Vietnam itself.

We can also give high marks to any number of excellent publications from the armed services' offices of military history, which are, in considerable measure, staffed by civilian historians (and thus have provided some real help for young scholars in the market for a job in history). As Stanley Sandler wrote, "Some of the most penetrating, documented criticism of U.S. Army policies and performance can be found in official Army histories."[11] They include Ulysses Lee's *The Employment of Negro Troops in World War II* (1966); W. E. Hermes's *Truce Tent and Fighting Front* (1966), about Korea; Ronald Spector's *Advice and Support: The Early Years* (1983); and William Hammond's *The Military and the Media* (both of the last two works are about Vietnam).

It may be useful to mention briefly three areas of concentration that turned up in the studies of our applicants because they were among the most innovative and most reflective of some of the recent trends alluded to earlier. First is technology, and here it is interesting to note that three of the applicants' dissertations were written in departments of the history of science and technology. Scholars in those fields are hardly running away from military history. The *History of Science Society Newsletter* publishes information on war and technology themes, and its annual "History of Science Society Employment Survey" tracks academic posts in military studies.[12] Whether it be examining the development of a fighter plane or a new class of battleships, dissertations and monographs in this area look at the relationship between strategic doctrine and technological decisions, at how each influences the other together with the political climate's impact on the entire process. Military hardware, viewed from multiple perspectives, sometimes seems more useful in winning the battle of Capitol Hill than in prevailing in overseas conflicts.

If technological studies are hardly novel at this time, they have, with few exceptions, rarely been so broad-gauged. One exception more than three decades ago was Walter Millis's *Arms and Men* (1956) which encompassed the whole sweep of American military history. It is still, to my mind, the best book ever written on the American encounter with war. In 1979 the *Journal of Modern History* devoted a special issue to "Technology and War." The 1980s alone produced three panoramic treatments of war and technology: by William H. McNeill, Martin van Creveld, and Robert O'Connell.[13] They will surely inspire more specialized undertakings like Jon T. Sumida's *In Defense of Naval Supremacy: Finance, Technology and British Naval Policy, 1898–1914* (1989), a model of masterly scholarship. During part of that period, when Sir John Fisher was First Sea Lord (1904–1910), "the Royal Navy was the largest department of the British government," and yet we still lack, according to Sumida, studies of the age of steam that "cover comprehensibly English naval material, personnel, finance, and governance."[14] Naval developments as well as land warfare in an earlier era are examined expertly in a 1990 collection of essays, *The Tools of War: Instruments, Ideas, and Institutions of Warfare, 1445–1871*, edited by John A. Lynn. The thrust of the volume, however, serves to remind us of the centrality of siege warfare in medieval and early modern history and of the improvement of military administration and the emergence of the professional army.[15]

Technology, of course, has its limits. Sir Michael Howard, in an afterword to *The Tools of War*, pointed out that the new instruments of conquest in the nineteenth century—railroads, repeating weapons, and heavy artillery—led the statesmen and generals in 1914 to conclude that hostilities would be short and decisive. This would not be the last time that technology failed to live up to expectations, as studies of bombing campaigns in World War II and Vietnam have demonstrated. George Raudzens advises us to be wary, in general, of stating what weapons accomplish in any given war since "weapons impact analysis, as distinct from hardware descriptions or assessments of theoretical capabilities, has not received more than marginal attention from scholars."[16]

Withal, the faith in the products of the military-industrial complex still remains unshaken in some quarters, fueled by the powerful linkage of the components of that complex: political, military, industrial, managerial, and (too often forgotten), academic. Dwight D. Eisenhower's warning notwithstanding, we have witnessed the proliferation of such projects as Trident, ABM (Anti-Ballistic Missile), Minuteman, and "Starwars" (Strategic Defense Initiative). As Thomas P. Hughes has reminded us, it was the World War II Manhattan Project, which resulted in the atomic bomb, that "became the model for these massive technological systems." Hughes's *American Genesis: A Century of Invention and Technological Enthusiasm, 1870–1970* (1989) places weapons' development within the larger framework of scientific change and systems of production and should serve as stimulus for shedding more light on these capital- and managerial-intensive mega-instruments of mass destruction.[17]

Van Creveld himself maintained that our obsession with scientific advances in weapons of destruction means that we are in danger of eliminating the human element from warfare, which brings us to our second area. Men and women both determine the outcome of wars. We refer not only to those who, in John Keegan's words, were exposed to the "face of battle," but also to those who remained at home and to the ways in which both veterans and civilians internalized the war at the time and after the guns fell silent. Vietnam and Afghanistan are recent reminders of the human factor, as was the war in the Persian Gulf. Many of the North Carolina candidates clearly were under the spell of John Keegan and Paul Fussell.[18] Some of their studies were social history, some intellectual history, and others a composite of the two, for example; dissertations on the northern mind in the Civil War; on World War I doughboys' perceptions of French culture; on attitudes of one French infantry division toward command authority during the "Great War"; on American images of the Japanese enemy in World War II; on the defenders of Wake Island in that same struggle; on formal war memorials throughout American history; and on the adjustment of American veterans to peacetime life, to mention only a partial list.

Some of these accounts owe something to Robert W. Johannsen's study of the Mexican War in the American imagination and to Gerald F. Linderman's account of the impact of combat on Civil War soldiers.[19] However, our candidates did not have the opportunity to draw on some stimulating contributions just off the presses, such as George L. Mosse's *Fallen Soldiers: Reshaping the Memory of the World Wars* (1990), which argued that "the Myth of the War Experience"—a vision that subverts its gore, consecrates its history, and finally justifies its aims—was not finally shattered until after World War II. Likewise, they did not have several seminal essays by Roger Spiller, who himself has obliterated a myth perpetrated by General S.L.A. Marshall in his 1947 book *Men against Fire*, in which Marshall contended that only about 20 percent of the GIs in some four hundred combat infantry units actually discharged their weapons during an entire engagement. Spiller's pieces collectively spell out as vividly as anything in print the grave psychological damages that combat does to men, including its postwar effects.[20]

None of our would-be colleagues wrote on women's role in things military, but there is a growing literature on the subject, some of it appearing in a relatively new journal, *Minerva*, which is devoted to women and the military. One of the most publicized books in this genre is Jean Elshtain's *Women and War* (1987), which examines their images in language and culture from Homer onward and the influence of those images on both women and men. The author persuasively contended that the portrayal of women as noncombatants and men as warriors helped the latter to maintain their dominance over the former in public decision making as well as elsewhere, although the concept of female purity enabled women to have a place in the polis as guardians of civic virtue. A very recent article by Drew Gilpin Faust attributed Confederate defeat in the Civil War in some degree to declining efforts on the part of southern women, who felt that their stalwart endeavors were unappreciated by their men.[21]

However, it is the impact of World War II on women that is particularly attractive in the field of American gender studies. The contributions of D'Ann Campbell rank among the most influential, especially her *Women at War with America: Private Lives in a Patriotic Era* (1984) and her invaluable survey of the secondary literature.[22] Figuring prominently in all these undertakings are questions of contemporary relevance, such as the degree of equality accorded women and their suitability for combat roles.[23]

The third and final area is national security studies, which is normally associated with political scientists as much as, or more than, with historians. However, historians need to deal with events that crowd in on our very safety and world stability, too—to give them a time dimension and to emphasize the part of individuals in the decision-making process. Several of our brightest job candidates were working here, in what is increasingly becoming known not only as national (or international) security undertakings, but also as strategic studies. These involve diplomacy, defense, the economy, and technology. Ernest May of Harvard, for example, has promising students probing this area: for example, focusing on North Atlantic Treaty Organization (NATO) problems and American defense policies. Historians are there cheek by jowl with political scientists, investigating the twists and turns of nuclear-era formulations in such organs as the *Journal of Strategic Studies*, to which historians contributed approximately half the articles in the 1989 volume.

A very recent collaborative venture of historians and political scientists is *The Origin and Prevention of Major Wars*, edited by Robert I. Rotberg and Theodore K. Rabb, in which the scholars of each discipline display their own approaches, with the former looking at the origins of specific wars and the latter generalizing about causation and conflict, with an eye to structural considerations within the international system. Most of the focus is on hegemonic wars, from the early modern era to the twentieth century, where Cold War influences seem to shape the thinking of the political scientists more than those of the historians. If Jack S. Levy, a political scientist, takes his own discipline to task for neglecting domestic political factors that contribute to war, he offers another observation that historians may want to acknowledge: "liberal or democratic states do not fight each other." As the decade of the 1990s opened with the West weighing the pluses and minuses to be derived from its involvement in a Middle Eastern conflict, historian John Guilmartin may have offered the wisest words of all: In an essay on the Ottoman Empire at war, 1453–1606, he noted that non-Europeans have often defined war very differently from Americans and Europeans.[24]

That is so even though we acknowledge the ways in which the West has militarily influenced the extra-European world. David B. Ralston (1990) in *Importing the European Army*, a study of that very process between 1600 and

1914, offered a persuasive account of how the refashioning of armed forces along European lines also transformed administrative, cultural, and economic patterns in Russia, the Ottoman Empire, Egypt, China, and Japan. All the same, Guilmartin is right in that these changes have scarcely transformed the *mentalities* of the peoples in question, including their definitions of victory and defeat and their conceptions of the military and political dimensions of warfare.

Another way of illustrating the truism that historians are not leaving contemporary history (however the term is defined) to the social scientists is to observe their participation in the growing number of interdisciplinary institutes, centers and seminars. At North Carolina, for example, there is the Curriculum in Peace, War, and Defense, and (in cooperation with Duke University and North Carolina State University) the Triangle Universities Security Seminar, both chaired by a historian. Ohio State University has its Mershon Center, and the University of Illinois its Program in Arms Control, Disarmament, and International Security. Another example based at the University of Maryland, is the Nuclear History Program, which promotes research and discussion of the development and management of nuclear forces and their place in the evolution of East-West relations. One can also mention the University of New Brunswick's Military and Strategic Studies Program and Centre for Conflict Studies. Both are headed by historians, as are Yale's Center for International and Area Studies and its International Security Programs.

Finally, military history has something to offer those who may be a bit too optimistic about the course of the world without the Cold War, an international scene which (as was being said before the Persian Gulf War of 1991) no longer requires national security programs and, perhaps by implication, can eschew military history itself. As historians, we know that the bipolar world after 1945 was itself the exception and not the rule in international affairs. Historically, definitions of security—of adequate numbers of arms and men—have always been in flux. However, those definitions have frequently been at odds with internal underpinnings of national strategy, especially economic and technological ones, as Paul Kennedy stressed in *The Rise and Fall of the Great Powers* (1982), a book both profound and disturbing in its implications for super states such as the United States and the former Soviet Union, which have engaged in "overstretch," as did once-powerful states such as Spain and Britain. During the initial weeks of the Persian Gulf crisis, however, historians were upstaged by a political scientist, John Mearsheimer of the University of Chicago, who speculated that a world without the Cold War may well be a more dangerous one than what we knew before the Mikhail Gorbachev era. Historians probably know better than he that a multipolar world awash with ethnic antagonisms and national rivalries is a prescription for tension, crisis, and conflict.

In any event, the military historian, whether a practitioner of the old or the new, and whether an academic, a free-lancer, or an employee of the armed forces, will always have a home in Clio's capacious mansion. That is, so long as what we write is good history.

NOTES

1. Whatever else may be said, these figures represent an improvement for the situation in 1958 when, according to a survey, only 4 percent of American colleges and universities included military history courses, Dexter Perkins and John L. Snell, *The Education of Historians in the United States* (New York: McGraw-Hill, 1977), p. 77.

2. Roger Spiller, Memorandum for the Director, Combat Studies Institute, 17 August 1990.

3. Four very useful surveys expertly analyze recent trends in military scholarship: Edward M. Coffman, "The New American Military History," *Military Affairs* 48 (January 1984): 1–5; and Peter Kaarsten, "The 'New' Military History: A Map of the Territory, Explored and Unexplored," *American Quarterly* 36 (Summer 1984): 389–418; Paul Kennedy, "The Fall and Rise of Military History," *Quarterly Journal of Military History*, 3 (1991), 9–12; Peter Paret, "The New Military History," *Parameters*, 21 (1991), 10–18. Two previous essays carefully examine the field for a slightly earlier period: John K. Mahon, "Teaching and Research on Military History in the United States," *Historian* 27 (February 1965): 170–184; and Allan R. Millett, "The Study of American Military History in the United States," *Military Affairs* 41 (April 1977): 58–61.

4. Leading critics of the new histories include Thomas Bender, "Making History Whole Again," *New York Times Book Review*, 7 October 1985, pp. 1, 42, 43; Theodore S. Hamerow, *Reflections on History and Historians* (Madison, WI: University of Wisconsin Press, 1987); and Gertrude Himmelfarb, "Some Reflections on the New History," *American Historical Review*, 94 (June 1989): 661–70. For a spirited counterattack, see Lawrence W. Levin, "The Unpredictable Past: Reflections on Recent American Historiography," *American Historical Review* 94 (1989): 671–79.

5. William E. Leuchtenburg, "The Pertinence of Political History: Reflections on the Significance of the State in America," *Journal of American History* 73 (1986): 585–600.

6. Richard A. Preston, "Review Essay: Canadian Military History: A Reinterpretation Challenge of the Eighties?" *American Review of Canadian Studies* 19 (1989): 102–3.

7. Martin Van Creveld, *Hitler's Strategy, 1940–1941: The Balkan Clue* (New York: Cambridge University Press, 1973), *Supplying War: Logistics from Wallenstein to Patton* (New York, Cambridge University Press, 1977), *Command in War* (Cambridge, MA: Harvard University Press, 1985), *Technology and War From 200 B.C. to the Present* (New York: The Free Press, 1989), and *The Transformation of War* (New York: The Free Press, 1991).

8. Peter Paret, *Clausewitz and the State: The Man, His Theories, and His Times* (Princeton, NJ: Princeton University Press, 1976), p. 392.

9. For comparative purposes, note the subjects that were most attractive to graduate students and their mentors prior to the last twenty years or so. Allan R. Millett and B. F. Cooling III, comps., *Doctoral Dissertations in Military Affairs: A Bibliography* (Manhattan, KS: Kansas State University Library, 1972).

10. I have charted the military's self-serving interpretations of the War of Independence in "American Historians and the Military History of the American Revolution," *American Historical Review* 70 (1964): 18–34. For a more comprehensive treatment of the military's flirtation with Clio, see also Carol Reardon, *Soldiers and Scholars: The U.S. Army and*

the Uses of Military History, 1865–1920 (Lawrence, KS: University Press of Kansas, 1990). Whatever biases the military displayed, it can at least be said of men like Upton and Ganoe that they addressed formidable questions that have run through American history, most notably the difficulties in creating a sizable peacetime establishment in a democracy.

11. Stanley Sandler, "The Army's Civilian Historians," *Perspectives: American Historical Association Newsletter* 24 (1986): 20–22.

12. A new essay by a scholar in the history of science field is Hugh R. Slotten, "Humane Chemistry or Scientific Barbarism? American Responses to World War I Poison Gas, 1915–1930," *Journal of American History* 77 (1990): 476–98.

13. William H. McNeill, *The Pursuit of Power: Technology, Armed Force, and Society since 1000 A.D.* (Chicago: University of Chicago Press, 1983); Van Creveld, *Technology and War*; Robert O'Connell, *Of Arms and Men: A History of War, Weapons, and Aggression* (New York, 1989).

14. Jon Sumida, "British Naval Administration and Policy in the Age of Fisher," *Journal of Military History* 54 (1990): 25, 1.

15. Another earlier collection of useful essays is Merritt Roe Smith, ed., *Military Enterprise and Technological Change* (Cambridge, MA: MIT Press, 1985).

16. George Raudzens, "War-Winning Weapons: The Measurement of Technological Determinism in Military History," *Journal of Military History* 54 (1990): 403–33.

17. Thomas P. Hughes, *American Genesis: A Century of Invention and Technological Enthusiasm 1870–1970* (New York: Viking, 1989), p. 442.

18. John Keegan, *The Face of Battle* (London: Jonathan Cape, 1976); Paul Fussell, *The Great War and Modern Memory* (New York: Oxford University Press, 1975); Paul Fussell, *Wartime: Understanding and Behavior in the Second World War* (New York: Oxford University Press, 1989).

19. Johannsen, *To the Halls of Montezumas: The Mexican War in the American Imagination* (New York: Oxford University Press, 1985); Gerald Linderman, *Embattled Courage: The Experience of Combat in the American Civil War* (New York: Free Press, 1987).

20. Roger J. Spiller, "S.L.A. Marshall and the Ratio of Fire," *RUSI Journal* 133 (1988): 63–71; "Isen's Run: Human Dimensions of Warfare in the Twentieth Century," *Military Review* 68 (1988): 16–32; "The Tenth Imperative," *Military Review* 69 (1989): 3–13; "Shell Shock," *American Heritage* 41 (1990): 75–87; "Man against Fire: Audie Murphy and History War," in Robert Calvert, ed., *The Texas Military Tradition* (College Station, TX, forthcoming); and "The Thousand Yard Stare: Psychodynamics of Combat in World War II" (unpublished essay). An important new work in this genre is Bill McAndrew and Terry Copp, *Battle Exhaustion: Soldiers and Psychiatrists in the Canadian Army, 1939–1945* (Montreal: McGill-Queens University Press, 1990). See also Bill McAndrew's essay in this volume. No historians concerned with the social results of World War II and the Korean War should miss the illuminating articles of sociologist Glen H. Elder, Jr., and his colleagues on the ways in which those conflicts affected the life trajectories of veterans. Their findings have appeared since 1986 in such journals as *Developmental Psychology*, *Journal of Personality*, *Psychiatry*, and *Sociological Forum*. See also "A Round Table: The Living and Reliving of World War II," *Journal of American History* 77 (1990): 553–93.

21. Drew Gilpin Faust, "Altars of Sacrifice: Confederate Women and the Narratives of War," *Journal of American History* 76 (1990): 1200–1228. The role of women in

southern society was scarcely changed as a result of the war, according to George C. Rable, *Civil Wars: Women and the Crisis of Southern Nationalism* (Urbana, IL: University of Illinois Press, 1989).

22. D'Ann Campbell, "Women in Uniform: The World War II Experiment," *Military Affairs* 51 (1987): 137–39.

23. For an influential champion of women's rights in the American military, see Janann Sherman, " 'They Either Need These Women or They Do Not': Margaret Chase Smith and the Fight for Regular Status for Women in the Military," *Journal of Military History* 54 (1990): 47–78. On women in combat, one can best begin with Nancy Loring Goldman, ed., *Female Soldiers—Combatants or Noncombatants? Historical and Contemporary Perspectives* (Westport, CT, 1982), and Paul E. Roush, "Combat Exclusion: Military Necessity or Another Name for Bigotry?" *Minerva* 8 (1990): 1–15.

24. John J. Mearsheimer, "Why We Will Soon Miss the Cold War," *Atlantic Monthly* 266 (1990): 35–50. See also Carl Kaysen, "Is War Obsolete? A Review Essay," *International Security* 14 (1990): 42–64.

Part II

Military History and the
Military Profession

10

Stress Lines and Gray Areas: The Utility of the Historical Method to the Military Profession

DOMINICK GRAHAM

Historical writing falls into one or more of the following in the spectrum of categories: entertaining, informative, descriptive, inspirational, critical, educational and prescriptive. Although our own work may lie nearer one end of the spectrum than the other, we like it to be judged both entertaining and educational. Readers who want to be educated favor subjects of current interest, for instance, syntheses that explain how we came to be in "the current mess" and that also suggest how we might escape from it. Paul Kennedy's *The Rise and Fall of the Great Powers* is a recent example of this genre: A prescriptive work that employs historical cases to illustrate the consequences of "imperial overstretch."[1] Because it concludes with an explicit warning that America should eschew policies beyond the country's capacity, Kennedy's book has sold well among Washington's political community, who felt that it was relevant for national leaders. *Thinking in Time: The Uses of History for Decision-Makers*, by Richard E. Neustadt and Ernest R. May, is more directly prescriptive, as its title suggests.[2] A study of policy decisions in which historical precedents were used, abused, or ignored as guides, it has become a useful text for officials, as its authors intended.

Both books are edifying because they suggest how the past may be useful as a guide in the present, as well as being merely entertaining. This, of course, runs counter to what most of us were taught: that history never repeats itself, and therefore, lessons cannot be learned from it. On the other hand, the eminent British military historian Michael Howard observed that one should study the past, not to find models for handling the next crisis but to gain the knowledge that will make one "wise forever." Historical method is an aspect of the wisdom to which Howard referred. What this chapter will attempt to show is that it is this method of determining what happened in the past, rather than our narratives of events, that makes the study of history relevant to the military professional of today.

More than any other profession, except perhaps the law, the military makes extensive use of history as a training and educational tool. That imposes a particular responsibility on those of us who write prescriptive military history, for if we regard ourselves as both educators and students of the military, then we must assume some responsibility for the way in which we present our subject. Certainly, we must strive to entertain as well as to inform, for unless we entertain, we will fail to reach and inform our audience. However, the most important point is that the relationship between historians and the military profession can be of greatest benefit when the former can demonstrate to the latter the practical relevance of applying the historical method of analysis to the military's studies. This does not mean a mere linear recounting of facts in a tidy cause-and-effect fashion, from the beginning of the plan to the end of the battle, whereby the historical account "proves" the "directing staff solution" and vice versa. Rather, historians should try to illuminate for the military professional the true "untidiness" of history: the dynamic processes whereby the conflicting influences of politics, events, decisions, personalities, and other factors (such as supply and weather) interact to guarantee that the outcome of the battle rarely, if ever, matches the original plan. They first must draw attention to the *stress lines* and *gray areas* that are endemic to the military's highly structured decision making, and second, ensure that the profession's historical writing and education are guided to and by those focal points.

This approach bears some elaboration, which will be developed in the following manner. First, the chapter will examine the junction (and the tension) between what might be called the *functional* and the *dialectical* planes, which run through both military planning and historical analysis. Second, it will consider the discontinuities in real time between policy, military strategy, operations, and tactics. Finally, it will highlight the organizations that are responsible for execution of these at all levels, for this is where the overlaps and discontinuities produce the gray areas which are areas that have not received adequate historical treatment.

FUNCTION AND DIALECTIC IN MILITARY ACTIVITY

A fundamental characteristic of military historical analysis is that it must approach its subject on the functional and dialectical planes simultaneously. The stress lines that occur within and between these planes are central to both the manner in which the military profession executes its tasks and the way in which historians portray the execution. Taking this conception a stage further, on the first plane, military staffs and units are organized (to carry out their missions) in a standard manner by function. Of course, the divisions between the functional elements (for example, between staff and line) are not—in practice—fully discrete. Between the hierarchical layers of people or branches responsible for planning and executing policy, strategy, operations, and tactics, there are fields of overlapping responsibility, and hence, the stress lines along which occurs much of the "friction" that fuels historical accounts. Nonetheless, these are common functions that transcend national experience. German, Canadian, and American forces are trained to do the same things in very similar ways; the purpose and organization of their staffs and units are similar.

On the other hand, the way in which each military institution is directed, trained, equipped, and staffed is influenced by factors on the dialectical plane: the political, social, cultural, and economic history of the nation it serves, as well as the characteristics of the political leadership and the current domestic and foreign trends acting on the leadership and the nation. As a result of the dialectical influence, there is a difference between armies when they meet, even if both are organized and equipped in a similar manner, have trained from the same texts, and have striven for the same results. If war is a test of functional efficiency, it is also a contest of these dialectical factors. The military professional is likely to be less familiar with the latter and to have little patience for them, because they are not amenable to definitive, empirical, "functional" analysis. However, if either the historians or the military consider only the functional plane, their judgments of decisions, events, and commanders may be too harsh. Furthermore, obsessed with function, they may overlook the peculiarities—even genius—in national styles of making war, for these often defy military logic and can only be understood in dialectical terms. Somehow, the two planes must be reconciled, and it is as much an art to accomplish this in historical accounts as it is in real time.[3]

Reconciliation is essential when historians judge very senior commanders. High-ranking officers are required to balance dialectical factors against functional considerations, and the higher their place in the chain of command, the more weight they must give to the former. Ironically, "supreme commanders" may be such in name only, for they seldom can do as they would wish. While more junior officers will expect the commander to devote time to their functional concerns, the political leaders will insist that the commander-in-chief adhere to their directives, which are inspired by national, and hence largely dialectical, imperatives. Indeed, the coalition commanders of the twentieth century have been nailed to a symbolic cross, with the vertical post representing the dialectical demands and the horizontal one the functional. In attempting to provide a full and fair rendering of command history to the military professional, the historian must understand the tension between these contradictory planes, which pull senior commanders in two directions at once, and write sympathetically of those in that position, particularly if they struggle honestly to resolve their dilemma.

Some applications of this dualistic approach may serve to illustrate it in concrete terms. Historians have tended to praise as progressive J.F.C. Fuller's writing about armor during the interwar period. However, his analysis was unsound from a functional perspective. German experience with antitank guns from 1917 and 1918 and French writing on the subject pointed directly to their mastery of the tank. On the other hand, British experience showed that while tanks were still mechanically unreliable and relatively blind, they could scatter enemy infantry caught in the open and that infantry accompanying the tanks could chase the antitank crews from their guns. This suggested a line of reasoning that was apparent in the military literature in the early 1920s: that the key to the future was to be seen in team action—combined arms operations—and in the improvement of each arm individually. Of course, this was not a new idea; it had been mentioned in the British Army's *Field Service Regulations* as early as 1909 and had almost materialized again in 1917 and 1918. Fuller himself had included it in his postwar writing among a list of "Principles of War." The difficulty, as always, was putting such an idea into practice. Neither Fuller nor B. H. Liddell Hart were enlightening on how to do that, for they had run up against the dialectical factors, which saved them from having to fully develop their ideas. It was British policy, rather than the stupidity of successive chiefs of the Imperial General Staff, that was the insuperable obstacle to the development of armored divisions and doctrine. Traditionally maritime and imperial, British foreign policy did not envision a "continental commitment" (and hence, a requirement for such formations) until February 1939. Other dialectical factors included the weakness of the British car industry (compounded by the Depression) which hampered the technical development of armored vehicles. These factors eluded Fuller's grasp, and he never appreciated their influence on his superiors. However, he was (and is) not alone in this; for the significance of these factors often has been lost not only on the military professional, but on the historian as well.

DISCONTINUITIES: POLICY, STRATEGY, OPERATIONS, AND TACTICS

However, in order to interpret the past correctly for the benefit of the military, it is essential for the historian to disentangle and understand the functional and dialectical elements and their relationship to each other. At the lower level of operations in the field, the functional dimension is of primary concern to the soldier, and historical investigation of this is not as complex as that for higher levels. At those higher echelons, command and staff records seldom reveal how compromises between functional and dialectical considerations were made. In those documents tracks are sometimes consciously covered, both to protect current participants and to thwart historical sleuths in the future. Whereas it is difficult to conceal the military events on the ground to which high-level decisions gave rise, the accounts of those decisions may be abridged in the official record; the right explanations for actions, rather than the real ones, tend to be recorded. It is here that the historian invariably encounters discontinuity between the plan and its execution.

These problems are not confined to the original documents, but are also to be found in the official histories and those commissioned by units themselves. Although the functional accounts (or events on the battlefield) may be the same in each, the dialectical influences are ironed out so that they appear to dovetail with the functional facts. This will leave the reader with an impression of tidiness, of a reasonable resolution of differences to the extent that any problems remaining did not have a detrimental effect on the soldier.

To challenge this orthodoxy, it obviously helps if the historian is familiar with the normal procedures of military decision making and the Standard Operating Procedures (SOPs) for carrying out operations. That is, the historian must understand the military functions of strategic, operational, and tactical planning. A study of the history of a plan, of the progressive but often unrelated changes in its object and its details, and of the alleged reasons for the changes is a useful preliminary to understanding the thoughts of the commanders who carried it out. In doing so, the historian may find that the political and military aims—the means provided and the methods employed—became variables that diverged progressively from each other, while the commanders on the scene struggled to keep them together.

The plan for BAYTOWN, the invasion of the toe of Italy, provides one example of this. As late as mid-June 1943, the plan was quite different from the operation that was carried out in September. First, in the original plan, British 10th Corps was to assault across the Straits of Messina while the fighting in Sicily was still in course. Eventually, 10th Corps went to Salerno with 5th Army, and BAYTOWN was carried out by 13th Corps, which had fought its way through Sicily while 10th Corps was still planning. Second, the aims of the operation also changed. Originally, it had two objectives: to knock Italy out of the war by a quick occupation of the south and to enable Allied ships to operate in the straits, thereby cutting supplies to the German troops still fighting in Sicily. What eventually occurred, the rapid move north after the landings in Calabria to link up with Mark Clark's 5th Army, was not part of the original plan but rather an improvization, provoked by the apparent crisis at the Salerno beachhead. Third, the date for BAYTOWN was changed several times to accommodate progress in negotiating Italy's withdrawal from the war. These changes did not take into account staff preparations, the shortage of landing craft, or the availability of transport for the assault divisions. Moreover, the Germans' success in escaping from Sicily had been concealed effectively until the crisis at Salerno. At that point it became politically advantageous to exaggerate the strength of German forces in southern Italy in order to explain Mark Clark's difficulties and to obscure the mismanagement of the Italian surrender, which was announced at a most inopportune moment.[4]

As the BAYTOWN example illustrates, a close study of high-level planning reveals discontinuities that are explicable only if one recognizes that plans are usually written back to front. That is, instead of first studying the conditions of the battlefield and then generating an intention and drafting an appropriate plan that matches intentions to conditions, it often appears that the general intention is declared first and a plan is then contrived. Consequently, the military conditions that prevailed at the plan's conception may have changed by the time the plan is executed—after a period of negotiation during which other factors have entered the equation. The circle of reasoning between a situation, a solution, and back to the situation is rarely completed in the fashion theoretically intended. Rather, a series of negotiations and compromises lead to frantic improvization by the commanders who execute the plan. This process reveals the stress lines that occur naturally in military planning within and between the policy, strategic, operational, and tactical levels. However, many historians prefer to adhere to the official version of events that glosses over these contradictions, when, in fact, they should regard the stress lines as the richest potential locus of research and insight.

Policy is promulgated at the strategic level, by the military, among other agencies, for policy has many branches; military strategy is but one arm of policy, and there is tension between it and the others. Historical interest at this level lies in showing how that tension influences policy decisions and their translation into strategy. The modern military has much to learn from accounts that explain this. In World War II, for example, the British had a great advantage in that their senior commanders had experience working in the intricate committee system (dating from the establishment of the Committee of Imperial Defence in 1904) that linked military and civilian agencies. After 1918, that system evolved further in recognition of the experience of the "Great War," which revealed unresolved stress lines between the military and the other sources of strategic planning. By contrast, the Americans, for reasons arising from the U.S. Constitution, kept civil and military matters separate. Consequently, the various agencies, including the military, had to rely on unofficial channels or "staged" forums to communicate with each other and to resolve differences. Success often depended on circumventing the rules, which was time-consuming and bad for interservice relations. Indeed, George Marshall, Chief of Staff of the U.S. Army, commented on several occasions on the marked contrast between the difficult relations of the Joint Chiefs of Staff with President Franklin Delano Roosevelt and the more workable relationship between Winston Churchill and the British Chiefs of Staff Committee.

The operational level, which is below that of strategy, has been neglected until recently in Anglo-American military thought, although not in German and Russian studies. This might be attributed to a certain intellectual laziness on the part of Western defense writers, who recognized only strategy and the tactical means by which strategy is executed. However, the gap between the general means by which the task delegated to the military should be carried out and the practical level of tactics required to do so remained too wide unless an extra level was introduced. That level is operations, which constitutes the true link between strategy and tactics. Operations have to serve the chosen strategy and be practicable in light of the current tactical situation. Obviously, there are tensions on either flank, and historians must take them into consideration. Likewise, the stress caused by the absence of an "operational" level of military thinking needs to be recognized in historical accounts.

Two examples should suffice here. In the first case, when Sir Douglas Haig seized the operational initiative for the first time by mounting the battle of Third Ypres (Passchendaele) in 1917, he undertook an operation based on a plan that was insecure both in strategy and in tactics. The weaknesses of the plan were apparent as early as 1915, when Brigadier General Frederick Maurice first considered it in a staff study. However, at the root of the problem was Haig himself; he was a loose cannon both on the battlefield and in the politics of the higher direction of the war. In London, where the land strategy loomed too large, even the high command doubted whether the plan for Third Ypres offered the best solution to the strategic problem on the Western Front or that it would fulfill the War Council's immediate goal, which was to solve the submarine crisis. However, domestic politics precluded any interference with Haig's execution of the limited land strategy that had been agreed to in Paris in May 1917. Politics thus proved to be the deciding factor that permitted Haig to continue.

At the front, the fact that army commanders had to share responsibility for operations with General Headquarters (GHQ) (that is, with Haig) was the source of considerable frustration and a number of disputes between GHQ and those commanders. Haig ignored the principle that commanders should be allowed to decide how to execute a commander in chief's (CinC's) directive; instead, he designed the operational plans himself. Even so, Third Ypres might not have been a decisive error had the operational plan matched the tactical situation. In that case, a series of limited tactical successes, the most that could be expected under the circumstances prevailing at that time, would have amounted to a successful operation. Of course, such a success would have served the Western Front strategy. The problem was that Haig habitually set operational goals that were impractical from a tactical perspective, and Third Ypres was no exception. General John Davidson, Haig's chief of operations in 1917, and generals Sir Henry Rawlinson and The Lord Plumer, the two army commanders directly responsible for carrying out the plan, objected that it was tactically unsound, as Maurice had shown in 1915. However, their objections were ignored, the operation went ahead, and the British army experienced yet another costly defeat.

Such an outcome is inevitable if a plan is tactically impracticable, and defeat obviously cannot serve strategy. The obverse is also true; even if they are practical, operations should not be undertaken if they do not advance the chosen strategy. In 1944 General Dwight D. Eisenhower made both errors simultaneously: He approved operations that were likely to fail on tactical grounds and that, even if they had succeeded, would have hindered the strategy that he and his staff had enunciated after the breakout from Normandy in August 1944. That approach had the American First army and the British Second Army fighting side by side north of the Ardennes. However, George Marshall, Omar Bradley and George Patton found that politically unpalatable. Therefore, to keep his American commanders happy, he allowed them to mount their own operations which split the Anglo-American advance into two parts. Through a mixture of deception and laissez-faire (evident in successive contradictory directives and in less-than-candid letters to Marshall), he passed this off as a "broad front strategy.'' Logistically starved and thus too weak for their tasks, each of the armies failed in turn, as Eisenhower's own staff had predicted. They had assumed that the intention was to defeat the enemy in the field, and the plan they devised took into consideration the available means. Eisenhower's real strategy, however, was to ensure—for ''political'' reasons—that the American army groups ''carried the ball.'' The resultant operations collectively represented a compromise between a plan that served Eisenhower's personal strategic agenda and that favored by his staff and the Combined Chiefs of Staff. To justify this strategy (if it may be flattered by that word), Eisenhower and Bradley convinced themselves in September that the German Army was near to defeat, and they clung to that illusion until the Germans' Ardennes counteroffensive shocked them out of it in December. As a result, the Allied armies, stalled along a wide front by logistical problems, exhausted themselves in small actions, while the Germans gained time to fight on.[5]

These cases illustrate the importance for historians of analyzing the structure of decision making at the joins, at the disjunctions that actually occurred in real time on the battlefield between strategy, operations, and tactics. The history of even successful operations has much to do with what happens along these stress lines, where function conflicts with dialectic and person with person. The role of personalities may be considered in light of whether they anticipated and prevented interpersonal conflicts or exacerbated them with negative consequences for operations and strategy.

When approached in the manner suggested above, the study of policy and strategy formation, and thence of operations is valuable to politicians and senior professional officers because it has a long historical half-life. The truths extracted from the method may help one become ''wise forever'' about the problems of high command. Junior ranks, on the other hand, find more to interest them in the junction between operations and tactics. At the tactical level, the contribution of historians is brought into question by the popular assumption that new weapons make old battlefield methods irrelevant. This view reduces military biographies and memoirs to museum pieces, to be read solely for entertainment, and relegates the study of past battlefields to a merely inspirational role. However, clearly this view is not shared by the military colleges and schools, which continue to use case histories to teach lessons; in fact, they often rely on the in-house historians to select and construct the cases. The most useful contribution that historians outside the military can make is to highlight and explain the dialectical elements that may show *why* particular tactics were used, rather than whether they were right or wrong in light of more modern teaching. After all, in theory at least, current tactical doctrine is based in some degree on what was done before; how it worked or how it was perceived to have failed. Unfortunately, in practice, the tactical picture is rarely so clear, either in real time or in the historical record, that the cause and effect of decisions, plans, actions, and reactions of people can be easily distilled and useful ''lessons'' can be extracted. John English's latest work *The Canadian Army and the Normandy Campaign*, which examined both preparation and performance in the crucible of battle, is a pioneering attempt at this.[6]

Wrestling with tactical problems requires considerable familiarity with military functions, but it is neither an impossible nor an unimportant subject of historical inquiry. The fact that it has taken historians a long time to tackle objectively the tactical level in World War I is due in large measure to the problems of the British official history series. First, it took thirty years to produce the series (it was not completed until 1948), and second, it homogenized strategy, operations, and tactics into a single, undifferentiated form of combat: trench warfare. Finally, although the official historians understood how the staff worked, what the duties in a headquarters were, the routine of a commander and his relations with his staff, and how these structural details affected the conduct of battles, they were writing for the cognoscenti and did not see a need to include this information in the histories, below the operational level. Consequently, later generations of unofficial historians have had to waste a lot of time trying to figure out exactly what much of the official writing implies, regarding these functions at the tactical level.

However, the weakness in Western Front historiography has also been methodological. Contrary to Clausewitz's advice in his chapters on "Method and Routine," "Critical Analysis," and "Historical Examples," writers seem to have started from a general assumption rather than analyzing the details at the sharp end and working upward. Simply stated, the assumption is that World War I was an unmitigated disaster, a failure of military function; the role of historical writing, therefore, has been to show how and why this was so. This approach, of course, has been the easiest and most popular, but it is the product of intellectual laziness. The truth of the matter is that to follow Clausewitz's dictum—working from the sharp end up—is slow, hard work. As Sir Ian Hamilton wrote in his observations on the Russo-Japanese War: "On the actual day of battle naked truths may be picked up for the asking; but the following morning they have already begun to get into their uniforms." Some of them remain scantily clad much longer, but the historian has to know enough about function and tactics in order to distinguish the partly-dressed from those in the new uniforms. That means that the historian must ask the right questions. However, those questions emerge only when one attempts to understand and describe a battle in detail from the ground up. This process will show how little one knows and how much one needs to learn. It is a chastening experience, but a much more thorough history is likely to result. In short, it is a mistake to begin historical research at the commander's chateau. The historian should reach that level only when he or she knows enough to ask the commander some awkward questions. The corollary to this is that the military professional, the official, and unofficial historians have a joint responsibility to record functional details, warts and all, before they are tidied-up, altered, buried, or forgotten.

ORGANIZATIONAL FRICTION: A HISTORICAL GRAY AREA

Historical *gray areas* are characterized by lack of obvious interest (often because they are not at "the sharp end") and hence, lack of demand; difficulty in research; lack of required expertise; or perhaps a failure to grasp the need to study them. In historical studies, politics is usually treated as the final arbiter of events. Thus, social and economic history, however important in their own right, are not regarded as mainstream until they are subsumed within political history. Likewise, within military history, certain aspects tend to be overlooked when the focus of attention is fixed on the last 400 meters of the battlefield; logistics is a case in point.

There is a strong case to be made that the story of Allied policy- and strategy-making in World War II is largely the story of the politics of managing logistics. Explicitly or implicitly, it lay behind every question discussed by the Combined Chiefs of Staff. Quite clearly, however, it has an impact on operations. For example, in order to make his office as Army chief of staff into an operational headquarters in 1942, General George Marshall absorbed within his Operations Planning Division all branches of the staff. However, there was friction between his own G4 (Logistics) staff and that of General Brehon Somervell who served simultaneously as commander of the U.S. Army Service Forces and as Marshall's chief G4 staff officer. In that position, with what amounted to a parallel army also under his command, Somervell was "Mr. Supply" and a power in his own right. The friction that ensued between Marshall's and Somervell's staffs explains in large measure the logistics problems that occurred in Northwest Europe in 1944–1945.

There are several points that follow from this. First, the military typically displays two reactions to situations that appear to be the result of friction between branches. One is to change the system, and the other is to change the personnel. There may be, in fact, something wrong with either or both. However, commanders and historians need to recognize that changing one or the other would not necessarily solve the problem of friction, because friction at overlapping functional points is natural and not simply the result of mismanagement or misbehavior. It is important for historians in particular to remember this when they investigate stories that center on logistical failures. Second, they may recount such stories satisfactorily as part of the history of logistics, but to integrate that with operations is more difficult. The fundamental question is, to what extent did it affect operations? Until they answer that question, logistics remains, like social history, outside the military historical mainstream, interesting in and of itself but contributing little to our understanding of the "big picture."

The same argument applies to a previously gray area that is now receiving more attention: the history of military intelligence. As Keith Jeffery points out elsewhere in this volume, the field is moving toward a maturity that will see intelligence fully integrated into the study of military history at all levels, but it is not there yet. For those seeking a model for integrating the gray areas into the mainstream, William McAndrew's chapter exemplifies this theme precisely. Using medical science and its various branches as a window, he has drawn through it morale, operational methods, training, and the supply of personnel and related them to specific operations, giving a wholly new perspective on the performance of soldiers and units under the stress of combat.[7] Making such connections is not easy, but it can and must be done if historians are to move closer to understanding what it means to be a commander in battle.

CONCLUSIONS: IMPLICATIONS FOR THE MILITARY AND THE HISTORIAN

The main purpose of this chapter was to expose some of the stress lines in military activity of which both professional soldiers and military historians need to be aware. These stress lines occur at the junctions of the functional and dialectical planes of military planning and action and in the discontinuities between policy, military strategy, operations, and tactics. Finally, they are implicit in the overlapping boundaries between the different organizations that are responsible for the execution of policy and plans at all levels. Wherever stress lines exist, friction occurs naturally. However, because of the difficulty of dealing with such sources of friction and their implications for operations, it is also natural that military professionals and military historians alike have tended to avoid them; in the historians' case, this overlooks gray areas in the historical record and leaves the story of strategy, operations, and tactics incomplete. However, it is clear that senior commanders expend most of their waking hours coping with friction at these junction points. Historians need to write about them with that fact in mind, for without this Clausewitzian concept, which points the historian to the structural sources of friction, the history of war will be either mechanical or formless, entertaining perhaps, but incapable of making the military profession "wise forever."

The application of the historical method in this way has important implications for the relationship between the military historians and the subject of his or her inquiry, the military profession. It also places the historian in something of a quandary. The professional ethic of the historical discipline demands detachment from the subject of study, but the approach to the subject described above requires a degree of intimacy that other historians might find unseemly. Nonetheless, it is essential, for the profession of "managers of violence" *is* different from all others. In order to understand fully how this institution functions, historians who write to educate both the public and the military itself have a responsibility to study it as closely as possible. This means studying the "living" institution and its members—individually and collectively—as well as the documents in the archives. They must learn what has been taught in the military and why—what is likely to work and what is not, in peace as well as in war. In this sense, they may find themselves of one mind with some military professionals and at odds with others. While a certain detachment is essential, historians who are not prepared to attain the intimate knowledge of organization and function and their interaction at all levels at headquarters and on the battlefield—the very stuff of which the military story is made—ought to restrict their work to intellectual history or unenlightening generalities; otherwise, they will write only military nonsense, and not military history. Those who do make the effort, however, are likely to have something very worthwhile to say to both professions.

NOTES

1. Paul Kennedy, *The Rise and Fall of the Great Powers: Economic Change and Military Conflict from 1500 to 2000* (New York: Random House, 1987).

2. Richard E. Neustadt and Ernest R. May, *Thinking in Time: The Uses of History for Decision Makers* (New York: Free Press, 1986).

3. See M. M. Postan, "Function and Dialectic in Economic History," *Economic Historical Review* 14 no. 3 (1962): 397–407, for a discussion of this conceptual approach.

4. Shelford Bidwell and Dominick Graham, *Tug of War: The Battle for Italy, 1943–1945* (New York: St. Martin's Press, 1986), part 2: "Salerno."

5. *The Papers of Dwight D. Eisenhower*, vol. 4, The War Years, ed. Alfred D. Chandler (Baltimore, MD: Johns Hopkins University Press, 1970); Letters to George Marshall mainly in September 1944, and directives to Army Group Commanders in September and October. "SHAEF Operations, 1944," Nevins Papers, Military History Institute, Carlisle Barracks, PA.

6. John A. English, *The Canadian Army and the Normandy Campaign: A Study of Failure in High Command* (New York: Praeger, 1991).

7. For a fuller discussion of the subject, see Terry Copp and Bill McAndrew, *Battle Exhaustion: Soldiers and Psychiatrists in the Canadian Army, 1939–1945* (Montreal: McGill-Queen's University Press, 1990).

11

History as Institutional Memory:
The Experience of
the United States Air Force

RICHARD H. KOHN

In late 1942, in response to a directive from the president of the United States to record the history of each wartime agency for future use, U.S. Army Air Forces Commanding General Henry H. Arnold established a historical program for the U.S. land-based air forces. It "becomes increasingly important that the record of our participation . . . be accurately recorded and preserved," he wrote to one of his commanders, "for the final analysis of accomplishments, as well as failures and responsibilities for each."[1] Historians during World War II served with units throughout the air forces, writing monthly an account that, together with the documents generated by their organization, recorded to an unprecedented degree the activities of the service during its most extensive wartime effort. The program continued after the war and, over time, was broadened and improved both in quality and usefulness. However, the purpose always remained as Arnold conceived it: to record what the forces did, how they performed their duty and accomplished their mission, and why they chose particular courses of action, in order to have a record to guide future activity.

The air force historical program, then and now, does not differ in concept from what other military establishments have done for over a century: that is, to create a special set of records for use in making the service more efficient and effective in combat. While the purposes are similar, official military history programs in the U.S. Department of Defense and in military establishments across the world vary in organization and focus. Some emphasize scholarly publication, officer education, or the most recent past, while others stress museums or the maintenance of archives. The range and mix of activities gives each of the programs a distinctive character. Where the U.S. Air Force effort differs from that of other military organizations lies in how it is organized and staffed and in its emphasis on the practical business of recording and using past experience.

First, the U.S. Air Force (USAF) has widened the concept of recording beyond combat operations to include virtually all aspects of its institutional life, in peace as well as in war. Its concept of usage has also expanded to include all aspects of policy- and decision-making, as well as professional military education, the writing of doctrine, and operations. Second, in organization and in execution, the program does not rely on uniformed or civilian people who spend a few days or hours at the end of a reporting cycle to create a brief compilation of information; instead, civilians, officers, and enlisted people who are professionally trained and who work full-time gather the most important material relating to mission activities and write a fully documented history that is as accurate, comprehensive, objective, and analytical as can be produced so soon after the events. Third, the air force deploys the vast majority of its historians in the field with its units, all the way down to the wing level and at virtually every headquarters above that level (at the numbered air forces and equivalent levels in support commands and at the highest field levels—the Major Command, and Field Operating Agency). In essence, the U.S. Air Force treats history as a staff function, which is fully integrated into the command and management of the forces. Nearly every commander above the squadron level has a full-time historian on his or her staff, who, along with the planners, operators, police, medical, public affairs, communications, and logistics people, help to manage the unit, train it, prepare it for battle, and employ it in combat. In the U.S. Air Force (USAF), the historian is integral to command, to the process by which staff work is accomplished, and to the functioning of the unit.

Day to day, and as a basis for operations, Air Force historians focus their effort on collection and dissemination: recording the history as it occurs by selecting documents out of the mass of paper generated, interviewing participants, attending meetings, and observing in every way possible the events that must be described, explained, and analyzed. From this evidence the historians support commanders and staffs in a variety of ways. The history and memorabilia of the organization can focus members on their mission and contribute to cohesion, morale, and efficiency. Individual bits of information and larger studies support the activity at all levels. The goal is to make a continuous and positive impact on policy, decision making, and operations, pervasively throughout the command.

The History Program across the air force consists essentially of three elements. The largest is in the field where, in the Major Commands, and Field Operating Agencies—those operating and support organizations that actually fly the aircraft or maintain and support them and the smaller, air force–wide agencies that provide support throughout the service—historians write an annual or semiannual history of what happened in that headquarters, unit, or organization. These documents are the vehicle by which historians collect the data. However, the histories are much more than aggregates of data; they are comprehensive, accurate, objective, and analytical narratives, often several hundred pages in length, and include one or more volumes of copies of the documents that are cited in the footnotes or are otherwise necessary to explicate events. Histories capture an enormous treasure of seemingly routine statistical, personnel, and logistical data, but they focus most heavily on the operations and mission efforts, detailing the accomplishments as well as the difficulties and problems encountered. At the lower echelons (the numbered air forces, research and development laboratories, logistical and training centers, and other organizations), the histories are reviewed and indeed "graded" by the major command history office as a way of assuring quality. At the wings, carefully recruited, specially trained noncommissioned officers write the histories and those are assessed and critiqued by the numbered air force historians. In forty years, these histories, with their documentary annexes, have proven to be the most satisfactory method of recording events. Most of these histories are classified. They are reviewed by the different staff elements from which the material came and by the commander (or his or her office) for accuracy, completeness, and verisimilitude. Almost never are they censored or vetted in any way; commanders largely understand the value and purpose of these documents and make every effort to help their historians create a reliable record.

The histories and other documents saved (each of the 200 or so history offices includes an archive of other useful sources retained over the years) comprise a data base. With other source materials, historians in the headquarters answer queries for information and prepare special studies, monographs, briefings, and other papers, which are usually requested by senior staff or by commanders but are also sometimes volunteered by the historian in the belief that they will be useful to decision-makers. These products help commanders and staffs in various mission areas, including negotiations with foreign governments, developing and integrating new weapon systems and aircraft; servicing or modifying equipment; deciding where to locate it at bases, experimenting with tactics in combat, and planning whole air campaigns. The usefulness and effectiveness of the historians depend on numerous factors, but over the years, they have increasingly come to be viewed as valuable staff members who can make unique and often indispensable contributions to the essential mission work of the organization.

The second element in the historical program is the Air Force Historical Research Agency (formerly the USAF Historical Research Center), at Maxwell Air Force Base, which is co-located with the library at the Air University in the center of an academic circle that includes the principal commissioned professional military education schools and associated research and war-gaming agencies of the service. The Agency houses a paper copy of every unit history, along with over 2,000 oral history interviews, 400 collections of personal papers, and other special records: altogether, over 60 million pages of documents going back to before World War I. The material grows each year by over a million pages, not counting special documentation from operations like Desert Shield and Desert Storm, which alone generated over a million pages of material.[2] The Agency accessions, stores, and makes available these documents to the service and, when unclassified, to the public. Virtually all the documents are microfilmed so that the units, almost all of which lack storage space, can jettison the paper copies of these multivolume documents. The Agency also provides bibliographical information and research help for the most difficult queries for information, those that require a broader document collection than an individual unit can support and those that come from outside the air force (from elsewhere in government, from foreign governments, and from the general public—an average of 5,000 queries a year). Air force units also turn to the Agency to update their lineage and honors data, or to change or create new unit emblems. As the air force began to shrink in the aftermath of the Cold War, the Agency undertook a large project to identify those flying units with the most interesting and distinguished lineage so that they could be retained. A small research staff answers requests for information and another small cell from this wealth of data writes reference books on bases, units, operations, and similar topics so that users have handy tools for finding information and historians can save time and effort answering questions for their clients. A computer index allows a researcher to find by means of key word search the documents pertaining to a particular issue or area; for example, if an air force commander needs information about B–52 landing gear problems in cold weather, the historian can tap into the data to ascertain which of those tens of thousands of different documents contain discussions of the problem. The Agency also supports Air University, helping with education in the various service schools and with research at Air University on doctrine, education, and operations. Likewise, the Agency supports the wider air force historical effort, hosting and administering courses on oral history and archives (and serving as the focus for expertise in those areas), and on historical method and airpower history, all for the ongoing education of historians, the military, and civilians.

The third tier in the system is the Center for Air Force History (formerly the Office of Air Force History) located in Washington, D.C., which has two missions. First, the Center researches, writes, and publishes books on air power and on the history of air operations and institutions, not only of the U.S. Air Force but of others as well, in order to broadcast a wider understanding of air power in the service, across the government, and among the public. Formed in 1969 to write the history of the Southeast Asia War and to improve the program as a whole by giving it a strong headquarters presence, the Center offers books on a range of topics, guided by a publication plan which is revised every three years after wide consultation within and outside the Air Force. At any given time, over two dozen volumes are being written, half on contract and half within the Center. The books, while meeting the highest standards of scholarship, target as their primary audience air force officers, who can use them for professional perspective as well as practical guides for policy and operational planning. The books provide the most practical method of disseminating the experience of air power to an institution that is determined to use every tool of analysis to accomplish its mission more effectively.

Second, the Center supports the headquarters of the air force in the very same way that a command history serves its commander and staff: through ongoing maintenance of a record and data base by means of an annual history and specialized archive and the provision of research services and analytical works in support of policy- and decision-making. In 1985, a small staff moved to the Pentagon to be closer to the Air Staff, and that group has grown continuously more active as Air Staff officers and civilians in the secretariat have learned to use historians in everyday business. To cite one example: In early August 1990, the special group created to help plan an air campaign in the Persian Gulf requested a historian, not only to record the very special planning project but to aid in the application of historical experience to the war.[3]

Finally, the entire Air Force history program is managed functionally by the Air Force Historian, who is located in the Pentagon. Formerly titled the Chief, Office of Air Force History, the Historian supervises the Commander of the Air Force Historical Research Agency and the Director of the Center for Air Force History, providing policy guidance and technical direction. The Historian provides what might be termed "functional management of the Air Force historical program: making policy for the system and setting the goals and professional standards for the historical work, assisting in the recruitment of the highest quality people and assuring their continued training and professional development, providing liaison and coordination with other historical programs in the United States and abroad, deploying historians to cover combat and contingencies, and advising the air force leadership on historical matters generally.

It is likely that this program is the most comprehensive and systematic among the world's military establishments. Its distinguishing feature is its practical character: applied history in the most direct sense of that term. Historians contribute frequently: answering queries, providing documents, doing special analytical studies, and writing broader analyses and works for the range of air force activity. Unlike many of the world's official military history efforts, that of the U.S. Air Force is largely peopled by civilian professionals and enlisted men and women rather than officers or ex-officers. The program does not include museums or art or photographic archives, which in the USAF belong properly in the public affairs function. Nor do the historians work directly in officer education or training; those activities are separately organized and staffed at Air University and in Air Training Command. However, historical work is used frequently in curricula, historical materials are often prepared or furnished by Air Force historians, and the faculties of the schools include professional historians. The USAF has chosen to embed its primary historical effort within the purview of the commander, thereby making history a function of command so that it can be integrated as closely as possible with the application and use of air forces. To the U.S. Air Force, the "lessons of the past" provide an ongoing guide to the present and future.

The system cannot merely be measured by its role and organization, however. Legitimately one may ask how frequently history is actually used, to what purpose, and with what result. Little doubt remains about the frequency of use. Over the last ten years, historical activity has grown across the service. Annually, historians answer 35,000 queries for information (not counting those that require no research and thus are not recorded), about 25,000 in the field and between 5 and 6 thousand each at the Agency and the Center; in the field almost all queries come from commanders and staffs, while at the Agency and Center half come from within the air force and the others from outside government agencies, foreign governments, scholars, and the public. At the Agency and Center, this query load has doubled in a decade. Other statistical indices have also jumped in recent years: the number of microfilm reels circulated and sold, the number of documents used at the Agency, the number of visiting researchers (over 1,000 each at the Agency and at the Washington Center yearly), involvement in professional military education, and Freedom of Information Act requests for documents. One senses from users that historians and historical analysis come more readily to mind than they did ten years ago; they are also more visible and have become more useful.

More difficult to evaluate is the extent to which history affects policy and decisions. Without question the program pumps out large quantities of books, documents, answers to queries, and other products. Across the system every year the history offices publish a half dozen new books and write up to 200 special studies and two dozen monographs. Anecdotal evidence suggests that historical material is the basis for major decisions or alterations in strategy, operations, tactics, or other activity. Clients praise the utility of historical data. Likewise, there seems, over time, to be less use of historians for naming streets or buildings on bases, producing photo displays for hallways, and other heritage activities which, while important and useful to the units, do not make the most effective use of the historian's time, the material he or she possesses, or the talent that he or she can bring to bear on an issue or problem. Frequently, historians save money for the government, for example in environmental suits, by identifying what occurred when, where certain materials are stored or buried, and who caused what. Once a group of former officers sued the air force for $35 million over inadequate quarters in Thailand during the Southeast Asia War; when historians found documents showing what the size of those quarters actually as, the suit was withdrawn. The NATO allies some years ago tried to persuade U.S. Air Forces in Europe to pay the entire cost of the new ground-launched cruise missile bases, but historians remembered that the host nations had agreed to pay a share. The result: $20 million in savings for the United States. New commanders often read the previous year's history before assuming their duties. Some years ago, one joined his wing immediately after it had failed an operational readiness inspection because of bombing inaccuracy; he researched the histories until he found the change in training procedures, altered them back to previous practice, and promptly won the Strategic Air Command B–52 bombing competition the very next year. In one fighter command, historical data discredited computer simulations indicating that jets could not penetrate surface-to-air missile belts, while in another, historical experience suggested changes in tactics to better assure the penetration of enemy air defenses. Time and again, historical data on pattern of operations, deployments, basing, and other activity have enabled staffs to plan better, to save time and money, and to better assure the success of a particular course of action. A study of the inquiries in one major command history office revealed that over half came from the operational units, the commander or his action group, the director of operations, or the director of plans. Deployments and exercises are often based on previous experience, testing and research are guided by earlier and similar events, and doctrine is formulated largely on the basis of historical memory. The air force uses experience to structure its forces, develop its weapons, and plan and execute its operations. One chief of staff stated that "airpower, as we know it today, has grown from the lessons we learned and the innovations we made" in World War II; "we are engaged in a process of evolutionary development that has roots in the framework that emerged from our victory in the air."[4]

Nonetheless, no statistical or anecdotal evidence can possibly measure history's impact on the institution. One secretary of the air force, a most thoughtful man who read the office's books and used history in his work, was once asked to give a specific instance of history affecting a decision. He could not at that moment cite a single example, despite his certainty of the value of historical perspective. Perhaps senior officials find it difficult or even impossible to isolate the reasons, by category of "input," for a particular decision.[5] Time and again, historians provide documents, information, special studies, or other help, yet never learn the result or the effect.

My own experience as Chief of the Office of Air Force History was probably typical in this regard. Invariably, our office had to ask its clients in order to learn how a study or a piece of information had been used or to find out the impact of our work. The office wrote a sixty-page analysis of major honor code violations at the U.S. Military and Air Force Academies since World War II at the request of the deputy chief of staff for manpower and personnel; the deputy chief, the chief of staff, and the secretary used it to assess and eventually to approve major changes in the Air Force Academy's honor system that had been proposed by the Superintendent. A recent incoming inspector general asked for a study of the evolution of the function of his office since its creation, set against the historic role of inspectors general in the American military; he used the document to clarify the role of the Inspector General in the air force and as the basis for a "white paper" delineating policy in the IG Department. Once, as I was leaving his office, the chief of staff stopped me to request a study of reform in Russian and Soviet history, mentioning an earlier paper I had done that he "had found so insightful." It took me several minutes to recall the earlier paper, not only because it was a short written addendum to a verbal exchange during his staff meeting six months before, but because he had not mentioned it since. That confirmed my earlier suspicion that if this particular chief scrawled his thanks on a paper and sent it back, it was helpful; but if he said nothing and the paper disappeared, it was likely to have been truly valuable, for he had used it in some fashion: sent it to someone for their edification, used it in the staffing process, or sent it elsewhere for action.

The commitment of the air force to the value and use of history arose again dramatically during the Persian Gulf War. Within ten days of the initial decision to intervene, historians began arriving in the theater to record the event. Eventually, some forty air force enlisted historians served in the Middle East. Two weeks after the operation began, the chief of staff tasked the office of Air Force History specifically to assure that the coverage would be comprehensive and complete. Upon arriving in Saudi Arabia, the air commander quickly formed a history office at his headquarters and gave his historian enormous support, urging and sometimes ordering subordinate commanders to make certain that historians had full access to all the people, information, and documents necessary for a full rendering of events. The general asked the Office of Air Force History for books and articles on desert warfare and recent conflicts in the area in order to read such recent experience personally and make it readily available to his staff. A few days before Iraq came under attack in January 1991, the chief of staff telephoned me to verify one last time that events would be well documented. Before the fighting ceased, air force historians had begun to assemble the documents, microfilm them, and research and write classified accounts of the deployment, buildup, planning, and combat.

None of this definitively proves the value of history to the military. There is no evidence that can be quantified or measured in such a manner as to verify history's usefulness. One can only marshal the familiar arguments about the benefit of perspective, the utility of previous experience, and the advantages of having available data that survives only because skilled, knowledgeable historians are present to keep track of events. Perhaps in the end, the most persuasive evidence comes from the users themselves. In the mid–1980s, when the U.S. Congress questioned the purpose and scope of the air force history program, Secretary of the Air Force Edward C. Aldridge responded vigorously with a powerful statement in defense of history's role and function. Several of his most senior generals spoke with equal force. "The Air Force program was established during World War II and has been in existence in its present form since then," Aldridge wrote. "The major purpose has always been to provide the Air Force information, ideas, and analyses that are relevant to current and future problems and issues pertaining to plans and operations." The Air Force program differed "from those of the other Services," he argued, "because it consists chiefly of an extensive, utilitarian, and productive field program that reaches two echelons below the programs in the other Services and serves commanders and staffs directly on a day-to-day basis." He pointed out that

"the top leaders of the Air Force and commanders at the various echelons feel strongly that this is a valuable and necessary program that has saved the Air Force money and time and helped avoid errors in judgment and operations . . . [C]ommanders choose to devote small amounts of money and people to the function. They regard it as a necessity, not a luxury.[6]

Thus, in the judgment of senior commanders, history indeed has value, and it is on their judgment, after all, that the success of the Air Force, in peace and in war, ultimately rests.

NOTES

1. Arnold to George Kenney, 8 November 1942, in the files of the Center for Air Force History, Bolling Air Force Base, District of Columbia.

2. See Richard H. Kohn "The Air Force," column in "Service Historians in the Gulf War," *Headquarters Gazette* 3, no. 1 (Annapolis, MD: Society for Military History, Spring 1991), p. 3.

3. Ibid.

4. Report to the Congress on the U.S. Air Force History Program, 10 March 1986, in the files of the Office of the Air Force Historian.

5. In her foreword to this volume, USAF Undersecretary Anne Foreman does provide a number of cogent examples of the practical application of history to decision making.

6. Aldridge to Senator John C. Stennis, 12 March 1986, in the files of the Center for Air Force History.

12

The Search for Principles and Naval Strategy

DONALD M. SCHURMAN

We often speak and write of *principles of war* or of *understanding* war. Scholars such as Peter Paret, Michael Howard, and Bernard Brodie view Clausewitz as a superior thinker and have averred that his superiority lies in the intelligent way in which he devised methods to create and elucidate concepts.[1] It is interesting to note that the judgments of Paret, who, in my opinion, knows more about Clausewitz than anybody, are based on an approach to his subject that is frankly modest and interpretive rather than severely critical.[2] This is a congenial approach and one that sees real value in taking the thought processes of, and influences on, Clausewitz seriously rather than moving in heavy artillery to bear on the weight and balance of his results. Paret has especially eschewed, where Michael Howard has not, the utilitarian value of Clausewitz's particular concepts and thoughts.

Why should a study of naval theory go back to the great army thinker, Clausewitz? It is true that he is generally regarded as the most profound thinker on war, to date. However, it is also true that, as Bernard Brodie observed, a thinker on war can hardly be regarded as universal who writes no lines on naval warfare, which is surely not an insignificant part of warfare as a whole.[3] On the other hand, Michael Howard stated that Julian Corbett was one of the few naval thinkers who employed Clausewitz in giving formality to his own notions of sea conflict, and with useful results.[4] Thus, although Clausewitz wrote almost entirely about land warfare, it is clear, in retrospect, that he has something to teach sea warfare specialists as well. The interesting thing is that the connection between Clausewitz and naval planning spans over a century and is not easy to trace. First, a word about Clausewitz and his "rival," Baron Antoine-Henri Jomini, is in order.

It is common knowledge that when American navalists, at the time of the steam revolution, began to look for guidelines and principles to both tactics and strategy they turned not to Clausewitz, but to Jomini. This was due to the fact that the second-class navy produced a literary naval man (Alfred T. Mahan) who married Jomini's thought to naval warfare. Whether this was because Jomini's "truisms" were easier for military minds to comprehend than Clausewitz's or because Americans, like Germans, looked for universal or root principles behind the world of action: principles that did no violence to their conception of history and were amenable to quantification. Clausewitz was resurrected as a great thinker by Helmut von Moltke the Elder, and Jomini was resurrected by Dennis Hart Mahan at West Point and then for sea power instruction by Dennis's son Alfred. For whatever reason, Jomini the quantifier suited the American military-naval mentality and Clausewitz suited the mind-set of the Great German General Staff. The British Army, a collection of regiments, was not philosophically inclined, and the British Royal Navy had no intention of fortifying its practices by calling in foreign justification. Furthermore, it must be said that neither Clausewitz nor Jomini, both writing under the shadow of Napoleon, had any sense that maritime thinkers might disinter them as reference points forty to eighty years on. Jomini's thought has proven useful as part of crammer packages for staff colleges all over the Western world and beyond. It has also proven useful as justification for the augmentation of military power in many countries. This reward must be sufficient for the Jominian idea. Clausewitz's thought has more claim to be a philosophy of war, quite apart from its utilitarian possibilities.

Paret claims that Clausewitz derived much in the way of method from the *Spirit of the Laws*,[5] that great work of Montesquieu, to which may be added the same author's *Perisan Letters*.[6] Montesquieu apparently impressed Clausewitz because of the succinct, almost episodic, nature of his divisions of thought.[7] Paret also noted, however, that the more mature Clausewitz was forced to the conclusion that the use of very tightly argued sections was inhibiting to the emergence of his real ideas.[8] In other words, Clausewitz took arms against Montesquieu's idea that brevity is the root of actuality, as well as of wit. He needed more space, and so his books got longer. However, it appears that there was another aspect of Montesquieu's thought that Clausewitz either ignored or did not *at first* grasp; this was the idea that the state was a unique and sovereign identity in a way that had something to do with culture, police, and language, but also with the rights and duties linking the governors and the governed. For instance, it would never have occurred to Montesquieu to suggest that any aspect of state policy, such as war, had an inherent right to stand on its own, or that it had philosophic justification apart from the state that gave it birth. Montesquieu was set in a much more historical mold. Why did the early Clausewitz question this mind-set and present his military thought in a much more particular, philosophic, or restricted manner?

Part of the answer, no doubt, lies in the fact that Napoleon had such a cataclysmic effect on accepted notions that were, generally speaking, French-dominated. He appeared to embrace in his person the god of war and the god of the state, and to contemporary Europeans this fusion of qualities and capacities seemed intertwined and equal. It is clear that nearly everyone was influenced by the Napoleonic phenomenon. It was only in the 1820s, as time distanced him from Napoleon, that Clausewitz began to realize that, after all, *plus ça change, plus c'est la même chose* was still an apt aphorism.

Thus, without for a moment detracting from the genuineness of the process by which Clausewitz came to subordinate war to state policy, it is a fact that this emphasis (pace Paret) is stronger in the later Clausewitz than in the pre-Jena, pre-Waterloo Clausewitz.[9] This is important because the mental uncertainties that were fundamental to the development of Clausewitz as a great thinker were soon passed on, because of his obvious genius, to his disciples and students. Thus, when moderns torture themselves with the contradiction that Clausewitz can be quoted as being in favor either of complete military freedom in wartime or the notion that war must be always subservient to state policy, they are responding to a problem that the young Clausewitz invented and the more mature Clausewitz tried to solve. Thus, the soldier who wants to justify his visceral feeling that in war, civilian outlooks and governance must give way to military ones, seems justified; and in the same way, civilians, horrified that the military should be given carte blanche at the beginning of a war and civilians kept on a short chain, also find justification for their objections in Clausewitz. Both sides had their fears justified in the wars of the twentieth century.[10] For instance, when World War I was over, and during the Cold War, the problems of civilian versus military control were debated. Quite apart from what happened in practice, the practical problem, as distinct from Clausewitz's final opinion on it, was still in existence; and people turn to the master for ammunition to justify their various points of view.[11]

Paret was clearly right to point out that just before his death, Clausewitz's powerful mind was attempting to adjust his views of the tendency of war to absolute violence with those that held the state to be in control of war's activities and policies. The triumph of state control was central to his thinking. This process returned Clausewitz to the main stream of European thought; back to the tradition of Montesquieu, Burke, Goethe, Immanuel Kant, Hegel, and Coleridge. Whether Clausewitz was a great philosopher, or even if he was a philosopher within the definition that philosophers might give of their own profession, is a moot point. However, his confusion between absolute war and war as an instrument of policy was likely due to the overwhelming influence of Napoleon, who blurred the distinctions between absolute war and controlled war in the minds of most of his contemporaries. That blurring did not seem to occur in naval affairs, and nineteenth-century naval thought was still firmly cast in pre-Napoleonic, eighteenth-century forms.

If Napoleon, the embodiment of the state and war combined in a single person, was one reason why Clausewitz strayed from the paths of continuity beaten by European development, another was the state of philosophy itself. Paret showed that Clausewitz had read Kant (1724–1824), who was publishing when Clausewitz was young.[12] Kant influenced most of his philosophical and literary contemporaries, and he influenced the immediate next generation as well. He was particularly interested in attempting to reconcile, through reason, particular prop-

ositions with general assertions. Crudely put, there was an ideal form, and a
practical form, and understanding depended on establishing connections between
the two. This problem of reconciliation had become particularly difficult after
the scientific ideas and discoveries of Copernicus and Newton (to name only
two) were fused and explained by René Descartes (1596–1650). Descartes made
a distinction between knowledge as information that came from the world of
ideas and that which came from material or natural sources. There was for
Descartes empirical knowledge, often founded on opinion and theological in-
ferences, and then there was material knowledge, which was based on scientific
evidence. At the end of the eighteenth century, the intellectual descendants of
Descartes were people like the Encyclopaedists, the Collectors (Linneus), the
Bibliophiles (Bayle), and the formalists. Such rigorous thought processes were
exemplified by the famous gardens of the English stately homes of the period.
The most famous of the gardeners, Capability Brown, can be thought of as
standing in the midst of classic plant layouts with a rose in one hand and a set
of compasses in the other. The romantic movement of the early nineteenth
century, to which Clausewitz belonged, was partly an attempt of the intellectual
world to break clear of a life dominated entirely by these forms and their almost
exclusively materialist base.[13]

Militarily speaking, it was in terms of materialist particularism that eighteenth-
century philosophy of war was written. In army terms, the aim was often to
bring the maximum firepower to bear on a foe. This required the most precise
movements of large bodies of men, and drill manuals on how to do it abounded.
In the same way, in England, such manuals on how, precisely, to stow men in
ship's boats to attack a hostile shore, were detailed. One was published in England
in 1759.[14] It informed everybody what to do in every situation, precisely. Everything was formalized; detailed and precise and not at all philosophical. It was
the nature of the age. Poetry was formalized, as was literature and painting. In
music the marching cadences of Joseph Haydn were typical. Only Wolfgang
Mozart, and perhaps Johann Goethe, who both defy categorization, were outside
the norms of the period. However, the cataclysmic events of the French Revolution and Napoleon corresponded to a new age that moved unsteadily along,
encumbered by tradition and yet looking to a new type of thinking called romanticism. Clausewitz perceived this. Warfare before Clausewitz was a thing
subservient to politics, precisely as Niccolò Machiavelli pictured it in *The Prince*.
The practice of war, in its deepest sense, was the practice of politics by intelligent
men, whose qualifications did not necessarily include moral vision. The actual
practice of war as an art or craft was subject to rules and regulations that could
be written down and learned. In the naval sphere these took the form of traditional
practice and professional expertise; that is to say, signal books and fighting and
command instructions. As for the army, there was a right and a wrong way of
doing things, and the discrepancies were codified. In the last decade of the
eighteenth century, British naval officers, and especially Lord Howe, had devised
a system for breaking the enemy line and concentration of force which Lord

Nelson carried to a high art in practice.[15] A nation that had always understood its developing logistic problems and its responsibilities for acting in deference to politics now possessed action manuals that matched its traditional instincts. It is not true to say that there was no naval strategy before Mahan, but it was generally not thought of in philosophical terms. Clausewitz changed the whole manner of looking at war by not only considering it in its actual military movements but also by looking keenly for the root principles behind military usage. Whether he was writing about defending a river crossing or about the conjunction of alliance forces for some grand purpose, he looked to the principles behind the action or the concepts. However, unlike eighteenth-century writers, Clausewitz deliberately did not attempt to write up precepts as a result of his studies, to be memorized and used as needed. He made it clear, as Paret emphasized, that his studies were designed to improve the minds of officers, especially staff officers. He wanted his readers to study the history and test the investigations with their own minds; to use his work as a guide to further investigations, not to come up with solutions. To do this he attempted to uncover the common principles that governed separate situations. He did not lay down maxims as to whether, invariably, the defensive or the attack was superior, but instead asked what are the special characteristics of the attack and the defense and how could they be used effectively? This involved thinking, like that of Kant, about the relation of the general to the particular. At their highest practical level, these questions related to politics.

This kind of approach meant that Clausewitz would always be interpreted differently by military scholars, on the one hand, and by utilitarian thinkers on the other. As his thought was investigated by different generations faced with different technological problems, he would be more ransacked than studied. Jomini, whom many regard as his rival, produced principles, maxims or rules that people *could* quote with the appearance of authority. Jominian thought customarily holds the military mind of the post-Napoleonic age and of our own. The reason for this is that Jominian thought is the only kind that staff or defense colleges really have the time or capacity to handle. Moreover, Jominian traditions are thoroughly American nowadays, and hence their respectability is taken for granted by America's imperial satellites on that account.

However, Clausewitz has been almost universally recognized as a great thinker as opposed to a coiner of military maxims. This was because he dabbled in the philosophical tendencies of the new Kantian or romantic age. Successful or not, he tried to ask the same kinds of questions about war that others asked about poetry, literary criticism, and the roots of ''pure philosophy.''

In England, Coleridge typified this conflict between the old and the new.[16] What was necessary to the new age was a way of thinking that broke the restraining manacles of materialism. The age of clocks had to give way, somewhat, to the age of emotional response to nature. Coleridge was a genius, an opium addict, a plagiarist, a diarist, and, of course a poet. The ''art of Memory'' is important enough in itself, but not a tool for distinguishing and understanding.

Thus, in retrospect, Coleridge came to see Linneus as a classifier. Now classification by the use of quantification is the main function of the computer, and Coleridge raised the question of whether quantification by itself added, or could add, to the main stock of real knowledge. Consequently, he turned from the mechanics of classification to the interpretation of thinking. In this investigation he included history, which he denigrated as mere classification unless some higher principle of divination could be used to interpret it. He eventually came to be famous for his distinction between the "fancy" and the "imagination." The first was a distant relative of Hartley's associationism, while the second was the shaping power of the mind that allowed for understanding of classified material (for example, history).[17] What was the understanding? It will be at once clear that although Clausewitz did not have a mind to rival Coleridge as an original philosopher, he did have the wit to see that if "principles" were elevated to philosophic formulae, then the result would be *not* understanding, but imprecise classification. He was much more down-to-earth and wanted his readers to not accept, but rather to *read* his evidence or construct their own evidence. Put another way, Coleridge and Clausewitz were wrestling with the same problem: to find, in a materialist world, the lodestone of discrimination to apply to lists of "facts."

What I have been trying to show, so far, was that when one speaks of military thinking before Clausewitz, both military and naval writings were mainly concerned with what we would call tactics—handbooks for proceeding, given the elements and equipment available—and that higher military thought (pace Machiavelli) was more the provision of policy and plans. This was the work of the state, to which the military was, in theory at any rate, subservient, and it was the profound effect of Napoleon's activities on people's minds, and the resultant nature and trends of philosophic discourse, that gave rise to Kant, Coleridge, and Clausewitz. Thus, it can be seen that the study of war, and land war in particular, quite aside from its practical and utilitarian value, had become a quasi-philosophical study in and of itself. This kind of thinking, represented by Clausewitz, was quite different from that of Jomini, or indeed from the whole prephilosophe tradition.

To turn more particularly to the sea, there were aspects of naval problems that made them different from problems of land war. In particular, naval activity never entirely divorced itself from sea activity, such as trade. A sailor was a sailor first and a naval recruit second because of the vastness of oceans, the rudimentary nature of navigational aids, and the frail nature of ships (relatively speaking). Also, while he learned to tune his constants in policy definition to known geographical features and ships' capacities, his customary physical separation from state control meant that every captain, or at least every admiral, had to be a strategist and define the balance between safety at sea, fighting, and sea purposes, notwithstanding that there were traditional responses built into most particular situations. Thus, the traditions of the past and the needs of the moment in some combination, together with codified instructions to naval fleet or station commanders, were the only naval strategy that existed.

Therefore, it must be said that writing about the sea was based largely on aspects of seamanship and fighting technique and on victories; it was not about the national purposes of sea power. This is less mystifying if one considers that sea power, undoubtedly, had a great influence on the Napoleonic phenomena, but it was, and is, hard to measure. There were ten years between Trafalgar and the Congress of Vienna. As Julian Corbett wrote, concerning 1805, "The sea had done all that the sea could do and, for Europe, the end was failure."[18] Nevertheless, in English eyes, subsidies and sea control had placed England in a place of honor at the Congress of Vienna. The British thought they had won and a basically naval strategy had paid off. However, while Germany produced Clausewitz and a philosophy of war (based, it is true, mainly on land warfare) as a by-product of that fighting, the British produced William James (d. 1827; this was the historian not the modern philosopher). James was one of those clergymen who is infected with intense feelings about fighting, death, patriotism, and victories. His history of the Royal Navy in the Napoleonic era showed how the British valor and skill overcame their foes.[19] His measuring stick was, crudely, a scale of wins and losses measured by victories and defeats. In his reckoning the balance was tipped overwhelmingly in England's favor. James examined encounters in detail, assessing them on the basis of results and what he thought was accepted tactical practice. There were, of course, more accomplished writers than James, like Southey and M'Arthur, who both wrote monographs on Nelson. Southey's work is still a classic. However, none of these works showed much interest in, or intelligence concerning, the deeper purposes of the state, of which Nelson was a mere professional agent. This was typical, no matter what might be thought in the precincts of the Board of Admiralty. When Nelson's letters appeared, as the century advanced, they were valued as a record of genius, victories, and revelations about Lady Hamilton more than as a repository of knowledge about how the great admiral interpreted the national purpose and his activities. The contrast with Clausewitz's methods and considerations could not be more stark. It is coincidentally interesting that there is no reason to suppose that jejune reasoning on the part of popular writers reflected the state of knowledge at the Admiralty. As Corbett observed, a century later, concerning the tactics of the 1815 period, the Admiralty did *not* support the dictum of "never mind maneuvers, always go at 'em"; this was the tactical wisdom of the mere fighting blockheads.

Before leaving this larger question of Admiralty policy in the hands of statesmen, it is worth noting that Britain's whole anti-slavery stance at the Peace Conference, an important part of its conference agenda, was posited on its capacity to exercise a measure of sea power on a wide scale. British political purposes were, of course, overwhelmingly economic, and to a much greater degree than any other power. It is well known that after the American war of

Independence, questions of free trade had to be balanced against such problems of the manning of the fleet and imperial responsibilities.[20] The navy and security were judged more important than free trade.

Coleridge was no thinker on war, and the British never produced, in the Napoleonic era, a quasi-philosophical writer about the navy of the stature of Clausewitz. It might be going too far to state that the British public did not demand or encourage such cogitations. However, if the British public were fixed on reading about victories rather than statecraft in its wider manifestations, it is also true that the practitioners of policy used the links between trade, empire, foreign policy, and national purposes with a skill that often amounted to genius. Napoleon was not the only example of war married to statecraft, as the careers of Marelborough, Chatham, Pitt, and Barham attest—not to mention Lord Nelson. They did not push Europe into cataclysmic spasms, but they allowed it to soothe its feverish excesses with the balm of trade and, in some measure, of cooperation. Britain grew very rich in the process. Thus, British naval traditions, unlike Continental ones, faced the advent of the age of steam with their presuppositions and ways of doing things, strategically speaking, intact.

Certainly Baron Jomini, whatever his influence on France and America, had no influence on the Royal Navy before 1900, and then only through Mahan, a connection that would be hard to document in detail concerning strategic policy and building programs. The Royal Navy may have found Jomini's concepts flattering, but they did not need or much heed his "principles." On the other hand, no one denies his influence on the United States Navy, despite the fact that his *subject* was the Royal Navy.

Nevertheless, it was not easy to escape the fact that changing technology, and indeed changing points of view, often altered definition of what a principle or a law was. What really differentiated the two kinds of thinking (Clausewitzian and Jominian) was the method of using the material. One was a guide to considering approaches to war problems, and the other was a prescription for action. Both methods would be useful in the future, not so much as opposing concepts or alternatives, but according to the cast of mind of the future investigator. No doubt the subtleties offered by the Clausewitzian method appeal to reflective minds, but that does not mean that anyone would wish to risk completely ignoring Jominian methods and precepts or pronouncing definitively for one method over the other. In fact, what emerged from the relatively new approach of Clausewitz at the end of the Napoleonic war was a technique to help *policy-makers* make decisions; whereas Jomini provided, as always, simply a variation on the law of averages as applied to military history. As Coleridge would say, the techniques were different in kind rather than degree.

Thus it was that as the naval revolution advanced in the nineteenth century, its underpinnings, at least in Great Britain, had nothing to do with philosophy in any accepted sense of the word, and certainly not with any accepted war theory based on a study of war in the late eighteenth century. Put more bluntly, the Royal Navy (and indeed, the French Navy as well) was not indebted to individual thinkers on war. At the very least, Jomini and Clausewitz were army thinkers and not naval ones, no matter how much they might be adapted by thinkers in the future. It was the fact that new technology seemed to demand new solutions that paradoxically sent navalists surrying back to history seeking traditional solutions to old problems. It must be said, furthermore, that these great pressures did not for a moment disturb the ingrained traditional responses of the Royal Navy to international situations that marine activities might influence. The Royal Navy was pragmatic. It was equally pragmatic in the seventeenth to the twentieth centuries. This pragmatism was grafted onto a corporate historical memory involving sea power, trade, and the great offices of State, of which the Admiralty was only one. There was a background to British behavior on and through the sea, but it was not philosophically grounded, nor was it German, French, or even American. It was emphatically British, even English, and therein lay its strength.

However, a change occurred after 1865, and that was a slowly developing urge to codify and arrange a very complex situation. The question was, were the same comforts and hazards that distinguished the age of sail applicable to the age of steam? Behind the quest was undoubtedly some (not much) sense of a decline of power and some (not much) sense of the complexity of colonial practicalities and relationships, but most of all, it was simply a sense that to maintain a fleet at sea that was driven by steam needed coal supplies that were both graded and strategically placed. This short-run precise practical problem of fuel supply was the basis for a plan of imperial military organization that bore relation back to the age of sail and ahead to the new age of oil. It even approached the age of nuclear fission.

All this had nothing to do with Clausewitz, or Jomini. It had nothing to do with Mahan, except as he took it into his mind to understand it. However, Sir John Colomb and Sir John Laughton marked the first British attempts to codify their own experience—*on which Mahan ultimately built*. However, while Mahan's work aimed at providing a philosophical umbrella for what happened, British navalists accepted the compliments gracefully but made no attempt to round out policy to Mahanesque prescriptions when they came across them. The materialist executives who ran the Royal Navy paid little attention to Colomb, Laughton, or Admiral Philip Colomb either, whom Jackie Fisher once dubbed, in a play on his name and his habit of filling up newspapers, "old column and a half."

Naval thinkers without naval executive training were indulged, rather than consulted, in Britain. It is true that Corbett became a War College fixture and an adviser to Fisher, but he was not acknowledged, except insofar as he ministered to that sense of corporate magnificence and self-sufficiency that admirals accept as their due. His ideas permeated slowly and penetrated, informally, the halls of Admiralty some thirty years later. People quoted him and Mahan when it suited them.

Was there a difference between Corbett and Mahan, from the Royal Navy's point of view? There was, though this difference did not lie on the philosophical level. Rather, the difference lay in the fact that Mahan's sources, for the most part, were secondary, and often French. Corbett's sources were the actual British state and Admiralty papers that detailed what was ordered, what was hoped for, and what happened. However, Julian Corbett attempted to marry Clausewitz and the documentary history of British sea power in *England and The Seven Year's War*, published in 1907. This book represented the first British attempt by a naval writer to both understand Clausewitz and adapt him to purposes of British naval analysis. Strange as it may seem, it is through Corbett's mind alone, before 1920, that any Clausewitzian method influenced the British preceptions of sea power in the ages of sail and steam. Captain S. W. Roskill informed the writer that it was Corbett's method, influenced by Clausewitz, that finally penetrated modern naval thought through the vehicle of history. Furthermore, this kind of thinking was a powerful tool in the desperate days of World War II. Mahan attempted to marry the published sources of British sea history with Jomini. By this time Mahan was aware of the fact that Corbett's approach was new, but the general public was not. The question of the influence of history on Mahan and Corbett, and then, as reflected, on the general public, remains to be assessed.

However, no matter how land and sea power were related, the material considered by Clausewitz and Jomini *was* preoccupied with land warfare. Although the Royal Navy in the mid-eighteenth century had been considered a part of general military statecraft and tradition, by the end of that century, after the testing time of the American Revolution, it was much more concerned with world wide problems resulting from the development of empire or imperial concerns. That was the measure of the change between 1745 and 1815.

However, the important new writing in the age of steam was not begun by Mahan, and of course Corbett came much later. The new strategy only partly came as a lineal descendant of activity of the wooden walls described by history. That was only one, and perhaps not the most important, strand. The other came from a consideration of the persistent needs of "Greater Britain." The navy was a major respondent to those needs, and of course the navy defined strategy in a traditional way.

The late 1860s saw new strategic thought emerge. It was initiated by two Englishmen who were not historians, even if they were to inspire a new historical school. They were Charles Dilke, who wrote *Greater Britain* in 1868, and John Charles Ready Colomb, who wrote his famous article on the defense of maritime trade in 1867.[21] Dilke's book was a futuristic estimate of the imperial situation and its possibilities, while Colomb's was an attempt to make the protection and enhancement of that empire, and particularly imperial trade, a practical concern. Dilke and Colomb were not philosophical. Referring to a work concerned with the civil service and the empire during these years, the late Jack Gallagher thought that imperial policy was not formed in Whitehall but by events east of Suez— or at least not entirely in Europe.[22] In his famous book, *Africa and the Victorians*, written with Ronald Robinson and Alice Denny, Jack Gallagher came to the

conclusion that imperial policy in the 1880–1900 period, and referring particularly to East Africa, was determined by Lord Salisbury according to the *ov-
erriding requirements* of the naval security of the Suez Canal and the naval
station at the Cape of Good Hope.[23] In other words, land grabbing, imperial
power, and trade were inexorably linked with naval policy. Naval policy was a
vital ingredient in the imperial mix. It is interesting that B. Semmel, in his book
Liberalism and Naval Strategy argued that only naked, blunt force can guarantee
the survival of Liberal principles, a point Gallagher made in *Africa and the
Victorians*.[24] The fact is that the problem of securing monetary cooperation within
the empire and financing such imperial policy, with that empire in various stages
of development and political sophistication, was what called forth the new naval
age, which was in place before 1890.

It is now fashionable to decry empire, and imperialists, (especially the British
empire and its servants), but the problems that concerned it, and them, were
what the rash of new naval writing, between 1860 and 1914, was all about.
Colomb, Laughton, Mahan, Richmond, and Corbett—all these naval writers, to
name but a few—were responding to an imperial situation that also generated
the naval support organizations, such as the Navy League and the Navy Records
Society. The problem was best understood by Joseph Chamberlain, who made
it clear, in the 1890s, that imperial organization or cooperation must occur or
the colonies would fragment and Britain herself would atrophy into an insignificant island off the Northwest coast of Europe. That imperial federation, as
imperial associationism with a strong monetary component, was essential to
British-imperial prosperity and power *in the long run*, he had not the slightest
doubt. Time has not lessened the prescience of Chamberlain's predictions.

Consequently, the new naval renaissance in England took place in response
to *imperial* questions, not merely as the shoring up of a supposedly rapidly
disintegrating patrimony—that decline celebrated by the Americans and accepted
in docile fashion by present British historians. Certainly naval writers turned to
the past (history) to highlight effective traditionalist approaches, but, at the end
of the nineteenth century, knowledgable people knew that traditionalist approaches meant imperial approaches. The fading vision flickered on from approximately 1867 to 1932. Mahan took the naval situation, applied a dose of
Jomini, and came up with salutes to both the British past and the American
future. It was not until after World War II that the British actually appeared to
enjoy basking in the reflected glory of American power and supposed accomplishments. Thus, the pressures and philosophical trends that prompted Clausewitz to write a seminal work on the nature of war in general, and land warfare
in particular, had little direct influence on naval theorists of the late nineteenth
century. Rather, those pressures and philosophies came to Corbett, Mahan, and
their contemporaries through Clausewitz's pen.

One might say: well, did not Julian Corbett bring a Clausewitzian approach
to the understanding of British Naval policy? The answer to that is yes, but the
number of Britons who read Corbett and who were involved in power politics

is insignificant. Semmel, coming to the problem recently, seems to have savored all the criticisms of Corbett that suited his purposes. Corbett was not immediately successful in providing a more philosophical base for naval policy decisions than that which already existed. What he did was provide a guide to decision making by writing documented British naval history that helped naval officers and states-men discover their actual naval past. His thinking about trade and the state was never as sophisticated as Sir John Colomb's. Richmond, his pupil, thought that there was not enough attention paid to trade problems by Corbett, but World War I interrupted his development of a sophisticated theory about the situation. After all, imperial planning involved looking at Britain and the empire as an amalgam of countries and not merely as a unitary state where all direction came from Westminster. However, Corbett was not an imperialist thinker so much as a writer on British naval power. It was the imperialist thinkers, particularly the Colombs, and later Richard Jebb, Lord Milner and his "kindergarten" (such as Leo Amery), Lionel Curtis, and the Round Table, who attempted to bring politics, trade, and empire together and who caused naval officers and statesmen to consider, and often to defer to, their naval opinions. This chapter does not claim that they achieved great results, but only that they tried to force strategists to see that imperial strategy was essentially naval strategy and to encourage them to base naval policy on imperial political and economic possibilities, not on realities. They were tough problems to wrestle with. However, it appears to me to be clear, as the British groped for policy, that their naval strategic concepts were imperial at base.

Finally, let it be said that while the origins of modern naval strategy can be traced, in part, to Clausewitz through Corbett, it remains true that in the Royal Navy, pragmatism ruled the roost both in the age of sail and the age of steam. The grand theories discussed by Mahan and later chewed over by Paul Kennedy appeal to the American military mind but were never a powerful influence in the Royal Navy. The same applies to Corbett's interpretations of Clausewitz. The plain fact is that the British resisted universalist doctrines with any esoteric tinge. What concerned the Royal Navy was its relation to empire. Naval policy was imperial policy, as the admirals all knew. As Gerald Graham has pointed out naval policy was a part, albeit an important part of imperial policy.[25] Chatham, Nelson, Lord North, Pitt, Palmerston, Disraeli, Gladstone, and Salisbury were the philosophers of empire, and hence of Naval Strategy.

NOTES

1. Karl von Clausewitz, *On War*, ed. and trans. by Michael Howard and Peter Paret; introductory essays by Michael Howard, Peter Paret, and Bernard Brodie; commentary by Bernard Brodie (Princeton, NJ: Princeton University Press, 1984).

2. See his Introduction to *On War* and, more particularly, his *Clausewitz and the State* (New York: Oxford University Press, 1976).

3. Brodie in Clausewitz, *On War*, p. 48.

4. Howard in Clausewitz, *On War*, pp. 38, 39.

5. Charles de Secondat, Baron de Montesquieu, *De l'esprit des lois* (Paris, 1970).

6. Charles de Secondat, Baron de Montesquieu, *Persian Letters* (London, 1923).

7. Paret in Clausewitz, *On War*, pp. 19, 20.

8. Ibid., p. 20.

9. Ibid., p. 22.

10. This is not to suggest that the civilians have always maintained control in the wars of this century. In World War I it is true that by 1916 the soldiers had such control, in both Britain and Germany, that the idea of civilian government was seriously at risk. I do not say that the soldiers were either better or worse governors than the civilians, but merely that they were no longer in absolute or undisputed control. Certainly this notion applies to Hitler; and Churchill and Roosevelt were not far behind in this line of development, if that is the right word.

11. For instance, Clausewitz could be brought in on the side of arguments about deployment and the use of nuclear fission or bacteriological warfare.

12. Paret in Clausewitz, *On War*, p. 15.

13. I have not attempted to identify the thought and activities of those mentioned just above; such information can be found in any reputable encyclopedia.

14. Thomas More Molyneux, *Conjunct Expeditions* (London, 1759).

15. Julian S. Corbett, *Signals and Instructions, 1776–1794* (Navy Records Society, London, NRS, 1908), pp. 69–74.

16. I simply use Samuel Coleridge, since his mind is congenial to me, as an example of the *kind* of thinking that went on in the age. He was no more a military thinker than Mozart.

17. I have used many sources for Coleridge's thought; more particularly the *Biographia Literaria*, ed. J. Shawcross (London, 1917), and Owen Barfield, *What Coleridge Thought* (London, 1972).

18. Julian S. Corbett, *The Campaign of Trafalgar* (London, 1910), p. 424.

19. William James, *The Naval History of Great Britain from the Declaration of War by the French in 1793, to the accession of George IV* (London, 1860).

20. This is raised in Vincent Harlow, *The Founding of the Second British Empire, 1763–1793* (London: Longmans, Green, 1952–64), vol. 2; Paul Kennedy, *The Rise and Fall of British Naval Mastery* (London: Allen Lane, 1976) and B. Semmel, *Imperialism and Navalism* (London: Allen & Unwin, 1986). Semmel did not mention Harlow, whose arguments are pragmatic and eighteenth century–based, in contrast to Semmel's modern liberalism.

21. Charles W. Dilke, *Greater Britain: A Record of Travel in the English-Speaking Countries, 1866–67* (New York: Harper & Bros., 1869); J.C.R. Colomb, *The Protection of Our Commerce and Distribution of Our Naval Forces Considered* (London, 1867).

22. Author's conversation with Gallagher. "Ronald Robinson and Jack Gallagher, with Alice Denny."

23. *Africa and the Victorians* (London: MacMillan, 1961).

24. B. Semmel, *Liberalism and Naval Strategy* (London: Allen & Unwin, 1986).

25. The essential link between naval and Imperial policy (and practice) was the major theme of all Gerald Graham's work. See especially, *The Politics of Naval Supremacy* (Cambridge, England: Cambridge University Press, 1965).

13

The Utility of History to Modern Navies

ERIC GROVE

"Why don't we learn from history?" enquired Vice Admiral Sir Peter Gretton in the late 1950s, remembering the Royal Navy's weaknesses in convoy escort forces and doctrine in the World War II. Now, however, some of his successors would say that there is nothing to learn. They argue that modern technology has so changed the face of naval warfare that it is useless to try to draw any conclusions or lessons from the past. Old concepts of "decisive battle" or "fleet in being" are now obsolete, they say, in the era of the nuclear-powered submarine. They assert that the technology of weapons, sensors, and tactical command and communications is now so fundamentally transformed from the days of the Napoleonic Wars or even the world wars of this century that naval history, even of the recent past, is of little more than antiquarian interest. Modern naval warfare is now highly dispersed and based on concepts with little apparent historical precedent, such as signature reduction and electronic warfare. The ability of frigates with towed array sonars to monitor thousands of square miles of ocean instead of a few tens of square miles is assessed as a fundamental change. It is also argued that both the ability of a single force to be controlled over a wide area by one officer in tactical command and the compression in the overall chain of command created by global instant communications make modern naval operations so different from those of the past that no previous experience is relevant.

This is especially true, the modernists go on, with the problem of the protection of merchant shipping. They admit that this remained the same from the days of sail to 1945; the same rules therefore applied throughout this period. Although technology evolved, there was no discontinuity; the relationship between the attacker and the defender in both speed and weapons range remained roughly similar. It was best, therefore, to put ships into convoy, thus emptying the ocean of targets and putting the defending forces in the most favorable situation to use their short-range sensors and weapons. Now, however, the argument goes, all is changed:

- The submarine has a passive acoustic performance that is two orders of magnitude better than the submarine of World War II, plus an ability to classify what its sonar operators are hearing;
- A nuclear-powered submarine has a submerged speed that is twice that of a convoy;
- Convoys can be detected by satellites and other "real-time" surveillance systems;
- Missiles and torpedoes can be fired at much longer ranges;
- Communications are now vastly superior; and
- Convoys seriously degrade the utility of passive sonars, the main modern antisubmarine sensors.

It thus makes sense, the antihistorians assert, to rely on independent sailings using neutral shipping and decoy technology to create a confusing environment for the attacker.[1]

We have, of course, been here before. At the end of the nineteenth century and at the beginning of the twentieth, the classics of modern maritime strategy were written to counter the arguments of the Jeune Ecole and others that technology had indeed changed everything. In the context of the extraordinary transformation that had overtaken naval warfare in the half century after 1855 Admiral Jackie Fisher made his famous comment, "History is a record of exploded ideas."[2] Others, however, disagreed. Although the two great masters, Julian Corbett and Alfred T. Mahan, were far from agreed on how one used history (the former regarded the latter's work as crude and unhistorical), both felt that there were lessons that could be drawn from the past. Corbett argued that useful strategic theory could be deduced from historical study. Such a theory could "at least determine the normal." He continued:

By careful collation of past events, it becomes clear that certain lines of conduct tend normally to produce certain effects; that wars tend to take certain forms each with a marked idiosyncrasy; that these forms are normally related to the object of the war and to its value to one or more belligerents; that a system of operations which suits one form may not be that best suited to another. We can even go further. By pursing an historical and comparative method we can detect even the human factor is not quite indeterminable. We can assert that certain situations will normally produce, whether in ourselves or our adversaries, certain moral states on which we may calculate.

Having determined the normal, we are at once in a stronger position. Any proposal can be compared with it, and we can proceed to discuss clearly the weight of the factors which prompt us to depart from the normal. Every case must be judged on its merits, but without a normal to work from we cannot form any real judgment at all.[3]

In this last comment, Corbett put his finger on the key point. History cannot prescribe actions to the modern naval officer. What it can do is to inform him or her of the likelihood of certain actions leading to certain results. The course of naval history clearly demonstrates that if ships are not convoyed, the odds are that they will suffer more serious losses than if they are. It should therefore be necessary for any proposal to substitute a new strategy for convoy to come up with some pretty convincing arguments that the alternative will work. Fisher was more right than he realized; there is no idea more exploded than the "too many eggs in one basket" argument with reference to convoy, although one still often hears it today.

Of course, new technology and techniques, can revolutionize naval warfare, not only tactically but operationally and strategically as well. Historical experience is not the only guide. For example, Mahan, in his later writings at least, was sound on convoy. He was, however, wrong to argue that the Dreadnought/ Invincible type had no future because long-range gunfire had never worked in the past.[4] It is perfectly rational to argue that modern technology does allow the historically based rules to be flouted—but one ignores the "normal" at one's peril. The very course of technological progress makes the pendulum swing back, as it is currently doing at sea with antisubmarine warfare (ASW). The halcyon days of long-range passive sonar are ending. As submarines become quieter, detection ranges are coming down once more; the sea is resuming its customary opaqueness. Naval planners now openly admit that they are going to have to concentrate their defensive forces around the assets, or "mission essential units" that they are actually trying to defend. We are "back to normal" again, or, as, the British Director of Concepts (Studies) put it to the Royal United Services Institute at the end of 1988:

. . . engagements of the future will tend to be localised, cued by external early warning but characterised by late detections and defensive systems with minimal reaction time but nevertheless a high probability of kill. True area defence may become increasingly difficult, which could lead to a demand for increased numbers of closer range systems with only a limited area coverage, together with some emphasis on passive defensive measures.[5]

Even as skilled and subtle a thinker as Corbett had difficulty with the influence of changing technology on defense of trade. He believed, like his contemporary naval colleagues, that the technical, commercial, and legal changes of the nineteenth century really had made convoy obsolete. He was not entirely wrong, of course. The kind of trade defense he prescribed proved effective enough against the limited German surface raider threat at the outbreak of World War I, but it could do nothing when the advent of unrestricted U-boat warfare (a further innovation) brought things "back to normal" once more. Then, the wheel of convoy had to be reinvented, but not before Britain had been almost brought to its knees.[6]

This apparently increased strength of the *guerre de course* in twentieth-century naval warfare might be taken to disprove Mahan's doubts about the utility of this form of warfare. However, further consideration justifies Mahan. The *guerre de course* has never been effective against a properly organized convoy system (which Mahan assumed). A *guerre de course* has never won a war. Even at its most effective, against Japan in 1945, it did not cause the enemy to cease fighting. Mahan's (and Corbett's) insistence on the main fleet as an essential component of naval power has stood the test of time. Indeed, when the American strategists developed their controversial "Maritime Strategy" in the 1980s, they were putting battlefleet doctrine into its latest form, explaining how one might use one's main naval striking force to neutralize the main striking force of an opponent, thus reducing the direct shipping defense task to manageable proportions.

The Maritime Strategy debate of the 1980s would certainly have benefited from more historically based analysis. Its supporters have been some of its worst enemies in that they have used some very bad history indeed. Rarely has there been a greater travesty of history than the "spots diagram" of shipping losses in the first half of 1942 that illustrated Admiral James D. Watkins's 1986 article.[7] This purported to show the dire results of not having a forward defense, but what it actually showed was the price paid for not having a convoy system off the American Coast and in the Caribbean. There had been "forward defense" in 1942 in the shape of the British Home Fleet, but this was of little avail to undefended merchantmen off Cape Hatteras. Similarly, the otherwise excellent book recently produced by M. A. Palmer of the U.S. Navy's Historical Section on the origins of a forward strategy—which very effectively shows that there was little "new" in it—contains some strange history on the reasons for Allied victory over the U-boat.[8]

A better historical foundation would have prevented forward defense being seen as an alternative to direct shipping protection or, for that matter, vice versa. Convoy escorts have always operated under the cover of the main fleet; the battlefleet has rarely been enough on its own to assure safety for shipping. The way the forward strategy has turned out in practice in northern Norwegian fiords could almost have been designed by Corbett, initiative at the outset of war (not to be confused with the offensive), creating a powerful defensive position and forcing the enemy to come to you, thus bringing on a major action under favorable conditions (in this context, the criticism was that there is no more potential for decisive battles looks rather strange). Of course, if the enemy chooses not to come and fight, he must remain at home to protect against possible attacks by the forward deployed forces (possibly leading to no more "fleet in being"). Moreover, the whole result is a threat contained, or as one might more traditionally say, "blockaded."[9]

Another aspect of the forward strategy that could have found historical justification is its emphasis on the use of maritime power to coerce Russia into a favorable settlement in limited war. As Andrew Lambert has pointed out, in 1855–1856, the British did just this to bring the Russian War to an end.[10]

Too often the debate over the Maritime Strategy has been clouded by "maxims" like those about which Corbett could be scathing. The desire has often been expressed to go "in harm's way," and the need to "seek out and destroy the enemy fleet" has often been reasserted. These have once more been used as substitutes for more rigorous thinking. Often such maxims are historically based—a quotation from some earlier naval hero perhaps, but they are classic misuses of history, not reflecting any real analytical thought and usually being quoted without any regard for context. This should not, however, discourage historians from trying to provide their own brief and epigrammatic guidance for action, if for no other reason than to refute or modify the more traditional "maxims." Corbett did so in the "Green Pamphlets" he produced for his doubting audiences at the Naval War College before World War I. For example:

In applying the maxim of "seeking out the enemy's fleet" it should be borne in mind:—
(1) That if you seek it out with superior force you will probably find it in a place where you cannot destroy it except at heavy cost.
(2) That seeing the defensive is the stronger form of war than the offensive, it is prima facie better strategy to make the enemy come to you than to go to him and seek a decision on his home ground.[11]

That advice is as good in 1992 as it was in 1906.

The course on which Corbett was lecturing has long since been abolished, which raises the question of how modern naval officers are to be educated to draw any benefits from the experience of their predecessors. Britain provides an interesting case study. Naval history suffered great damage in Britain by association with Sir Geoffrey Callender's *Sea Kings of Britain*, the standard text for many years in the Royal Naval Colleges at Osborne and Dartmouth. Written for 13–14 year-olds at Osborne, it was only intended to enable small boys to acquire an acquaintance with the naval past by introducing them to Britain's naval heroes. Sadly, its uncritical approach became identified with the whole subject. To naval officers of the mid-twentieth century "naval history" was knowledge of a few great names, if that. In the 1970s things were even worse; "naval history" for almost all Dartmouth students had become a few lectures that were known as a time when they could get some well earned rest. Sir Peter Gretton's article was available in an offprint made available by some thoughtful member of the staff but it lay largely unread in the book store.

An attempt was made in the early 1980s to resurrect a properly examined history course for new entry officers, but too much was attempted in too little time and the course was offered for only a few years.[12] It has been replaced by a new "Defence Studies" course in which there is a small history component that survived after press comment about the continued value of the subject. The Royal Naval College Greenwich moved away from naval history in its continuing education of the naval officer corps. However, under the latest head of the Department of History and International Affairs, Geoffrey Till, there has been an encouraging renaissance and a real attempt to restore a historical perspective, notably in the so-called "Theatre Case Studies" undertaken by the Staff Course.

If naval officers do not receive much education in naval history what of the facilities to provide historical advice to the Naval Staff? This has had a historical section since 1919 and, despite lack of resources and attempts to limit the extent of its criticism of decision-makers, it has been responsible for some excellent work. The "Staff Histories of World War Two" are models of their kind, and the most important, D. W. Waters and F. Barley's *The Defeat of the Enemy Attack upon Shipping*, is the best justification of convoy ever written.[13] The current head of the Naval Historical Branch is naval aviation historian J. D. Brown who is a fully integrated member of the Naval Staff with the title "Assistant Director (Data and Doctrine)." This means that his advice is sought as a matter of course, but the resources of the department are stretched thin and it must perforce concentrate on answering specific inquiries, compiling and keeping records, and similar tasks. Despite a most helpful staff, the sheer lack of funds means that it is only able to give limited assistance to academics and other outside researchers. Other countries have invested more heavily than Britain in both the serious academic study of naval history and historical facilities available to naval policy-makers: For example, Canada is a model of its kind. In Europe the Service Historique de la Marine in France has lavish facilities and staffing and close links with the French academic historical community.

The perennial problem of integrating historical advice with operational policy was illustrated by a study of trade defense undertaken about a decade ago in Britain by a special working group of officers at the Maritime Tactical School. The study looked at the implications of new technology on the problem and was dubious about the advantages of convoy, for reasons similar to those quoted at the beginning of this chapter. However, the drafters of the report had never read the Staff History. Their research was confined to publicly available secondary sources. This illustrates a fundamental problem with staff histories; they are not available to those interested, at least for some time, while those who do have access generally have insufficient time to read them or even apprise themselves of their existence. The histories are thus rarely read, even by those who should.

This illustrates an important point: What usually happens is not that history is ignored but that arguments are often made from bad history rather than sound analysis. Even relatively trivial errors (how often is Trafalgar explained by senior officers at Trafalgar Night dinners on the basis that the battle "saved Britain from invasion"?) display an attitude to history and naval historiography that can have serious consequences. Equally, of course, naval historians must have a sound grasp of modern naval tactics, operations, and technology if they are to give credible and useful advice to the modern officer.[14]

One special area of contemporary naval interest on which history can shed light is that of naval arms control. From Rush-Bagot in 1817 to London in 1936 there is a rich source of possible precedents, lessons—and warnings. Never has there been a greater need to be careful about context. There is a good argument that the technological conditions of the interwar period made structural naval arms control as possible then as modern conditions make it difficult now—but perhaps that is a useful point worth making in itself. Certainly, however, historians must stamp on some of the stranger arguments that surround the naval arms control debate, that "navies do not start wars" (1941? 1917? 1905?) or that the German pocket battleships somehow tell one something about naval arms control. Again the danger is bad history, not the utility of good history.

Despite all the technical transformation of the last few decades, and perhaps also because of them, a proper understanding of the professional past remains of vital importance to naval officers, both individually and collectively. Wheels can be reinvented, but often at an unnecessarily high price. History seems to show that certain patterns of behavior do recur, if not automatically, then with a high degree of probability. History tells you what *not* to do: It saves time and trouble, and it may even save lives. Prince Philip put it well:[15] Too often, he said, history is studied to explain how we won the last war. Instead, it should be studied with the much more uncomfortable purpose of finding out the mistakes we made at the start. One of those mistakes is to pay too little attention to naval history. The seas are littered with the wrecks of ships that were sunk because hard-won experience was forgotten or misinterpreted. Naval history is far too important for naval practitioners of any generation to ignore.

NOTES

1. Vice Admiral Sir Peter Gretton, "Why Don't We Learn from History?" *Naval Review* 46 no. 1 (January 1958): 13–25. A copy of this article was sent over to the United States by Lord Mountbatten as part of his First Sea Lord-Chief of Naval Operations private correspondence with Arrleigh Burke. The two navies' ideas on the effectiveness of convoy were diverging further at this time and Mountbatten was anxious to bring history to his aid; See Public Record Office (PRO), Kew, England, File, ADM205/173.

2. R. F. McKay, *Fisher of Kilverstone* (Oxford: Clarendon Press, 1973), pp. 265–66, gives the origins and meaning of Fisher's famous remark.

3. Sir Julian Corbett, *Some Principles of Maritime Strategy*, new ed. (Annapolis, MD, 1988), p. 9.

4. Mahan fully recognized the importance of convoy in his *Sea Power in Relation to the War of 1812* (Boston: Little, Brown, 1905). His earlier writings had tended to overemphasize fleet actions. For a good assessment of Mahan's influence, see R. A. Bowling's "The Negative Influence of Mahan on the Protection of Shipping in Wartime: The Convoy Controversy in the Twentieth Century" (Ph.D. dissertation, University of Maine, 1980).

5. Commodore R. Cobbold's lecture to the Royal United Services Institute, 16 November 1988, printed as "Future Maritime Needs and Means," *RUSI Journal* 134, no. 3 (Autumn 1989): 29–30.

6. Corbett, *Some Principles*, ch. 4, part 2, pp. 261–81. He wrote, "It now becomes doubtful whether the additional security which convoys afforded is sufficient to outweigh their economical drawbacks and their tendency to cause strategic disturbance." Instead, he advocated a system of defended areas using cruiser patrols.

7. Admiral James D. Watkins, "The Maritime Strategy," supplement to *U.S. Naval Institute Proceedings* (January 1986): 11.

8. M. A. Palmer, *The Origins of the Maritime Strategy: American Naval Strategy in the First Post-War Decade* (Washington, D.C., 1988). On pages 26–27, Palmer asserts that "defensive" convoy escorts did not inflict sufficient attrition on U-boats and that

more "offensive" measures such as the Bay of Biscay campaign were required to defeat the German submarines. This was not the case. The significant damage was done by the convoy escorts and supporting forces.

9. For a description of NATO Striking Fleet operations in the late 1980s, see the author's forthcoming *Battle for Fiords* (Shepperton, 1991). This book is based on firsthand observation of Exercise Teamwork '88.

10. See A. Lambert, *The Crimean War* (Manchester, 1989).

11. Quoted in Appendix 1 of Corbett, *Some Principles*, pp. 324–25.

12. The author brought the idea of an examined naval history course for new entries back to Dartmouth from Annapolis in 1981.

13. Waters and Barley's work is *The Defeat of the Enemy Attack Upon Shipping: A Study of Policy and Operations*, vols. 1A and 1B, BR1736 (51) (1A & B). It can be seen at the Public Record Office, and a new edition is in preparation for the Navy Records Society.

14. The author's two and a half weeks at sea observing "Teamwork '88" were some of the most professionally valuable he has ever spent.

15. The author has been unable to run down the precise reference but has confirmed Prince Philip's authorship.

14

Military History in the Federal Republic of Germany and the *Bundeswehr*

ROLAND G. FOERSTER

As far as the cognitive interest and scholarly approaches are concerned, military history in Germany has generally undergone similar development as in other Western countries during the past two centuries. There were always the systematizers and theoreticians who looked for immutable rules and principles of war that could, with enough study, be learned and universally applied. On the other hand, there were always those who argued against the utility of history for the simple truth that history does not repeat itself. Moreover, there were always the pragmatics, who combined both the didactic and purist approaches. It is not at all surprising, therefore, that, in order to set things straight, a renowned military historian such as Sir Michael Howard titled his 1961 lecture at the Royal United Services Institute, "The Use and Abuse of Military History," thereby indicating that there must be some ways of "using" military history and there is no unbreachable division between academic research and military use of history, but also admitting that there is a definite possibility of "abuse" as well.[1]

On the other hand, a different development of military historiography in Germany can doubtlessly be observed in more specific ways. One is a delayed academic approach toward the subject compared to other Western nations, in a curious way connected and interrelated with the development of the political and social conditions of the German state in the nineteenth and early twentieth centuries, particularly in Prussia. The other trend will become quite clear when one looks at the dominant role of the military in German history before 1945. Both aspects show that the critical mind has to use great care to understand how military history was conceived, understood, and employed in Germany's past; otherwise, it will find itself at a razor's edge rather quickly, whether intellectually, militarily, politically, or ideologically. It is doubtful, therefore, that military history, as an unalienable part of the academic as well as the military world, has been exposed to such a wide span of controversial discussion as in Germany after World War II. History has become a wide field of disagreement, and even of ideological friction, over its role in society as well as in the military and academic worlds.

Few nations in modern history find themselves in the bizarre situation of carrying a great deal of guilt for the most disastrous wars on the one hand, and on the other hand to be known for some of the most brilliant military theoreticians and pragmaticians, thinkers, and leaders. In trying to dissolve this ambiguity— in order to determine if the German military past is worthwhile understanding, if it is "usable" for society and the military, to which degree it can form the basis for national and military tradition, very critical standards will have to be applied today. It will not be sufficient, therefore, to judge such questions by measures of political opportunism or military pragmatism alone ("My country, right or wrong!") or even by the most convenient and indolent of all historical criteria: success.

With these issues in mind, discussions on the relative value and respectability of military history began right after 8 May 1945 and they still prevail. In order to shed some light on the state of the art of military history in Germany in present times and its role in the Federal Armed Forces, the *Bundeswehr*, it is necessary to look at three different aspects of military history.

1. Academic research and publication of military history proper, which today are certainly not a field for only the military, but rather for the entire academic community;
2. The didactic task of teaching military history within the forces, requiring a wide spectrum of approaches; and
3. The difficult and rather touchy question of military tradition. For obvious reasons, this has become a subject for high-level political decision making rather than a historical or military subject.

This chapter tries to look at these points and at the rather complicated interrelation of military history, the military profession, and society in present-day Germany.

RESEARCH AND PUBLICATION OF MILITARY HISTORY IN GERMANY AFTER 1945: REBIRTH OR BURIAL?

Kriegsgeschichte or "Military History": A Contradiction?

The Story up to 1945. Research, application, and publication of military history in Germany for roughly the past 200 years has to be looked on under the following conditions:

1. From its beginnings, the subject suffered from a "congenital defect," a semantic conceptual restriction caused by the German term *Kriegsgeschichte* (war history) which intellectually constrained academic and practical approaches to the mere phenomenon of war. Where *military history* or *histoire militaire* emerged early in other cultures, including social, political, and economical criteria of history and their inter-

relations with the military, German historians started to use the much broader term *Militärgeschichte* only in the early twentieth century. Therefore, the term *Kriegsgeschichte*, in connection with its exclusive, as well as confining, conception, restricted the comprehensive and complex historical politico-military subject to a highly skillful and intricate, yet academically limited description and analysis of war from the middle of the eighteenth century on.[2]

2. *Kriegsgeschichte* before 1945 was, in most cases, *amtliche* or "official" history. Although this should not be principally harmful, in Germany it left *Kriegsgeschichte*, particularly during periods of predemocratic or suppressive political systems, wide open to censorship and restrictive considerations, which lacked critical and political utility.[3]

3. *Kriegsgeschichte* until 1945 was the legal and approved educational instrument of the General Staffs and military academies, documented, researched, published, taught, and applied by mainly military officers, with the prime purpose of making the lessons of war teachable and applicable.[4]

4. The writing of *Kriegsgeschichte* primarily did not serve the principles of general knowledge and cognition but rather was a matter of utility and raison d'état.[5]

Such principles and intentions were naturally directed toward the perfectly acceptable and logical purpose of making military experience usable for the future. They were, stated modern historian Heinz Hürten, "doubtlessly existent within all rationally organized and operating societies," and they presented themselves "for the military in a very specific way, because everyday life, peaceful normality, does not permit any efficiency control for that kind of action which after all constitutes the raison d'être of the military."[6] Moreover, this approach, at its time, was by no means only accepted by the military, but was embraced as well by leading historians like Friedrich Meinecke.[7] From the times of the ancient chronicler to the world wars, *Kriegsgeschichte* was used and applied as nothing else but an early—and, by its very nature, uncritical—form of "operations research."

It was no one less astute than Gerhard von Scharnhorst, who, in Prussia, founded a department of history within the new Great General Staff in 1816 after the end of the Liberation Wars.[8] "Historia vitae magistra," he is quoted to have said, and it was his notion that this "mistress" would not tell a person *what* to think but rather *how* to think: a surprisingly modern approach to history. The historical work of the Great General Staff from then on was indeed marked with an honest and serious struggle for historical accuracy: Clausewitz could not have developed his revolutionary theories toward an overall understanding of war without a true scholarly approach.[9] The historical oeuvre of the Great General Staff in the years to follow, especially under the direction of Field Marshal Count Helmuth von Moltke, reached a high degree of reliability, despite harsh contemporary and later criticism.[10] However, the methodical approach was limited in subject, width of perspective, and standards of criticism. Even the *Reichsarchiv*, the historiographical successor of the Great General Staff after its dissolution in 1919, was principally unable to shed the tight skin of the *Kriegsgeschichte*[11] and the organizational restrictions of the Great General Staff.[12]

There were exceptions. Before the turn of the century, Max Jähns combined military conditions with political, constitutional, and social aspects in his writings. The first, however, to consider *Kriegsgeschichte* a constituent part of general history was Hans Delbrück, who became involved in heated arguments over that topic with the General Staff historians as well as with civilian university academicians before World War I. After the founding of the Weimar Republic, even well-known professors dealt with military history: Scholars like Fritz Meinecke, Hans Delbrück and Herman Oncken served on the "Historical Commission" of the Reichsarchiv, among others, and in 1928 a retired army captain, Walter Elze, became professor of and founded a *Kriegsgeschichtliche Abteilung* at the Historical Department at the Berlin University.[13]

After 1933, *Kriegsgeschichte* in Germany slowly but surely fell victim to the influence of the National Socialist (NS) system. Disliked or politically "unreliable" scholars were retired or had to emigrate. *Kriegsgeschichte* again became a domain for the military profession and was set to work in a craftsman-like applicatory manner. Under these circumstances, it once more lost its chance for an intellectual penetration of questions of the interdependence between state, society, and war and fell into hopeless stagnation during those years. What was even worse was that *Kriegsgeschicte*, during the time of the NS regime, became a vehicle of NS ideology and propaganda. In due course of the perennial military request to put a certain "use" to military history, some Wehrmacht historians were requested to "forge" *Kriegsgeschichte* as an intellectual weapon and to convey this "means of combat" shortly and simply "to those who have to use it in all of its versatility."[14]

There were few who tried to uphold the scholarly standards of historiography, at least at the universities. One such scholar, Gerhard Östreich, in 1939 presented a new theoretical approach, which was supposed to overcome the General Staff-type *Kriegsgeschichte* but not leave the research of war history and the military simply to the general historians. In addition to the term *Kriegs- and Militär-geschichte*, he introduced a subject called *Wehrgeschichte*. Despite its clear commitment towards the Arts and the historical-critical method, it was to be understood as a *Wehrwissenschaft*, a military science. *Wehrwissenschaften*, in concurrence with the definition of science during the rule of National Socialism and its terminology, had a carefully calculated political determination, however, in order "to serve the political and military leadership of people and state by means of their scientific findings."[15] According to Heinz Hürten, this meant nothing else but the "ultimate militarization of the historiography in its entirety," although the idea as such remained more or less programmatic.[16] Nevertheless, the term *Wehrgeschichte* left a very strange aftertaste in the years after 1945 because it expressed an unholy alignment of history and NS ideology and subverted history to an intellectual instrument to promote the unscrupulous intentions of an inhuman political system.

Military History from the End of World War II to 1957

In view of the unspeakable misery of World War II and the horrendous crimes committed on behalf of the German people, the Potsdam Agreement (1945) provided that German military power be destroyed and its alleged indigenous source, German militarism and imperialism, be eradicated. Among the measures of reeducation was discrimination against anything military, including a directive that forbade the teaching of military history at German universities.[17]

Above all, the German people themselves were absolutely fed up with anything military: with millions killed and numerous cities bombed to ruins, a quest for survival had become their foremost and imperative interest. Looking for a scapegoat for the inhumane and cynical abuse of goodwill, personal sacrifice, and national pride committed by the NS regime, military leaders of all ranks were blamed for having supported Hitler. Moreover, quite subtly, the military was, in the eyes of many, also seen to be at fault for losing the war, leaving it culpable in a double sense. In addition, the Nuremberg trials and their sentences had a devastating effect on the militarily-minded.[18] It all resulted in a deep-rooted and fundamental syndrome of suspicion and dislike of the military. One has to understand this very clearly in order to fully conceive the reasons for the political and social development during the years to come, during which Germany has faced a long-term and more or less unconcealed crisis of acceptance relating to everything military within German society. From the end of World War II on, and even today, anything military is looked upon with suspicion and rejection, particularly by intellectuals, and ironically including such academic subjects as military history.

With the German past a shambles, the military profession dishonored, and *Kriegsgeschichte* discredited for both methodological insufficiency and political as well as ideological abuses, the year 1945 meant a turning point for military history in Germany. The ancient "official" *Kriegsgeschichte* of the General Staffs came to a full stop for a limited time, with one exception, however. Directed by the Historical Division of the U.S. Army, a group of former high-ranking German officers, then prisoners of war (POWs), started in 1946 to evaluate their experience of World War II by writing a series of studies at a POW camp at Königstein/Taunus; they were known as the "Operational Historical (German) Section" and provided a treasure of material for later research, although their findings at times revealed apologetic undertones.[19]

Otherwise, public and individual military historiography in Germany developed in a curiously ambiguous way after the war. On the one hand, for a number of reasons, military history as an academic and university subject was never able to establish itself after 1945, contrary to a veritable boom in numerous countries in both the East and West. This even applies to the two Universitäten der

Bundeswehr (Armed Forces Universities) which do not have a department of history, not to mention an institute of military history.[20] There was a unique and finally successful attempt by Werner Hahlweg to establish a professorship of military history at the University of Münster/Westf in 1969, but it turned out to be more or less a "lex Hahlweg," directed at a meritorious and well-known scholar.[21] However, at the conferences of the German Historical Association (the *Historikertag*) or the *Haus der deutschen Geschichte* in Bonn you will look in vain for a section of military history.

On the other hand, among general historians there developed considerable interest in military history in a broader sense. Questions concerning the relation of war and society and the interrelation of the military with politics, economy, culture, and ideology were discussed. Scholars such as Werner Hahlweg, Gerhard Ritter, Hans Rothfels, and Rainer Wohlfeil, to name but a few, started quite early to work toward an understanding on a new academic basis of the phenomenon of NS, the *Wehrmacht* in World War II, and the role of the military in the industrial age. However, what constituted a real problem in those years of serious research in the field of military history was a severe lack of archival documentation, as most of the German sources were either destroyed during the war or confiscated by the Occupation Forces.[22] Nonetheless, there was a veritable flood of literature written by the wartime generation in order to free itself from the trauma of the ordeal they had survived. Because it was virtually impossible—and probably too early—to research and publish reliable and comprehensive historical accounts on World War II, during the immediate postwar years a wide range of military historiography from this period— academic, biographical, or trivial—was later subject to harsh criticism, with much emotion involved. Where one side claimed such literature to represent the "historiography of the victors," bemoaning undue condemnation and demonization of the Germans and their history, the other side spoke of a "literature of exoneration," and the dust has not yet settled.

With the prospect of building up new German forces, an official interest arose in military history as early as 1952, when a directorate was established within the *Dienststelle Blank*, the organizational forerunner of a future Ministry of Defense.[23] Its head was Lieutenant Colonel (GS) (ret.) Dr. Hans Meier-Welcker, a trained historian and student of professors Hans Rothfels and Rudolf Stadelmann. He represented a perfect combination of the true virtues of an experienced General Staff Officer and the mind of a educated scholar. He headed the directorate under various denominations until in 1958, when he became chief of the *Militärgeschichtliche Forschungsamt* [Military History Research Office] (MGFA) and moved with the office to Freiburg.

Meier-Welcker represented a stroke of luck to the organizational and intellectual reconstruction of official military history in Germany. From 1952 on he systematically prepared the ground for a scholarly concept of research, publication, and teaching of military history for and within the new forces, the *Bundeswehr* (established 1955). From the beginning he stressed three major prerequisites for the future work of the MGFA:

1. Military history (he still used the term *Kriegsgeschichte*, very likely out of custom) is an integral part of general academic historiography, if one with a particular objective.[24]

2. Freedom of research is guaranteed for all scholars of military history by Art. 5 (3) of the *Grundgesetz* (Basic Law, i.e. the German constitution).

3. The experience of joint operations in modern warfare excludes a separate history of each of the three services.

Thus, in 1957, "official" military history was reinstituted in the Federal Republic of Germany under the responsibility of the minister of defense—but under entirely different political, legal, and academic conditions than *Kriegsgeschichte* before 1945. After its establishment, the MGFA was—and remained—the only historical research institute attached to a federal ministry. Therefore, "Kriegsgeschichte" of the old kind was entombed after World War II in the Federal Republic, but military history emerged from the ashes with a brilliant new academic understanding, despite a few adverse conditions at the first glance.

Research and Publication at the MGFA after 1957

There were a few contradictions and ambiguities that from the beginning which accompanied the MGFA's work and self-determination:

• Although deliberately claiming freedom of opinion and an academic approach to history, the MGFA was not solely dedicated to pure research.[25] It always had to serve, at the same time and by virtue of its existence, the Ministry of Defense, and had to support the troops. This was done by preparing purpose-oriented studies for planning and command and supplying aids and textbooks for teaching military history to the Officer Corps.[26]

• Although the "new" military history had said farewell to the *Kriegsgeschichte* and the *Bundeswehr* had intentionally cut ties with most of the traditions of the Wehrmacht and the Reichswehr, the MGFA at least *institutionally* was still the successor of official historiography (like the *Reichsarchiv*).

• By decree of the Ministry of Defense, the MGFA was not an entirely independent research institute but rather an *Amt* (office).[27]

However, as time proved, these apparent contradictions have never posed a serious threat to the scholarly approach of the MGFA. One reason was an uncompromisingly high standard of qualification with respect to the staff. The scholars hired by the MGFA were about half military and half civil servants, which meant a new approach compared to earlier times. While every researcher, military or civilian, was required to hold at least a master's degree, the civilians were expected to have military experience or, better still, reserve officer status. This solution was supposed to secure a sound methical standard and instigate a continuous flow of information between civilian historians and scholars with military experience.[28]

Another reason was a strong and unyielding adherence to the scholarly standards of the historical profession from the very beginning and an almost unanimous consent among all members of the MGFA about this. It was the agreed intention "to conduct research of military history as a special branch of history by the methods, objectives and standards of scholarly historiography, and therefore to examine military facts and proceedings in all of its complex conditions with respect to a comprehensive frame of reference," as stated by a study group of the MGFA much later, in 1976.[29] This conception of military history comprised as its subject of research the entirety of military life and conditions as well as their relation to society in general. In doing so, it went far beyond the limits of traditional *Kriegsgeschichte* or other rather limited approaches to military history. It is remarkable, in this context, that such intentions were summarized as early as 1955–1956 in a series of essays and presentations by Hans Meier-Welcker, who was, of course, not the only originator of such fundamental theses, but certainly a visionary thinker who at least started to make them work.[30] Most important, these principles virtually materialized in cold print in the Table of Organization for the MGFA, which was issued by the Ministry of Defense in 1956.[31] In essence, they have not yet changed.

The third component of sound research conditions in the MGFA from its beginnings was the unalienable right to freedom of research and opinion. Integration of the armed forces into society and the primacy of politics required the strictest observation of human rights, particularly within the armed forces. Therefore, it was never a question of principle that Art. 5 (3) of the Basic Law ("arts and sciences, research and teaching are free") would unconditionally apply to the activities of the MGFA.[32] As a result, acceptance and encouragement of a widespread plurality of opinion have become a distinctive feature of the work of the MGFA, even to the extent where at times teamwork research becomes a bit bothersome.

Starting in 1957–1958, the MGFA's research was first directed at a reliable analysis of the causes and the course of World War II, based on documentary material. Basic conceptions had already been developed in the early 1950s at the Ministry of Defense. This project was not intended to serve as instructional material only for the forces, it was rather meant to be *the* official German account of this most disastrous event, which, for reasons of mere quantity, had to be researched and written by a major group of scholars over an extended period of time. The tackling of this task was therefore only possible with the organizational and financial support of a government agency, in this case the MGFA. The original intentions, to get away from a purpose-oriented military history and attempt the over all general approach toward a comprehensive history of World War II, had to be deferred for want of archival material at that time as well as a shortage of manpower.[33] It was not before 1962 that a project group broke ground by working out the first conceptual ideas of how to tackle this enormous task. One of the first decisions of this committee was to formally replace the term *Kriegsgeschichte* with *Militärgeschichte* for this project (for obvious reasons).[34] When work finally started in the early 1970s, discussions on subject and methods for *Das*

Deutsche Reich und Der Zweite Weltkrieg had been following more or less all the puzzling trends of those years to reach a new understanding of history in general. Full consent was never reached, but the results so far show that streamlined consent is not absolutely necessary for a great teamwork. To the contrary: Too much consensus might even be counterproductive in view of a desirable plurality of conceptions in history, which are indispensable indicators for freedom of research and opinion in a democratic society.[35]

Another early plan of the MGFA was the research and presentation of the beginnings of German defense policy and German rearmament after World War II, which was, in fact, the stunning story of Germany's reintegration into the community of the Western nations.[36] Since this problem could only be solved by examining a highly complex tissue of political, economical, and cultural facts, causes, and interrelations on a national and international basis, the level of abstraction and comprehension in defining what was military history had to be set even higher. Starting research in 1972 (a long time after first conceptions were drafted), volume 1 of *Anfänge westdeutscher Sicherheitspolitik* appeared in 1982, followed by volume 2 in 1990.[37] Again, this project went way beyond an outdated conception of military history, offering comprehensive insight into essential historical developments during the period of the Cold War.

A third major project of research of the MGFA stemmed from the conviction that the newly conceived approach toward military history need not necessarily be restricted to the immediate past or to contemporary military history alone. Never before had there been a handbook of German military history, and when Colonel Meier-Welcker conceived this idea in the early 1960s, he thought of creating a work that would serve the military profession, especially with the educational aspect in view, as well as academic historiography. It took fifteen years to finalize the project, and the first of five volumes of *Handbuch zur deutschen Militärgeschichte 1648–1939* appeared in 1964.[38] The *Handbuch* in itself constitutes a document of the process of a year long serious quest for a modern approach to military history. The team of authors finally arrived at the conception that, "besides an effort to deliver a typological description of war and the 'Art of War,' it was not so much their intention to examine war, battles or campaigns, but the 'Personenverband'—the 'association of people'—the military."[39]

After the late 1950s, neither the popularity of military history nor the number of military historians dealing with it outside the MGFA significantly increased. Certainly, there were a number of scholars in the Federal Republic who, out of professional interest, looked at the phenomenon of war or the military and its relations to government and society from a general, and often abstract, point of view: historians such as Fritz Fischer, Karl Demeter, Werner Hahlweg, Eberhard Kessel, Fritz Herre, Andreas Hillgruber, Gerhard Oestreich, Gerhard Ritter, Hans Rothfels, Rudolf Stadelmann, and Rainer Wohlfeil. However, academic military history remained sparse in Germany, and was usually restricted to less than a half dozen specialized periodicals. One of them, the *Militärgeschichtliche Mitteilungen (MGM)*, was published by the MGFA from 1967 on. It soon became a platform for the publication and discussion of demanding papers concerning military history, even on an international level. The *MGM* served as a bridge to overcome the deeply rooted mental reservations between official and public historiography, a gap that has closed only slowly. The days have passed, however, when military historians in Germany were christened "historians of annihilation" (*Vernichtungshistoriker*),[40] but you can still hear statements such as, "Military history is much too important as to leave it to the military historians."[41]

TEACHING MILITARY HISTORY IN THE ARMED FORCES AFTER 1957

Conceptions and Definitions

It was another story, however, to solve the approach to military history in its didactic role, namely, for the education of cadets (*Fahnenjunker*) and officers within the new German armed forces after 1955. When it became obvious in the early 1950s, that German forces were to be built up in the near future, it was logical to ask if military history was still useful or necessary and thus to be included as part of the education of cadets and officers. There was a wide span of opinions, but it was unanimously agreed that instruction of *Militär- und Kriegsgeschichte* ("military and war history") was absolutely necessary. Concerning the problem of which subjects and methods to use, however, the discussion resulted in the perennial question of whether there was "ein innerer oder ein praktischer Nutzen der Kriegsgeschichte" (an *intrinsic* or *pragmatic* utility of military history), forming two distinctly different groups.[42]

The pragmatists, more or less following the tradition of the classical *Kriegsgeschichte*, believe in the existence of an immediate utility of historical experience and, therefore, in its teachability and applicability. This holds true even under the impression of World War II and in an age of potential Nuclear, Biological and Chemical (NBC)- warfare. The other group, relying on the "intrinsic" value of a broad historical education as offered by general *Militärgeschichte*, emphasizes individuals' development of all their mental and intellectual abilities, enabling them, in any given military situation, to act and react in a most effective way. While both factions agree on the premise that there is definitely a utility in military history, if one defines "utility" with the assumption that history enables a person engaged with it to learn from it as far as conduct and behavior are concerned, they still disagree in several other aspects. The quarrel continues today in Germany, although all permissable arguments in this respect have already been presented in the past and logical conclusions were drawn in the 1960s.

There are three further essential inconsistencies that separate the respective groups:

1. One is the question of the *historical period* from which the historical subject should be selected. While the pragmatists, as in the time of Clausewitz and

Helmut von Moltke the Elder, wish to employ historical examples from the nearest possible past,[43] their antagonists—searching for the timeless elements of historical cognition—do not care from which period such educational exemplifications are drawn.[44]

2. Another point is the conviction of the pragmatists that military history can provide *immediate* advice for practical purposes during the uncertainties of war or in its preparation. The school of "intrinsic values" is only willing to accept a *mediating* utility of historical events after critical reflection within an overall perspective.[45]

3. The pragmatists are afraid that too much involvement of cadets and young officers in critical and analytical historical approaches will cause an unnecessary "intellectualization," which will make them unfit for quick decisions and therefore weaken the forces.[46] The other faction will not permit the assumption of any contradiction between the ability to act, on one side, and intelligence on the other, in other words, it will not comply with an "antithesis of character and intellect," rather assuming a causal connection instead.[47]

Altogether, even the pragmatists concede the possibility and accept the advantages of an intrinsic utility of military history, although in their opinion it will be achieved anyway and instrumentally by their own approach. They also admit that regulations, rules, or directives for the present or the future cannot be expected from military history, even with respect to its pragmatic utility.

This leads us to a short evaluation of the question of the "intrinsic or pragmatic utility" of military history. Friedrich Forstmeier, former chief of the MGFA, principally and brilliantly answered it already when he wrote not of two different opinions but of *two different levels of approach*. Military history—and its intrinsic values—are directed at a far-reaching, comprehensive, and profound *education* of the entire personality. It enables a person "to employ the knowledge and cognition received not only in a narrow professional way, but for his whole life." On another level, historical experience is conveyed by a pragmatic approach for an everyday tactical or operational use which provides the necessary *training* of the military profession. The approaches do not contradict but rather complement each other.[48]

The logical consequence of this conception should be that, although the latter approach is admittedly indispensable for the training of military officers, we do not deal with military *history* proper at this level but with something else which should not be called history at all. Different levels of officers ought to be introduced for this kind of training, such as *Militärkunde*, which would translate as "military studies."[49] The difference between the two levels—between "military history" and "military studies"—pertains to the *methods of teaching* alone. In both cases the historical material taught must be unconditionally subject to the criteria of scholarly history.

For teaching military history in the *Bundeswehr*, it was again Meier-Welcker who made two more things perfectly clear. First, in order to convey cognitive abilities, it does not matter from which historical period the examples are taken;

teachers were given a wide berth of discretion. Second, "above and beyond any utility ranks the discourse with history proper, which leads us to unalienated cognition."[50] This has been, in concurrence with the conviction of an "intrinsic utility" of military history, unmistakably a creed for the essential insights of history as a whole, and *not* for short-lived application or questionable "lessons." It was a testimony in favor of an allover humanitarian education: Military history should teach what is of lasting significance, he wrote, because "he who learns from history should walk a path on which he will not experience practices for one or the other opportunity only, but he should—which means infinitely more— learn how to see, to recognize and to judge."[51] It was this philosophy that was to characterize all concepts of teaching military history in the *Bundeswehr* there- after, and it was this understanding that led Minister of Defense Bonn to introduce the subject *Militär-* and *Kriegsgeschichte* for all three services as early as 1956. Meier-Welcker's conceptions and opinions were materializing to a high degree and are still valid today, at least as far as the understanding and scholarly approach of military history are concerned.

Establishing the Directorate of Education, Information, and Special Studies

From Producing Studies to Conducting Historical Education. Since the found- ing of the MGFA in 1957–1958, some of its scholars were always assigned to work on military studies, answer inquiries, prepare instructional material, and support the instructors of *Militär- und Kriegsgeschichte* at the educational in- stitutions of the *Bundeswehr.*[52] Much time was consumed in these more pragmatic and necessary aspects of military history, but until the late 1970s there was, with the exception of a small reference section, no organizational establishment to an obvious administrational demand. After the general "crisis of history" had been called off in the late 1970s, the *Bundeswehr* followed suit. In 1978, the Armed Forces Chief of Staff, General Harald Wust, urged a revival of historical education in the forces. In a directive to the MGFA he stated that historical knowledge and traditions in the forces were suffering because the results of historical research were not sufficiently conveyed in the *Bundeswehr.* According to this directive, historical education in the forces was meant to enable a military person

- by way of a realistic and comprehensive view of history to understand his or her role in a democratic society and recognize the purpose of military service,
- via the presentation of selected events and personalities of general and, particularly, of military history to train his or her political and military judgement, to found decisions on historical experience, and to obtain standards for conduct, and
- to deal properly with historical problems under guidance.[53]

As a consequence of these wide-ranging directives, a new directorate was added to the MGFA under the somewhat cryptic denomination, Directorate of

Education, Information, and Special Studies'' (*Abteilung Ausbildung, Information, Fachstudien* or AIF), which was officially established in 1980.[54] For the first time, the MGFA had an institution responsible for the "improvement of the historical education within the armed forces" in its own right, as the Armed Forces Chief of Staff called it: an educational didactic branch, with a wide spectrum of tasks. In 1991 the directorate was renamed Directorate Historical Education (*Abteilung Historische Bildung or AHB* for obvious reasons).[55] The AHB does not itself teach, but it is instrumental in developing general conceptions for teaching military history throughout the armed forces. The target groups and teaching objectives are manifold, but may be roughly divided into three major divisions:

1. Teaching the instructors: enabling military leaders of all ranks to establish historical interrelations between current political events and their historical background during weekly instruction hours, that are mandatory by law[56] for all men, and particularly for young conscripts, in concurrence with the principle of *Innere Führung* (Principles of Leadership and Civic Education).[57]
2. Shaping the personality and the historical conscience of officers and NCOs in a social, anthropological, and cultural context in order to qualify them for and identify them with their profession.
3. Training the military mind and judgment of present and future commanders in order to found their decisions on established historical knowledge.

All this did certainly *not* mean a relapse into the ancient *Kriegsgeschichte*, or even a second-rate military history, as some critics would have it.[58] Even if the directorate started to research operations of World War II on a new critical basis, it did so strictly within the comprehensive scholarly approach established at the MGFA and with the "intrinsic utility" of history in mind. Military strategy and operations, sometimes to the level of tactics, are definitely legitimate subjects of military history. Observing the methodological standards of general history, including these events, in a comprehensive historical frame of reference with regard to their complex conditions, such approaches to *Operationsgeschichte* (operational history), as it has been called lately by the MGFA, are fully acceptable. They can convey historical facts, conditions, and interdependencies of the past, providing knowledge and the ability for critical analyses. They show a multitude of possibilities to act and leave potential room for maneuvering. They school intellect, judgment, and awareness of problems; they can move, excite, upset, and shock, and they should, in addition, be fun to read. They *cannot* and *should not* do two things, however:

• First, operational history cannot provide rules, regulations, or directives. History does not repeat itself and cannot, therefore, develop inherent laws. Uncritical adherence to alleged "lessons of history" may easily lead to catastrophe.
• Second, as with any other kind of history, military or operational history cannot deliver

a unique or compulsory view of history. Such views are clear signs of oppressive political systems and a time-tested means of indoctrination.

For AHB, it was actually not too difficult to stick to these principles, although there are always the odd attempts by the advocates of "lessons learned" to bend the rules a little. The only prerequisites necessary to avoid this are unwavering adherence to the standards of scholarly history and, in view of the knowledge of how history was corrupted militarily and ideologically not too long ago, a strong belief in the power of human rights.

MILITARY HISTORY AND TRADITION

In 1951, Gerhard Ritter, at the time one of the elder statesmen of critical military history, asked in despair, "What, however, could still be certain, concerning politico-historical convictions and traditional values of German history, after the ignominious abuse of their noblest ideals, their most dignified traditions, the nation's faith in herself and in her future?"[59] Only one year before, a group of former high-ranking *Wehrmacht* officers had, during a secret conference at a Monastery at Himmerod (Eifel), concluded that, with respect to the new German forces, German military traditions had to be given up, at least partially.[60]

Although it is true that "tradition and history are unseparately related with each other," in Germany the problem has become much less a question of history than one of ethics and politics.[61] It is extremely difficult, even today, to satisfactorily answer questions such as: Did military tradition in Prusso-Germany support a historical development toward Hitler and the Third Reich in the long run? Was there to be an entirely new start of tradition after 1945 or could some lines of tradition be accepted, even including the *Wehrmacht*? Is tradition, in a philosophical way, divisible into "good" and "bad" parts, particularly with respect to a historical personality? Finally, which values could serve as an orientation for acceptable, worthwhile, or valuable traditions, with guidelines for the forces in mind? All these questions and many more were over the years discussed publicly in a most controversial manner, with rocks and molotov cocktails replacing arguments in some incidents.

Because "tradition" in the *Bundeswehr* is legally a responsibility of the Ministry of Defense, the MGFA has honestly tried to approach the problem from a strictly historical point of view.[62] Nonetheless, tradition has many powerful facets. During the years that the *Bundeswehr* existed—and, indeed, formed its own tradition—there were three official attempts by the Ministry of Defense to solve the dilemma.[63] Although contradictory in some aspects, the three directives agreed on the stipulation that *all* tradition honored in the *Bundeswehr* had to correspond with the values and the democratic fundamental order of the Basic Law. This is quite acceptable. It only poses the question of to which degree traditional military elements that have proven valuable but have developed over the centuries under entirely different social and political (i.e., undemocratic) conditions, can stand up to such demands.[64] This is very difficult for prede-mocratic periods of German history, such as the Wars of Liberation (1812–1815) and the Wars of German Unification (1864–1870/71) and their protagonists: Gerhardt von Scharnhorst, Carl von Clausewitz, and Helmut von Moltke the Elder, for instance, just were no democrats. Moreover, it proved particularly critical in the case of military leaders, who were, for example, brilliant military minds during World War II but had supported Hitler unconditionally and were possibly involved in war crimes.

The problem of military tradition in the *Bundeswehr*—and in the Federal Republic—has thus not been solved satisfactorily. The spectrum of opinions and ethical objections is too wide. In this respect, quite a few foreign countries have a high esteem for the *Wehrmacht* and do not understand the Germans. It is true, there were admirable examples of prowess, effectiveness, chivalry, and courage; millions of men did their duty unblemished. However, there were also, as grad-ually comes to light after more intense studies, horrid examples of cruelty, inhumanity, and murder. Therefore, the *Wehrmacht* cannot be an overall shining example for the soldiers of the *Bundeswehr* or be glorified in a *general* way. On the other hand it must not *generally* be condemned as "unworthy for tra-dition" simply because it was Hitler's instrument of power, without which he could have never realized his criminal war of occupation and racial annihilation.[65] All in all, there is a very clear and difficult obligation for historians to differentiate carefully in each individual case.

NEW PERSPECTIVES: THE "FALL OF THE WALL"

Changing Tasks for the Forces and the Role of Military History

The fall of the Berlin Wall on that memorable 9 November 1989 was a first step toward the long-hoped-for unity of the two Germanies and the most telling indicator of a general worldwide political change in East-West relations. Within an amazingly short time the threat potentials in Europe began to deflate, and the political and social preconditions that had led to the formation of the Western Alliance and the buildup of German forces in the 1950s had begun to funda-mentally change. In addition, it signaled the collapse of communism as an idea and as a basis for organizing mega-societies.

For the relation between military history and the military profession in Ger-many, this meant entirely new perspectives and substantial new tasks. If we accept a utility of military history (within the limits and conditions pointed out before this chapter), there arise three major objectives in this respect. One is the obvious necessity to once more explain and define the purpose of armed forces within a democratic society from a historical point of view. Refraining from a lengthy legitimation by the perception of more than forty years of severe threat from the Warsaw Pact, the purpose and role of the *Bundeswehr* in the Federal

Republic and within the Alliance will now have to be justified by the more "classical" function of any military force, as a guardian of sovereignty and political self-determination. In an era of more readiness for peace, the military will have to learn to stand *for* something rather than *against* something. This would certainly not exclude a new role within a peace-securing and -keeping supranational organization like the United Nations.[66] To convey and explain this message to the public and the military—as an integral component—will be a most important mission for military history as an essential educational instrument, particularly with respect to the acceptance of the armed forces in society as well as the morale of the military profession.

The second aspect is that military history will have to play a much more important role in the educational process of all professional soldiers. This has to occur in a process almost like the restructuring of the educational system for the military profession under Scharnhorst began in 1807, in a period of far-reaching political upheavals, because, according to him, "history alone provides the material, which educates the living intellect." Military history indeed powerfully supports the efforts to shape military educators, instructors, and leaders, who are well grounded in a sophisticated, humanistic way, able to think analytically and in context, true to the ideals of the constitution, but also willing to risk their lives in its defense—their outstanding military training being a matter of course. It is this ideal for which military history in the *Bundeswehr* should strive.[67]

There is one more urgent task for military history in Germany as an unalienable component of political education. In the former German Democratic Republic which is now part of a united Germany, there is a vast backlog of demand for the development of a consciousness of liberty among a great majority of the population. There is also a lack of knowledge about the ways and means of democratic decision making in general, and in particular, for explaining the rules of the game for running armed forces in a democratic way. History provides the material to explain the interrelations of this problem from our own past to the former soldiers of the *Volksarmee* ("People's Army") who have now joined the *Bundeswehr*, particularly the young conscripts. There must be no patronizing complacence on our side, however. Forces like the *Bundeswehr* that were lucky enough to have had an almost forty years headstart on freedom have every reason to pass along this experience firmly but with tact and considerate understanding. Military history will be able to render excellent services in this respect.

NOTES

1. Michael Howard, "The Use and Abuse of Military History," *Parameters*, no. 11 (March 1981): 10–15, repr. in *The Evolution of Modern Warfare* (Ft. Leavenworth, KS: Combat Studies Institute, 1989), pp. 2–7.

2. A very thorough examination of the emergence and development of this term by Wolfgang v. Groote is in his "Militärgeschichte," *Militärgeschichtliche Mitteilungen*

(hereafter *MGM*) 1 (1967): 5–19; see also Rainer Wohlfeil, "Wehr-, Kriegs- oder Militärgeschichte? *MGM* 1/(1967): 21–29.

3. Michael Salewski, "Zur preußischen Militärgeschichtsschreibung im 19. Jahrhundert," *Militärgeschichte in Deutschland und österreich vom 18. Jahrhundert bis in die Gegenwart*, Vorträge zur Militärgeschichte no. 6 (Herford/Bonn, 1985), pp. 54–56. This statement does not contradict Martin Blumenson, "Can Official History Be Honest History?" *Military Affairs*, 26 (1962): 153–161, and his opinions in favor of "official history," since he analyzes conditions within a modern democratic society.

4. See Hans Umbreit, "The Development of Official Military Historiography in the German Army from the Crimean War to 1945," In Robin Higham, ed. *Official Histories* (Manhattan, KS, 1970), pp. 160–209. Umbreit presents a comprehensive bibliography of "official" publications in this context; see pp. 169–204.

5. See Michael Salewski, "Militärgeschtsschichtreibung," p. 51.

6. Heinz Hürten, "Militärgeschichte in Deutschland: Zur Geschichte einer Disziplin in der Spannung von akademischer Freiheit und gesellschaftlichem Anspruch," *Historisches Jahrbuch* 95 (1975): 375–76.

7. Ibid., p. 376.

8. See Detlef Bald et al., eds., *Tradition und Reform im militärischen Bildungswesen: Von der preußischen Allgemeinen Kriegsschule zur Führungsakademie der Bundeswehr* (Baden-Baden, 1985), pp. 20–32.

9. See Hew Strachan, *European Armies and the Conduct of War* (London, 1983), p. 6.

10. See Eberhard Kessel, "Moltke und die Kriegsgeschichte," *Militärwissenschaftliche Rundschau* (hereafter *MWR*) 6 (1941): 120–22, and Umbreit, "Military Historiography," pp. 162–63.

11. For history and structure, see Umbreit, "Military Historiography, pp. 165–67.

12. Hans Meier-Welcker, "Über die Kriegsgeschichte als Wissenschaft und Lehre," *Wehrwissenschaftliche Rundschau* (hereafter *WWR*) 5 (1955): 7.

13. See Hürten, "Militärgeschichte," p. 386. Meier-Welcker, "Kriegsgeschichte," p. 6, pointed out that this was the only research institute of *Kriegsgeschichte* of importance in Germany between the world wars.

14. General Herhudt v. Rohden, last chief of the Kriegswissenschaftliche Abteilung des Generalstabs der Luftwaffe, in an essay of 1944, quoted from Hans Meier-Welcker, "Entwicklung und Stand der Kriegsgeschichte als Wissenschaft," *WWR* 6 (1956): p. 7. About further aspects of Rohden's understanding of history, see Manfred Masserschmidt, *Die Wehrmacht im NS-Staat* (Hamburg, 1969), pp. 339, 441.

15. Gerhard Östreich, "Vom Wesen der Wehrgeschichte," *Historische Zeitschrift* 162 (1940): 233, 235, 245, 248. Cf. Wohlfeil, "Militärgeschichte," pp. 22–23.

16. Hürten, "Militärgeschichte," pp. 387–88.

17. Friedhelm Klein, "Militärgeschichte in der Bundesrepublik Deutschland, *Vorträge* 6: 184.

18. See Roland G. Foerster et al., *Von der Kapitulation bis zum Pleven-Plan*, vol. 1 of Militärgeschichtliches Forschungsamt, ed. *Anfänge westdeutscher Sicherheitspolitik 1945–1956* (München, 1982).

19. See Charles Burdick, "Vom Schwert zur Feder," *MGM* 2 (1971): 69–80.

20. There are history courses taught at these universities, but within the departments of Social or Educational Arts, respectively. As of October 1990, the Hamburg University offered a program to earn an M.A. in history but *not* military history. See Wilhelm Deist,

"Militärgeschichtliche Forschung in Freiburg i.Br.," *Mitteilungsblatt des Verbandes der Historiker Deutschlands* 1 (1990): 24.

21. See Dermot Bradley and Werner Hahlweg, *Militärgeschichte, Militärwissenschaft und Konfliktforschung*, Studien zur Militärgeschichte, Militärwissenschaft und Konfliktforschung no. 15 (Osnabrück, 1977).

22. Hürten, "Militärgeschichte," pp. 388–90.

23. Norbert Wiggershaus, "Die amtliche Militärgeschichtsforschung in der Dienststelle Blank und im Bundesministerium für Verteidigung 1952 bis 1956," *MGM* 2 (1976): 115–21.

24. Meier-Welcker "Über die Kriegsgeschichte," pp. 1–8.

25. "Zielsetzung und Methode der Militärgeschichtsschreibung," in *Militärgeschichte: Probleme—Thesen—Wege* (hereafter *Militärgeschichte*) (Stuttgart, 1982), pp. 57–59.

26. Klein, "Militärgeschichte," pp. 188–189.

27. BMVg Fü B IV, dated 29 July 1957. Bundesarchiv-Militärarchiv (hereafter BA-MA), Bw 2/1051.

28. Wiggershaus, "Militärgeschichtsforschung," pp. 118–19.

29. "Zielsetzung," pp. 48, 58. The study group was convoked by the former chief of the MGFA, Captain (N) Dr. Friedrich Forstmeier. Chaired by Prof. Dr. Heinz Hürten, it concluded its task in 1976. Its findings still comprise the valid and comprehensive conception of military history at the MGFA.

30. Meier-Welcker, "Über die Kriegsgeschichte," pp. 1–8. Hans Meier-Welcker, "Entwicklung und Stand der Kriegsgeschichte als Wissenschaft," *WWR* 6 (1956): 1–10. Hans Meier-Welcker, "Über den Unterricht in Kriegsgeschichte: Entwicklung and Auffassungen," *WWR* 6 (1956): 539–46.

31. BA-MA, Bw 2/1058; STAN [Table of Organization] Nr. 202–8, Stand 19.01.1956.

32. Karl Carstens, "Militärpolitik und Militärgeschichte," *MGM* 2 (1967): 5–13, esp. pp. 6, 10.

33. The intention was "to show to posterity, to history altogether, an image as objective as possible of the processes and interrelations of that time," BA-MA, BW 2/1419. BMVg—Fü B III 4—Az 10–87–05 v. 20.07.59.

34. See Klein, "Militärgeschichte," p. 191.

35. Militärgeschichtliches Forschungsamt, ed., *Das Deutsche Reich und der Zweite Weltkrieg*, vols. 1–6 (Stuttgart, 1979). The English language edition is, *Germany and the Second World War*, vol. 1 (Oxford: Oxford University Press, 1990). The work is planned to consist of ten volumes and will be based on all available source material in Germany.

36. As early as 1957. BA-MA, BW 2/1054. Fü B IV A5—Az 557—81 TgbNr. 161/57 v. 29.07.57. Betr: Militärgeschichtliche Forschungsstelle.

37. Militärgeschichtliches Forschungsamt, ed., *Anfänge westdeutscher Sicherheitspolitik*. The work earned a national award in 1985. Vol. 2 Lutz Köllner et al., *Die EVG-Phase*, (München, 1990).

38. Militärgeschichtliches Forschungsamt, ed., *Handbuch zur deutschen Militärgeschichte 1648–1939* [hereafter *Handbuch*], 5 vols. (München, 1979), repr. Deutsche Militärgeschichte, 6 vols. (Herrsching, 1983).

39. Manfred Messerschmidt, Chief Historian MGFA, in his introduction to Militärgeschichtliches Forschungsamt, *Handbuch*, I: vii.

40. Deist, "Militärgeschichtliche Forschung," p. 22.

41. Remark addressed to the author at a discussion in Freiburg in July 1990.

42. A comprehensive summary of this discussion is offered by Gerhard Göhler in "Vom Nutzen der Kriegsgeschichte, Parts I and II," *Wehrkunde* 13 (1964): 591–96, 648–52. The term *innerer Nutzen* (intrinsic utility) was reintroduced in 1960 by Hans Meier-Welcker in "Unterricht und Studium in der Kriegsgeschichte angesichts der radikalen Wandlung im Kriegswesen," *Wehrkunde* 9 (1960); 608–12, quoting Karl Wenninger in 1902.

43. On the pragmatists, see, for example, Hermann Heidegger, "Kann Kriegsgeschict*sunterricht heute noch einen praktischen Nutzen haben?" in *Militärgeschichte*, pp. 30–31.

44. Meier-Welcker, "Unterricht und Studium." Cf. Friedrich Forstmeier, "Sinn und Wert des kriegsgeschichtlichen Unterrichts, 'Innerer Nutzen' oder 'Applikatorische Methode?' " *Wehrkunde* 10 (1961); 372–374; repr. in *Militärgeschichte*, pp. 33–37.

45. Controversial positions are exemplified by Heidegger, "Kriegsgeschichtsunterricht," on one side, and Meier-Welcker, "Unterricht und Studium," and Forstmeier, "Sinn und Wert," on the other. For a full account, see Göhler, "Kriegsgeschichte," p. 593.

46. Heidegger, "Kriegsgeschichtsunterricht," p. 32.

47. Gerhard Papke, "Was ist Kriegsgeschichte?" *Wehrkunde* 10 (1961): 417–22; repr. in *Militärgeschichte*, pp. 38–47.

48. Forstmeier, "Sinn und Wert," p. 37; cf. Göhler, "Kriegsgeschichte," part 2, p. 652.

49. Papke, "Kriegsgeschichte," p. 46, calls it *Kriegskunde* (war studies), as he still speaks of *Kriegsgeschichte*. Cf. Göhler, "Kriegsgeschichte," part 1, p. 595.

50. Meier-Welcker, "Über den Unterricht," pp. 544–46, and Meier-Welcker, "Über die Kriegsgeschichte," pp. 1–8.

51. Meier-Welcker, "Unterricht und Studium in der Kriegsgeschichte angesichts der radikalen Wandlung im Kriegswesen," *Wehrkunde* 9 (1960): 608–12; repr. in *Militärgeschichte*, p. 23.

52. In the beginning, more than half the personnel worked for these purposes, although research was to have had priority. See Wiggershaus, "Militärgeschichtsforschung," 119–20.

53. BMVg—GenInspBw—dated 17.08.78.

54. STAN [Table of Organization] MGFA of 1980 (restricted). MGFA, Freiburg, Germany.

55. Jahresweisung Amtschef MGFA 1991 (Directive 1991, Chief MGFA), MGFA, Frieburg, Germany.

56. No. 17, Soldatengesetz (Military Law).

57. ZDv 12/1 (Central Field Manual 12/1).

58. See Detlef Kotsch, "Zur Entwicklung der militärgeschichtlichen Forschung in der Bundesrepublik Deutschland," *Militärgeschichte* (DDR) 2 (1990): 161.

59. Gerhard Ritter, *Geschichte als Bildungsmacht: Ein Beitrag zur historisch-politischen Neubesinnung* (Stuttgart, 1946), p. 7.

60. Hans-Jürgen Rautenberg and Norbert Wiggershaus, "Die 'Himmeroder Denkschrift' vom Oktober 1950: Politische und militärische überlegungen für einen Beitrag der Bundesrepublik Deutschland zur westeuropäischen Verteidigung," *MGM* 1 (1977): 135–206.

61. Günter Roth, "Einführung: Tradition in deutschen Streitkräften bis 1945," in

Militärgeschichtliches Forschungsamt, ed., *Entwicklung deutscher militärischer Tradition*, vol. 1, *Tradition in deutschen Streitkräften bis–1945* (Herford, 1986), p. 11.

62. Militärgeschichtliches Forschungsamt, *Entwicklung deutscher militärischer Tradition*, vol. 1, *Tradition in deutschen Streitkräften bis 1945*; vol. 2, *Tradition und Reform in den Aufbaujahren der Bundeswehr* (Herford, 1985); vol. 3, *Symbole und Zeremoniell in deutschen Streikräften vom 18. bis zum 20. Jahrhundert*, 2d ed. (Herford, 1986). (Also see Militärgeschichtliches Forschungsamt, ed., *Von der Friedenssicherung zur Friedensgestaltung: Streitkräfte im Wandel* (Frieburg, 1991).

63. (1). BMVg—Fü B I 4—Az 35–08–07 dated 01.07.65, "Bundeswehr und Tradition," = "Traditionserla" dated 7 July 1965, canceled 20.09.1982. (2). BMVg GenInspBw—Fü S I 3—Az 35–08–07 dated 20.09.82, Information für Kommandeure Nr. 1/82: "Richtlinien zum Traditionsverständnis und zur Traditionspflege in der Bundeswehr." (3). *Weißbuch 1985* [White Paper 1985], ed. by Orders of the Bundesregierung by BMVg (Bonn, 1985), pp. 313–16.

64. See Heinrich Walle, "Tradition—Floskel oder Form? Neue Wege zu alten Werten," in Militärgeschichtliches Forschungsamt, *Streitkräfte im Wandel*. Walle has analyzed the latest development in this field from a number of different angles.

65. This is the opinion of Manfred Messerschmidt, former chief historian of the MGFA, among others, and was first expressed in an article, "Das Verhältnis von Wehrmacht und NS-Staat und die Frage der Traditionsbildung," in: *Das Parlament. Beilage: Aus Politik und Zeitgeschichte*, no. 17 (1981): 11ff.

66. Political decisions in this respect have not yet been made by the German government.

67. See Günter Roth, Chief MGFA, in a draft, "Denkschrift zur Bedeutung der historischen Bildung in den Streitkräften" (unpubl. manuscript, 18 May 1990).

15

The Napoleonic Paradigm: The Myth of the Offensive in Soviet and Western Military Thought

DAVID R. JONES

This chapter developed as a result of a number of considerations which emerged when I began teaching courses in general military studies as opposed to the narrower field of Russian and Soviet military history. As I surveyed the overall Western experience of war, I became increasingly convinced that the success accorded the style of offensive warfare waged by the armies of Revolutionary and Napoleonic France was essentially an aberration when compared with the norm of western experience. I concluded further that despite this fact, this Napoleonic aberration had become accepted as the norm by most later thinkers, and that this misperception, in turn, has had a number of unfortunate and painful consequences for those soldiers who have attempted to follow in Napoleon's footsteps.

In some part, my reflections on this matter were provoked as well by the doctrinal problems that confronted the Soviet military in the latter half of the 1980s. One outcome of Mikhail Gorbachev's "new thinking" on matters of security was that Moscow's "military doctrine" became "defensive" in style as well as in intention.[1] As the former Defense Minister Dmitri Yazov explained, the peacetime deployments and stance of the Soviet Armed Forces had to be such that they provided only a "reasonable and reliable sufficiency" of armed force, or a level "determined by the minimum requirements of defence." Since this clearly "does not pose a real threat of war to other countries," it naturally "ensures equal mutual security."[2] In contrast, the Soviet forces earlier had been configured so as to mount a strategic-operational, theater-level offensive during the initial period of any "defensive" conflict waged against the West.[3]

This shift in emphasis has left Soviet (and now, Russian) military planners debating the best practical model on which to structure their forces. In the process, they already have turned repeatedly to models provided by their own recent military history (e.g., Gankin-Gol, Kursk, etc.).[4] However, what follows suggests, first, that their recent doctrinal shift in fact represents an important, if unintended, rejection of the aberrant Napoleonic paradigm and that the results may well accord better with the more enduring "lessons" of military science and history than did their former belief that the only sure defense was a successful offence. Second, some of the issues raised also explain why many Soviet (and other) military men instinctively opposed the adoption of a "defensive" defense posture.

THE OFFENSIVE IN POSTWAR SOVIET
MILITARY THEORY

Although soldiers of most times and places have paid at least lip service to the value of studying military history, many nonmilitary thinkers have had their doubts. However, as Michael Howard once pointed out, for the professional warrior such studies have a number of practical uses. Not the least of these is to inculcate the military and patriotic traditions that so frequently have helped sustain soldiers in battle. Even more important is the fact that if "there are no wars at present in which the professional soldier can learn his trade, he is almost compelled to study the wars of the past." However, he also warned that these efforts will be largely fruitless unless they have breadth or width in terms of scope and time, depth in terms of the detailed examination of particular campaigns, and a sense of context (i.e., sociopolitical environment).[5]

This approach parallels that taken to military history by Soviet military thinkers. As practitioners of the Marxist-Leninist school of social science, they had long believed in the utility of military history for solving problems of contemporary military doctrine. "By analyzing the history of the Soviet Union and of other states, and exploring the experiences of past wars," wrote Marshal V. G. Kulikov in 1976, "military history reveals the way in which military events have tended to obey the fundamental laws of war. This understanding permits military science to interpret present problems and approach future ones correctly." In addition, "military history is an effective tool in the ideological and historical-patriotic education of the people."[6]

This is not meant to suggest that military history was the sole ingredient in military science or that it was necessarily by itself a reliable guide to the nature of "future war." Rather, as one eminent Soviet military historian noted, the "practical significance of history consists above all else of the fact that since it is the preserved accumulated experience of mankind, it assists in the correct resolution of contemporary problems." As for military history per se, it was concerned "with both the social sides of war and with the military art—with the means and forms of armed battle; that is, with deciding which of many factors are the ones on which depend the course and outcome of all battles, operations and wars."[7]

For our purposes, the significance of this view is that until Gorbachev forced a change of emphasis, Soviet writers agreed with A. A. Sidorenko that many centuries of military history, including the history of the Soviet Armed Forces, are convincing proof that in an armed conflict of any scale . . . —only the offensive permits one to attain victory over the enemy. The offensive is the only type of troop combat activity which can be employed to attain the complete rout of an enemy and the capture of important objectives and areas.[8]

All also agreed that the offensive mode of combat had appeared at the very dawn of warfare, but they accepted that the Revolutionary and Napoleonic Wars (1789–1815) brought "a deep transformation in the organization of armed forces and the means of conducting an offensive." Now mass armies were equipped with better weapons, divided into permanent divisions and corps, and supported by developed logistical systems, and so were believed to have acquired the capability of fighting much more decisive battles. As a result, "the main aim of the offensive became the destruction of the enemy army in battle."[9]

Sidorenko therefore argued that while "the military doctrine of our state never had and cannot have an aggressive character with regard to its political goals," any attack on the USSR would nonetheless unleash "the most active and decisive offensive that utilizes full combat might."[10] Like the majority of their Western colleagues, Soviet military theorists also argued that as "a type of combat activity, the offensive has incontestable advantages over the defense." These included conferring on the attacking troops such widely recognized military virtues as the initiative and ability to achieve surprise, raised morale, the use of captured enemy supplies and resources and, frequently, sustaining fewer losses.[11] Given the constant repetition of these assumed advantages, it is not surprising that training and practice revealed what Nathan Leites termed "a Soviet inclination to indulge in the offensive to excess," and even a tendency to "abuse" the offensive in efforts to avoid suspicions of *passivnost* (passivity).[12]

As good dialecticians, Soviet military men of course recognized the continuing existence of the defense, the antithesis of attack, in battle in particular and war in general. However, until recently, Soviet military men of course recognized the continuing existence of the defense, the antithesis of attack, in battle in particular and war in general. However, until recently, Soviet writers rarely presented the defense as a coequal of the offensive, even though both forms of combat "seek to destroy the enemy."[13] In practice, however, since 1945 they have tended to treat the defense as a sometimes unavoidable prelude by which "troops repulse an offensive by superior enemy forces, inflict significant losses upon him, hold the position they occupy, and create the conditions for transferring to a resolute offensive."[14] Thus, while Soviet commanders were taught how to assume operational and tactical defensive positions when absolutely necessary, they were urged to assume the attack as soon as possible since only resolute offensive actions could bring about the primary aim of battle: the destruction of the enemy's armed forces. Moreover, at the strategical level of waging war, most Soviet writers long followed Marshal V. D. Sokolovskii in urging that "strategic defense and defensive strategy should be decisively rejected as being extremely dangerous to the country."[15]

The extent to which these views have dominated Soviet military literature is evident from even a brief review. For example, Sidorenko introduced his study with a wide-ranging (thirty-two page) discussion of the factors that have promoted offensive action since Napoleon transformed Western warfare.[16] While space does not permit an analysis of his arguments here, I should note that his approach is typical. Similar discussions can be found in any number of Soviet works such as V. A. Semenov's history of the operational art, V. E. Savkin's work on the principles of operational and tactical combat, A. A. Yamonov's study of encounter or meeting battles, and S. P. Ivanov's important examination of offensive operations during the initial period of a war. All stress the rise of mass armies after the French Revolution, the creation of larger troop formations (divisions, corps, armies, and fronts), the technological advances made in mobility, firepower, and shock, and the resulting increased importance of offensive action at all levels of combat.[17]

In proposing these conclusions, Soviet military historians were guided by the lessons they drew from military history and also by the classical teachings of Marxism-Leninism on war and military affairs. "The offensive against the enemy," wrote V. I. Lenin in 1905, "should be the most energetic attack; attack and not defense should become the slogan of the masses."[18] While the Bolshevik leader was here speaking as much of political as of military matters, this spirit infused Communist military writings during the Civil War (1918–1920), as well as the latter writings of M. V. Frunze. "It must be clear," wrote the man some have called the Soviet Clausewitz, "that the side which holds the initiative, the side controlling the feature of surprise, frequently will frustrate the will of the opponent and thereby create conditions which are more favorable for itself." For this reason, he concluded, "attack and the offensive, other things being equal, will always bring more benefits than the defense."[19]

THE OFFENSIVE IN IMPERIAL RUSSIAN AND WESTERN ARMIES

On the basis of such statements, some Western analysts have argued that it was Frunze who "established the necessity for the offensive as the policy of the Red Army."[20] Nonetheless, like the search for a "unified military doctrine," the requirement for an offensive military doctrine predated World War I. Then, despite the warnings of Y. S. Bliokh, the experiences of Plevna, Manchuria, and Port Arthur, as well as the musings of A. A. Neznamov and others, the Imperial Army had joined its French allies in adopting offensive plans for the war against Germany and Austro-Hungary.[21] While tactically and operationally this offensive tradition could be justified by the examples of Peter the Great and A. V. Suvorov, as well as the tactical teachings of M. I. Dragomirov, in the operational sphere the Napoleonic model remained dominant.[22] While this reflected the fact that Russian theoretists shared a European heritage, this had been mediated through the works of such leading Russian military thinkers as N. V. Medem, G. A. Leer, E. I. Martynov, and A. A. Neznamov, among others.[23]

As suggested, such Russian military theories have had their counterparts in the West and, since 1945, "offense-mindedness" has pervaded the Western military as well. A prominent, recent example is the U.S. Army's *Field Manual No. 100–5, Operations*, which laid down the fundamentals of "AirLand Battle." In the same manner in which Soviet writers invoke the ghosts of Peter I, Suvorov, and A. A. Brusilov, this manual claimed for the U.S. Army "a long history of offensive campaigns" and cited Generals William T. Sherman, "Stonewall" Jackson, Douglas MacArthur, Omar Bradley, and George Patton as "American leaders who were expert in the attack." It defined the offensive as "the decisive form of war, the commander's only means of attaining a positive goal or of completely destroying an enemy force." The attacker "concentrates quickly and strikes hard at an unexpected place or time to throw the defender off balance," and, with the attack launched, he "must move fast, press every advantage aggressively, and capitalize on each opportunity to destroy either the enemy's forces or the overall coherence of his defense." In this regard, the Vicksburg Campaign of General U.S. Grant, "who understood the essence of offensive operations," was held to be "the most brilliant campaign ever fought on American soil" and to exemplify "the qualities of a well-conceived, violently executed offensive plan."[24]

The universal quality of this trend is equally clear from a brief review of the so-called "Principles of War" through which officers are introduced to the essentials of their profession. For example, the U.S. Army first adopted a set of principles into its training regulations in 1921. In so doing, it drew on the eight principles developed by Major General J.F.C. Fuller for the British Army during World War I, which, in 1923, were adopted for that force's *Field Service Regulations*. At present, the U.S. Army's list has been expanded to nine, and some sources list as many as ten. Moreover, while few analysts would suggest that any commander should attempt to rigidly follow these rules, they would probably agree with Hew Strachan that "at the very least they provide an insight into the military brain."[25]

Among these principles one commonly finds that of "offensive action" (although it sometimes is subsumed under that of "initiative"). *Field Manual 100–5*, for example, combines the two by defining the "offensive" principle as: "Seize, retain and exploit the initiative." Its authors go on to note that while the principle of "objective" directs all action toward a common goal, that of "offensive suggests that offensive action, or maintenance of the initiative, is the most effective and decisive to pursue and to attain that common goal." Further, they stress that this is "fundamentally true in both the strategic and technical senses." In the end, whatever the level, "the side which retains the initiative through offensive action forces the foe to react rather than act."[26]

Earlier, another American authority defined this principle as meaning simply that ''victory can never be won by passive defense; only sustained offensive action, or the threat of unfailing offensive action brings success.'' This means, Rear Admiral Henry E. Eccles (USN) explained, that a commander must strive ''to exploit at every practical opportunity the initiative inherent in offensive action; to bring vigorous, timely concentration of forces against a weaker concentration; to create favorable conditions for attack''; and so on.[27] As summarized by Hew Strachan, this principle quite simply asserts that the offensive ''is the stronger form of warfare as it affirms morale and only it can lead to victory. The defensive,'' he continued, ''is weaker because it disperses resources, yields the initiative to the enemy, and is therefore acceptable only as a prelude to a counter attack.'' This principle is thus closely allied to that of ''morale,'' as well as to those of ''concentration on the decisive point,'' ''surprise,'' and the ''flexibility and mobility'' that permit realization of the other principles mentioned.[28]

In such expositions of the value of offensive action, the value of the defensive—passive or otherwise—is usually muted. True, some writers do hasten to warn ''that the one thing that this principle does not teach is a Foch-like doctrine of 'Attack! Attack!' '' However, despite this caveat, the same author directed the offensive principle explicitly at a commander who has been forced on the defensive since ''it highlights the fact that ultimate success can only be gained by eventually reverting to the offensive,'' a fact that must be considered when planning the defensive.[29] Indeed, the U.S. Army's *Field Manual 100–5* makes this same point even more strongly: ''While it may sometimes be necessary to adopt a defensive posture, this should be only a temporary condition until only the necessary means are available to resume offensive operations.'' Meanwhile, however, an ''offensive spirit must be inherent in the conduct of all defensive operations—*the defense must be an active, not a passive one. This is so*,'' the manual continues, ''because offensive action, whatever form it takes, is the means by which the nation or a military force captures and holds the initiative, achieves results, and maintains freedom of action.''[30]

Symptomatic of the dislike of Western professionals for purely defensive measures was the Strategic Air Command's indignant rejection as useless '''Maginot-line thinking'' of proposals that it protect its bombers with blast-proof shelters in the 1950s.[31] Consequently, it is clear that Soviet and Western military personnel are as united today on the utility of the offensive at the tactical and operational, and often at the strategic, levels of war as they were in 1914. At that time the ''cult of the offensive'' found its most eloquent proponents in such French soldiers as Ferdinand Foch and his pupil Loyzeaux de Grandmaison. This latter was responsible for a new and extreme doctrine, proclaimed in the name of Chief of the General Staff Joseph Joffre, that the

French army, returning to its traditions, no longer knows any other law than the offensive. . . . All attacks are to be pushed to the extreme. . . . [The goal is] to charge the enemy with the bayonet in order to destroy him. The result can only be obtained at the price of bloody sacrifice. Any other conception ought to be [seen] as contrary to the very nature of war.[32]

In general, this was a logical conclusion to be drawn from the line of French military thought that ran through the writings of Charles-Ardant du Picq, who had stressed to his own teacher, Foch, the impact of the attack on the maintenance of morale.[33] Arguing that "any improvement in firearms is bound to strengthen the offensive," Foch had gone on to insist that waging war always meant to attack, and that a commander must always strive to impose his will upon the enemy by destroying him in "the decisive battle."[34] It was left for Grandmaison to pull all these strands together in official form. "We are rightly told," he pronounced, "that psychological factors are paramount in combat. But this is not all: properly speaking there are no other factors, for all others—weaponry, manoeuvrability—influence only indirectly by provoking moral reactions. . . . The human heart is the starting point in all questions of war," and it responds best to offensive action.[35]

While the military organizations of other nations drew on different traditions, the overall result was the same. Faced with the probability of a two-front war, the German General Staff had adopted a plan, originally drafted by Count Alfred von Schlieffen, that called for a rapid mobilization, concentration, and offensive against France in the west and advocated an offensive doctrine to match.[36] Generals like William von Blume, Baron Colmar von der Goltz, and Friedrich von Bernhardi all insisted that "the strategical offensive is the more effective form of warfare." They then extended this superiority to the tactical field as well, while Sigismund von Schlichting urged the virtues of maneuver and mobility.[37] This spirit even reached pragmatic Great Britain. There, before he witnessed the losses inflicted by the Boers in 1900, Colonel G.F.R. Henderson upheld the virtues of massed attacks as a means of maintaining morale, and in 1905 his colleague F. N. Maude still insisted that the "chances of victory turned entirely on the spirit of self-sacrifice."[38]

ROOTS OF MODERN OFFENSIVE DOCTRINES

In 1914, of course, the offensive doctrines of all the European powers proved incapable of dealing with the powerful new weapons provided to the defense, and for four years Europe became a killing ground. In the search for causes, scholars have proposed a number of diverse explanations. The French radical Joseph Monteilhet charged that the offensive of 1914 "springs fatally" from the nature of the professional army, since it is "a theory linked in origin and in object to [that organization's] destiny."[39] In some ways this view seems supported by more recent social scientists like Jack Snyder and Barry Posen. The former, for example, has argued that institutional considerations such as prestige, conceptions of necessity, and the chance to simplify complex calculations, among other factors, naturally bias military planners toward offensive options.[40] Posen has basically agreed, suggesting that many civilians and most soldiers "are intuitively attracted to the offensive as somehow the stronger form of war." In addition, he believes that military organizations "will generally prefer offensive doctrines because they *reduce uncertainty* in important ways"; namely, by facilitating "standard scenarios," denying the opponent his "standard scenario," enhancing military autonomy, increasing organizational size and wealth, and so on.[41] In addition, he suggested that another set of factors (desire to conquer, to pass costs on to the enemy, to prevent the military balance shifting against one, etc.) help further to explain the adoption of offensive strategies by some countries.[42] Most recently of all, the classicist Victor Hanson has argued that the traditions of Greek infantry warfare have entered our cultural traditions to make the offensive "the Western way of war."[43]

While such factors undoubtedly had their influence, military historians generally remain unconvinced by such social scientific hypothesis. Indeed, as Snyder admitted, in each specific case, "the degree, direction and cause of bias in thinking about offense and defence are likely to be shaped by a highly particular set of factors—that is, threats, predispositions and strategic circumstances rooted in the peculiarities of the case."[44] Moreover, it is precisely the "particular set of factors" that interests most historians. As Douglas Porch remarked with regard to Monteilhet, "any army as driven by political and social strife and internal doubt as the post–1900 French army was simply not capable of formulating and applying a tactical doctrine" developed by professionals at the *école de guerre*. However, while he quite correctly attributed the adoption of an offensive doctrine to the growing influence of the republicans, for whom it had "been part of the ideological baggage" for a century. Monteilhet's belief that it resulted from the professionals' historical approach to military science and revived interest in Napoleon was a major contributing factor.[45]

THE NAPOLEONIC WATERSHED

Anyone reading the military literature of the period 1815–1914 must recognize the dominating presence of Napoleon Bonaparte, either in his own right or through Antoine Henri Jomini, Karl von Clausewitz, or other interpreters. True, the doctrine of theorists like Grandmaison was, as B. H. Liddell Hart later charged, "a travesty of Napoleon's."[46] Nonetheless, while this British critic of pre–1914 military doctrines charged that the military planners of the day had been "obsessed with the Napoleonic legend," he lay the real blame on the great Prussian philosopher of war. It was Clausewitz, he insisted, who "analyzed, codified and deified the Napoleonic method" he was "the master at whose feet sat for a century the military students of Europe."[47] Thus, Liddell Hart charged that the fault of men like Foch was that in concentrating on will and the moral aspects of battle, they had followed Clausewitz "in underestimating the material factors, such as armament."[48] Other writers have agreed. J.F.C. Fuller, for example, argued that when one regarded "Foch's offensive *à l'outrance*, we see Clausewitz throughout.''[49] However, his defenders have pointed out, the great German philosopher actually taught that, strategically at least, the defense is a ''stronger form of war'' than the offense.[50] Even so, by the late 1800s theorists like Frederich von Bernhardi openly disagreed. Most of his disciples considered this view to be an embarrassment, and ''every aspect of his work that *could be taken* as offensive advocacy has been so taken.''[51]

''What,'' Barry Posen asked, ''accounts for such systematic misinterpretation?''[52] His own hypothesis has been noted, and there can be little doubt that his stress on ''will'' and the activism implied by his concept of battle appealed to both the century's romanticism and later Social Darwinism.[53] Similarly, his style was frequently difficult, so that many chose only isolated quotations. These, in turn, easily became doctrinal slogans that distorted the real essence of his work. Thus, in dealing with his influence on Foch, Fuller defined the latter as ''not the contemplative student of war, but a Clausewitz drunk on violence.''[54]

However, the real reason for the perversion of Clausewitz's teachings is probably much simpler. Despite the extensive study of his works and those of others, and despite the lip service paid to their influence, the real significance of men like Jomini and Clausewitz was as symbols of the new style of war brought about by the French Revolution and Napoleon. Although the term *revolution in warfare* has tripped so lightly off the tongues of analysts in our century that it is almost meaningless, the fact remains that for contemporary soldiers, the years 1792 to 1815 brought about dramatic changes in their profession. Moreover, regardless of Clausewitz's relatively moderate views on the attack, his and Jomini's works clearly documented this watershed.[55]

Jomini's classical teachings on lines of communications, maneuver, concentration, and offensive action, for example, codified one aspect of the Napoleonic legacy.[56] Clausewitz, on the other hand, called attention to the vital significance of actual battle as the ''centre of gravity'' of any operation. It was, he believed, ''a struggle for real victory, waged with all available strength'' with the aim of securing a decision.[57] The implications of his teaching that success could be gained through a ''decisive battle'' only becomes fully evident when we add his latter comment that we ''are not interested in generals who win victories without bloodshed.''[58] While this last statement initially appears to be a gratuitous example of Germanic brutality, its real significance only becomes clear when compared to the style and teachings of the ''great commanders'' of the previous (pre–1789) era. For example, despite his obvious recognition of the value of seizing the initiative and attacking under favorable conditions, Frederick the Great also noted that the ''greatest secret of war and the masterpiece of a skilful general is to starve his enemy. Hunger exhausts men more surely than courage, and you will succeed with less risk than by fighting.''[59]

An even greater contrast emerges if we compare the apostles of Napoleon with Marshal Maurice de Saxe, the great French commander of the previous century. Rather than rushing to seize the initiative and go on the offensive, he scorned those who ''believe that it is advantageous to take the field early.'' After all, what difference if the enemy should lay siege to a few fortresses? Rather, this marshal argued "that there is no need to hasten and that one should remain in winter quarters longer than usual" while one's opponent wasted his resources. After all, "a single campaign reduces an army by a third, and sometimes by a half, and . . . the cavalry especially is in such a pitiable state by the end of October that they are no longer able to keep the field." He therefore counseled that one remain in quarters, harass the enemy and, if "towards the end of a good siege" you attack with a "well-disciplined and well-ordered army, you will ruin him."[60]

As for the value of battle, de Saxe believed that when circumstances were favorable (e.g., "when an opportunity occurs to crush the enemy"), it should be joined. The defeated enemy should be pursued and, if possible, destroyed. Nonetheless, he wrote in one of his most famous comments, "I do not favor pitched battles, especially at the beginning of a war, and I am convinced that a skilful general could make war all his life without being forced into one." As indicated above, he preferred instead to dissipate the enemy's forces by small engagements.[61] Here the views of Frederick initially seem more congenial to the post-Napoleonic generation. "War is decided only by battles," wrote the Prussian warrior-monarch, "and it is not finished except by them."[62] However, while this contains the germ of Clausewitz's battles of decision, Frederick still carefully avoided maneuvers like those made by Napoleon, deep into the enemy's territory, on the grounds that it would weaken his army and endanger his communications, and so force him into battle on unfavorable terms. For a successful offensive campaign that brings "assured conquests," he taught, "it is necessary always to proceed within the rules: to advance, to establish oneself solidly, to advance and establish yourself."[63]

It is true, of course, that Napoleon prided himself in following in the footsteps of the great Frederick. "I think like Frederick," he once remarked, "one should always be the first to attack." On another occasion he instructed: "Make war offensively, like Alexander, Hannibal, Caesar, Gustavus-Adolphus, Turenne, Eugene, and Frederick." However, as indicated, the style of Frederickian war was still closer to that of de Saxe than Napoleon. This is clear if we compared the Prussian's advice on a step-by-step process of conquest with the later teachings of his self-professed student. "Once one has decided to invade a country," Napoleon noted, "one must not be afraid to deliver battle, and should seek out the enemy everywhere to fight him."[64] Here in reality is a search for the type of decisive battle celebrated by Clausewitz, and with him, most of the military thinkers of the nineteenth century.

THE FAILURE OF MILITARY HISTORY

The principles comprising the Napoleonic paradigm, J.F.C. Fuller argued, can be summed up as including: (1) his "invariable reliance on the offensive; (2) his trust in speed to economize time, and (3) to effect strategic surprisals; (4) his insistence on concentrating superiority of force on the battlefield, particularly at the decisive point of attack; and (5) his carefully thought-out protective system."[65] That military men of Napoleon's own and later ages should be mesmerized by his spectacularly successful employment of these principles should not be surprising. In comparison with his meteoric campaigns, the wars of the eighteenth century seemed stylized minuets or ritualistic ceremonials that few soldiers sought to emulate. As a result, Napoleon's style and diverse comments were molded into theories of war by Jomini and Clausewitz, then were justified by successive generations of military historians, and finally were enshrined in the doctrines that guided Europe's armies as they marched bravely off to the killing fields of 1914.

Many military theorists quite naturally reacted to the bloodbath that was World War I by condemning adherence to the Napoleonic model and its associated offensive-mindedness. In France the reaction was greatest and brought about a new defensive doctrine which became flesh in the much-derided Maginot Line. Elsewhere, however, other thinkers quickly turned to the new technology of armored warfare as a means of reviving the seemingly moribund offensive.[66] The result was once again spectacular: the Blitzkrieg with which Hitler conquered most of Europe between 1939 and 1941. These victories, along with the use of armor in the series of powerful counteroffensives that carried the Red Army from Stalingrad to Kursk and then to Berlin, have seemed to confirm the validity of the offense in contemporary warfare. So, too, have subsequent Israeli victories in 1956 and 1967 and, most recently, the victory of the U.S.-led coalition over Iraq.

Despite the doubts of some dissident-successors to Ivan Bloch, military historians long have been virtually unanimous in upholding the Napoleonic paradigm, and with it the value of the offensive. However, as Michael Howard pointed out, military historians are no less prone to "myth-making" and to using selective history to support a priori bias than are other historians.[67] Obsessed with the "Napoleonic Revolution in War," military historians have only recently begun to examine seriously the professional European military experience before 1800. Such neglect of a pre-revolutionary era is common enough, and it has been repeated in our time in the tendency to ignore the traditions of the Russian Imperial Army in treatments of its successor, the Red Army.[68] In our case, neglect of the pre-Napoleonic period means that military historians generally have accepted the principle of "offensive action" as a given law of war and have viewed warfare of all ages accordingly. When this is joined with a widely shared interest in technological innovation and "problem solving," the tendency has been to confirm the primacy of the offensive in conventional land warfare.

Nonetheless, there is good reason to suggest that the proposition that an initial offense is the best defense is, in fact, a myth. This is not to argue that wars can be won by remaining passive. Rather, it means that a long-term view of military history supports Clausewitz's proposition that strategically, and possibly operationally and tactically, the defense is indeed the stronger form of warfare. Space does not permit such a review here, but certain highlights deserve mention. Thus, recent scholarship suggests that European warfare from the medieval period to the French Revolution remained a slow and painful process in which dreary sieges were punctuated by battles in the open field. However, such battles were rarely decisive in the Clausewitzian sense, and an able commander could usually avoid fighting if he felt the circumstances were unfavorable.[69]

The one break in this pattern was brought about by the new siege artillery introduced by France into Italy in 1495. Nonetheless, within a bare twenty years, military architects had developed a fortress style (the "Italian trace") that largely nullified the advances in artillery.[70] Warfare again bogged down until Napoleon's genius combined new tactical ideas, the use of such subordinate independent formations as divisions and corps, and the manpower provided by conscription to again wage offensive warfare. Even so, as the lessons of Spain and Russia should have indicated (and to Clausewitz, perhaps they did), this new primacy of the offensive was again a temporary phenomenon. That this might indeed be the case was indicated by the siege of Sebastopol in the Crimean War (1853–1854), the bloody battles of the American Civil War (1861–1865), the sieges of Paris in 1870–1871 and of Plevna in 1878, Britain's experiences in the Boer War (1899–1902), and the Manchurian battles and siege of Port Arthur in 1904. All pointed to the resurgence of the superiority of the defense, a superiority that became self-evident in 1914–1918.[71]

As noted, however, the myth of the efficacy of strategic and operational offensive power was revived by the application of the internal combustion engine to the battlefield. However, if the new mobility provided by armored and mechanized forces on the ground and support aircraft overhead brought the *Wehrmacht* its early victories, after 1943 the renewed power enjoyed by a well-prepared defense was evident in the battles before Kursk and the defensive war waged by the Germans in the East, Italy, and France during 1943–1945. For a time, this fact was obscured by the "scientific-technical revolution in military affairs" wrought by nuclear weapons and ballistic missiles. However, the power of these systems became sufficient to "negate" the military utility, and many close observers of military matters have again begun to question the value of an operational-strategic offensive. Indeed, given the experience of the Yom Kippur War of 1973 and the long Iran-Iraq conflict of the 1980s, the same is true of the offensive at the tactical-operational level as well. However, proponents of this latter view continue to be vocal, and their expectations seemed justified by the U.S. coalition's success against Iraq in 1991. Even so, the weapons that did so well recently could prove equally deadly in the hands of a skillful defense. Thus, like Hitler's victories of 1939–1941, the desert battles in south Iraq may only indicate the modern offense's superiority over a less well-conducted and technologically modernized enemy. For this reason, Chris Bellamy may still be correct in predicting that in a future conflict, the "attacker would be worn down by a process of attrition, constantly surprised by the force and form of the defender's attacks." Moreover, he pointed out, this "is not the image of a future war which many would have predicted: it is the Dragon Variation."[72]

CONCLUSION

On this basis, then, let us again consider Gorbachev's insistence that the Soviet military devise a doctrine that was defensive in style as well as purpose. Trained in the rituals of the myth of offensive action, his military planners probably found the task initially distasteful. Nonetheless, if the above analysis is correct, Gorbachev may well have forced a needed revision on his soldiers. Moreover, once they have been liberated from the influence of the myth of the offensive promoted by the Napoleonic paradigm, which itself is an aberration in the overall trend of Western warfare, military historians of the former Soviet Union, will find much to support the new doctrinal orthodoxy. At the very least, the resulting research may prove refreshing as history, and at best, it may help strengthen the tendency toward a similar reassessment among Western military scholars.

NOTES

1. Dale R. Herspring, "The Soviet High Command Looks at Gorbachev," *Adelphi Papers* no. 235, *The Changing Strategic Landscape*, part 1 (Spring 1989): 48–62. We should note, however, that in the eyes of Soviet theorists, their "military doctrine" and resulting "military strategy" has always pursued the "defensive" goal of protecting the Socialist Commonwealth and USSR from the "imperialist aggressors." Until recently, however, the means of doing so have been predominantly offensive in nature; see the entries "Doktrina voennaia" and "Strategiia voennaia" in S. F. Akhromeev, ed., *Voennyi entsiklopedicheskii slovar'*, 2d ed. (Moscow: Voyenizdat 1986), pp. 240, 711–12.

2. Dmitri Yazov, *"The Supreme Goal of the Soviet Armed Forces is to Prevent War"* (Moscow: Novosti, 1989), p. 4.

3. On the development of the *strategic-operational theatre defence*, see N. V. Olgarkov's *Vsegda v gotovnosti k zashchite Otechestva* (Moscow: Voenizdat, 1982), and his *Istoriia uchit bditel' nosti* (Moscow: Voenidzat, 1985). For a discussion of the implications of Ogarkov's writings, see Mary Fitzgerald, *Changing Soviet Doctrine on Nuclear War* (Halifax, Canada: Centre for Foreign Policy Studies, Dalhousie University, 1988), and Dale R. Herspring, *The Soviet High Command 1989: Personalities and Politics* (Princeton, NJ: Princeton University Press, 1990).

4. See, for example, A. Kokoshin and V. Larionov, "The Battle of Kursk in Light of Today's Defensive Doctrine," *Mirovaia ekonomika i mezhdunarodnye otnosheniia* no. 8, (1987): 32–33.

5. Michael Howard, "The Uses and Abuse of Military History," in M. Howard, *The Causes of Wars and Other Essays* (London: Temple Smith, 1983), pp. 189–90, 194–97.

6. V. G. Kulikov, "Aktual'nye problemy voennoi istorii v svete peshenii XXV s'ezda KPSS," *Voenno-istoricheskii zhurnal*, no. 12 (1967): 11–15.

7. P. A. Zhilin, *O voine i voennoi istorii* (Moscow: "Nauka," 1984), p. 534. Also see M. M. Kir'ian et al., *Istoriia voennogo iskusstva* (Moscow: Voenizdat, 1986), pp. 3–6, for a more expanded description of the content of the military art.

8. A. A. Sidorenko, *Nastuplenie* (Moscow: Voenizdat, 1970), p. 3. For a brief review

of the Soviet practice and literature on this topic, see David M. Glantz, "Soviet Offensive Ground Doctrine since 1945: Historical Overview," *Air University Review* 34, no. 3 (1983); 25–35.

9. A. A. Sidorenko, "Nastuplenie," in N. V. Ogarkov, ed., *Sovetskaia voennaia entsiklopediia* (Moscow: Voenizdat, 1978), 8:519; I. Kh. Nagramian et al., *Istoriia voin i voennogo iskusstva* (Moscow: Voenizdat, 1970), pp. 5–6.

10. Sidorenko, "Nastuplenie," p. 5.

11. Ibid., pp. 3–4.

12. Nathan Leites, *Soviet Style in War* (New York: Crane Russak, 1982), pp. 221, 208.

13. I. A. Grudinin, *Dialektika i sovremennoe voennoe delo* (Moscow: Voenizdat, 1971), p. 54.

14. P. I. Skuibeda, comp., *Tolkovyi slovar' voennykh terminov* (Moscow: Voenizdat, 1966), p. 268.

15. V. D. Sokolovskii et al., *Military Strategy*, ed. Harriet Fast Scott (London: Macdonald and Jane's, 1975), pp. 283–84; Leites, *Soviet Style*, pp. 237ff.

16. Sidorenko, "Nastuplenie," pp. 7–39.

17. V. A. Semenov, *Kratkii ocherk razvitiia sovetskogo operativnogo iskusstva* (Moscow: Voenizdat, 1960); V. E. Savkin, *Osnovnye printsipy operativnogo iskusstva i taktiki* (Moscow: Voenizdat, 1972), pp. 5–51; A. A. Yamanov, *Vstrechnyi boi* (Moscow: Voenizdat, 1959); and S. P. Ivanov, ed., *Nachal'nyi period voiny (Po ipytu pervyk kampanii i operatsii vtoroi mirovoi voiny)* (Moscow: Voenizdat, 1974).

18. V. I. Lenin, *Polnoe sobranie sochineny*, ed. Ya. Gladkov et al (Moscow, 1958–65) 55 vols., 13: 376.

19. M. V. Frunze, *Izbrannye proizvedeniia*, 2 vols. (Moscow: Voenizdat, 1957), p. 49.

20. Walter Darnell Jacobs, *Frunze: The Soviet Clausewitz, 1885–1925* (The Hague: Martinus Nijoff, 1969), p. 111. Although the case for the strategic offensive was made by A. A. Svechin, *Strategiia*, 2d ed. (Moscow: Voennyi vestnik, 1927), pp. 182–189, his concerns were largely drowned in the enthusiasm that was roused by prospects of mechanized warfare. On Soviet offensive doctrine in the interwar period, see David R. Jones, *The Advanced Guard and Mobility in Russian and Soviet Military Thought and Practice*, SAFRA Papers, no. 1 (Gulf Breeze, FL: Academic International Press, 1985), pp. 89–94; Karl S. Shultz, "The Revolution Rearmed: Development of Soviet Mobile Warfare Doctrine, 1920–1941," in Jacob W. Kipp et al., *Historical Analysis of the Use of Mobile Forces by Russia and the USSR* (College Station, TX: Center for Strategic Technology, Texas A & M University, 1985), pp. 115–58; and Richard Simkin, *Deep Battle: The Brainchild of Marshal Tukhachevskii* (London: Brassey's, 1987).

21. Western surveys of Imperial Russian military thought are still limited to Walter Pintner's essay "Russian Military Thought: The Western Model and the Shadow of Suvrorov," in Peter Paret, ed., *Makers of Modern Strategy from Machiavelli to the Nuclear Age* (Oxford: Clarendon, 1986), pp. 354–74; and Peter von Wahlde's pioneering *Military Thought in Imperial Russia* (Ph.d. dissertation, University of Indiana, 1966). Notable Russian studies of the power of the defense in pre–1914 Russia are A. A. Neznamov's *Oboronitel'naia voina (Teoriia voprosa)*, one volume of which appeared in St. Petersburg in 1909, (*Strategiia*), and Y. S. Bliokh's famous *Budushchaia voina v. tekhnicheskom, ekonomicheskom i politicheskom otnoshenniakh*, 3 vols. (St. Petersburg: Sytin, 1898).

22. Von Wahlde, pp. 121–29. On Suvorov, see Philip Longworth, *The Art of Victory: The Life and Achievements of Generalissimo Suvorov, 1729–1800* (London: Constable, 1965), pp. 213–21. Dragomirov's debt to Suvorov is evident in his version of *The Art of Victory*: "O nauke pobezhdat Suvorova," in M. I. Dragomirov, *Sbornik orginal'nykh i perevodnykh statet M. I. Dragomirova, 1856–1881*, 2 vols. (St. Petersburg: Tip. V. A. Balasheva, 1881), I: 222–43.

23. Dragomirov, "O nauke pobezhdat Suvorova," pp. 131–48. Russia's prewar planning is outlined in detail in Jack Snyder, *The Ideology of the Offensive: Military Decision Making and the Disasters of 1914* (Ithaca, NY: Cornell, 1984), pp. 157–98. It is discussed critically in D.C.B. Lieven, *Russia and the Origins of the First World War* (London: Macmillan, 1983), pp. 101–16, and David R. Jones, "Imperial Russia's Forces at War," in Allen R. Millett et al., *The Effectiveness of Military Organizations*, 3 vols. (Boston: Allen and Unwin, 1988), I: 285–90.

24. United States, Department of the Army, Headquarters, *Operations*, Field Manual No. 100–5 (Washington, DC, 20 August 1982), pp. 8–10. Its "historical" comments are comparable in tone with K. Basilevich, *The Russian Art of War* (London: Soviet War News, 1945), pp. 11–12, 20–22, 37–40.

25. Hew Strachan, *European Armies and the Conduct of War* (London: Allan & Unwin, 1983), pp. 1–2. Slightly different listings of the American principles can be found in Field Manual No. 100–5, pp. B–1–B–5, and Samuel B. Payne, Jr., *The Conduct of War: An Introduction to Modern Warfare* (Oxford: Basil Blackwell, 1989), pp. 153–54. Fuller's are listed in D. K. Palit, *The Essentials of Military Knowledge* (London: C. Hurst, 1963), pp. 129–50.

26. Field Manual No. 100–5, p. B–2.

27. Henry E. Eccles, *Military Concepts and Philosophy* (New Brunswick, NJ: Rutgers, University Press 1965), p. 109.

28. Strachan, *European Armies*, pp. 1–2. Also see Archer Jones, *The Art of War in the Western World* (Urbana, IL: University of Illinois, 1987), p. 670.

29. D. K. Palit, *War in the Deterrent Age* (London: MacDonald, 1966), pp. 103–6, esp. p. 104. Also see his *Essentials*, pp. 134–37.

30. Training Manual 100–5, p. B–2. Italics in original.

31. Barry R. Posen, *The Sources of Military Doctrine: France, Britain, and Germany Between the World Wars* (Ithaca, NY: Cornell, 1984), p. 15.

32. Quoted in B. H. Liddel Hart, *The Ghost of Napoleon* (London: Faber, 1933), pp. 136–37. On doctrinal developments in the French Army at this time, see Douglas Porch, "The French Army and the Spirit of the Offensive," in Brian Bond and Ian Roy, eds., *War and Society: A Yearbook, of Military History* (London: Croom Helm, 1975), pp. 117–43.

33. Ardant du Picq, *Battle Studies. Ancient and Modern Battle* (Harrisburg, PA: Military Service Pub. Co., 1943), pp. 149–68; Fernand Schneider, *Histoire des Doctrines militaries* (Paris: Presses Universitaires de France, 1964), pp. 63–69.

34. Ferdinand Foch, *The Principles of War* (New York: H. K. Fly, 1918), pp. 310–15; Liddell Hart, *Ghost of Napoleon*, p. 135; Michael Howard, "Men against Fire: The Doctrine of the Offensive in 1914," in Paret, *Makers*, pp. 510–26; and Jay Luvaas, "European Military Thought and Doctrine, 1870–1914," in Michael Howard, ed., *The Theory and Practice of War: Essays Presented to Captain B. H. Liddell Hart* (London: Cassell, 1965), pp. 71–91.

35. Quoted in Porch, "French Army," p. 120.

36. Gunther E. Rothenberg, "Moltke, Schlieffen, and the Doctrine of Strategic Envelopment," in Paret, *Makers*, pp. 311–19; Gerhard Ritter, *The Schlieffen Plan: Critique of a Myth* (London: Oswald Wolf 1958).

37. Baron C. von der Goltz, *The Nation in Arms: A Treatise on Modern Military Systems and the Conduct of War* (London: Hodder and Stoughton, 1914), pp. 151–63; F. von Bernhardi, *How Germany Makes War* (London: Hodder and Stoughton, 1914), pp. 125–44; S. von Schlichting, *Osnovy sovremennoi taktiki i strategii*, 2 vols. (St. Petersburgh: Sytin, 1902), II: 66–84.

38. G.F.R. Henderson, *The Science of War* (London: Longman's, 1905), pp. 147–64; F. N. Maude, *The Evolution of Infantry Tactics* (London, 1905), p. x.

39. Joseph Monteilhet, *Les Institutions Militaires de la France (1815–1932)* (Paris: Plon, 1932), pp. 271–72, 351.

40. Snyder, *Ideology*, pp. 18–40, 205–16.

41. Posen, *Sources*, pp. 47–50. Italics in original.

42. Ibid., pp. 69–71.

43. Victor Davis Hanson, *The Western Way of War: Infantry Battle in Classical Greece* (New York: Knopf, 1989), pp. 9–18, 222–28.

44. Snyder, *Ideology*, p. 216.

45. Quote from Porch, "French Army," p. 117; see also Monteilhet, *Institutions*, pp. 321–30.

46. Liddell Hart, *Ghost*, p. 137.

47. B. H. Liddell Hart, *Paris, or the Future of War* (New York: Dutton, 1925), pp. 8, 10.

48. Quote from Liddell Hart, *Ghost*, p. 135; see also Foch, *Principles*, pp. 8–9; Stefan T. Possony and Etienne Mantoux, "Du Picq and Foch: The French School," in Edward Mead Earle, ed., *Makers of Modern Strategy. Military Thought from Machiavelli to Hitler* (New York: Atheneum, 1970), pp. 222–23. On Clausewitz in France after 1870, see Eugene Carrias, *La Pensée militaire française* (Paris: Presses Universitaires de France, 1960), pp. 278–302.

49. J.F.C. Fuller, *The Conduct of War, 1789–1961* (Westport, CT: Greenwood, 1961), p. 128.

50. Quote from Ibid., pp. 71–73; See also Clausewitz, *On War*, pp. 357–76.

51. Quote from Posen, *Sources*, p. 47; see also Frederich von Bernhardi, *On War of Today*, 2 vols. (New York: Garland, 1972), II: 2. On the misinterpretation of Clausewitz on defense, see Michael Howard, *Clausewitz* (Oxford: Oxford University Press, 1983), pp. 60–64.

52. Posen, *Sources*, p. 47.

53. Michael Howard, "Jomini and the Classical Tradition in Military Thought," in Howard, *Theory and Practice*, pp. 13–14.

54. Fuller, *Conduct*, p. 128.

55. Ibid., pp. 71–73. On the revolution in warfare, see Peter Paret, "Napoleon and the Revolution in War," in Paret, *Makers*, pp. 123–42.

56. Howard, "Jomini," pp. 16–17; A. H. Jomini, *The Art of War* (Westport, CT: Greenwood, 1962), pp. 65–129; see also Strachan, *European Armies*, pp. 61–64, and John Shy, "Jomini," in Paret, *Makers*, pp. 145–46, 153–55, 163–68.

57. Clausewitz, *On War*, p. 248.

58. Ibid., p. 260.

59. Frederick II (the Great), *Instructions for His Generals* (Harrisburg, PA: Military Service Pub., Co., 1944), p. 31.

60. Maurice de Saxe, *Reveries on the Art of War* (Harrisburg, PA: Military Service Pub., CO., 1944), pp. 85–86.

61. Ibid., p. 121.

62. Frederick II, *Instructions*, p. 95.

63. Ibid., p. 24. On the eighteenth-century style of campaigning, see Strachan, *European Armies*, pp. 8–22, and Christopher Duffy, *The Military Experience in the Age of Reason* (New York: Atheneum, 1988), pp. 151–97, 254–67.

64. All the quotations in this paragraph are cited in Fuller, *Conduct*, p. 49.

65. Ibid.

66. On these developments see Posen, *Sources*, chs. 3–5; Strachan, *European Armies*, ch. 10; John Weldon, *Machine Age Armies* (London: Abelard-Schuman, 1968), chs. 1–5; and Lord Michael Carver, *The Apostles of Mobility* (London: Weidenfeld and Nicholson, 1979).

67. Michael Howard, "The Use and Abuse of Military History," pp. 188–95.

68. On the similar tendency of military writers to accept claims of novelty after 1917 see David R. Jones, "Russian Military Traditions and the Soviet Military Establishment," in K. M. Currie and Gregory Varhall, eds., *The Soviet Union: What Lies Ahead? Military-Political Affairs in the 1980s* (Washington, DC: USAF/GPO, c. 1985), pp. 21–22.

69. Philippe Contamine, *War in the Middle Ages* (Oxford: Basil Blackwell, 1984), pp. 219–37.

70. Michael Howard, *War in European History* (Oxford: Oxford University Press, 1976), pp. 30–31, 34–36; J. R. Hale, *War and Society in Renaissance Europe, 1450–1620* (London: Fontana, 1985), pp. 46–51; and Geoffrey Parker, *The Military Revolution: Military Innovation and the Rise of the West, 1500–1800* (Cambridge: Cambridge University Press, 1988), pp. 6–24.

71. The trend outlined here is done so at greater length, and with considerable analysis, in Archer Jones, *The Art of War in the Western World* (Urbana, IL: Illinois University Press, 1987), a work to which I am greatly indebted. Also see William McElwee, *The Art of War: Waterloo to Mons* (Bloomington: Indiana, 1974).

72. Christopher Bellamy, *The Future of Land Warfare* (London: Croom Helm, 1987), p. 290. For a Soviet view of the "negation" of nuclear weapons, see Ogarkov, pp. 35–47. Since completing this essay, I have discovered Williamson Murray's "The Strategic View: Napoleon's Flawed Legacy," *MHQ: The Quarterly Journal of Military History* 2, no. 1 (Autumn 1989): pp. 101–2. In this article, Murray pointed out the elusive nature of Clausewitz's "decisive battle" and the costs entailed by pursuing this objective.

Select Bibliography

The list that follows is not intended to be exhaustive. Rather, it is a brief introductory guide to literature on the writing of military history and the relationship between military history and the military professions of selected Western nations.

Alger, John I. *The Quest for Victory: The History of the Principles of War*. Westport, CT: Greenwood Press, 1982.

Ball, Col. Harry P., USA (Ret.). *A Responsible Command: A History of the U.S. Army War College*. Carlisle, PA: Alumni Association of U.S. Army War College, 1983.

Barnard, Henry. *Military Schools and Courses of Instruction in the Science and Art of War*. Westport, CT: Greenwood Press, 1969. reprint, 1972.

Barnett, Correlli, Shelford Bidwell, Brian Bond, and John Terraine. *Old Battles and New Defences: Can We Learn from Military History?* London: Brassey's, 1986.

Beckett, Ian. F. W., ed. *The Roots of Counter-Insurgency: Armies and Guerrilla Warfare, 1900–1945*. London: Blandford Press, 1988.

Bittner, Lt. Col. Donald F., USMCR. *Curriculum Evolution: Marine Corps Command and Staff College, 1920–1988*. Washington, DC: History and Museums Division, HQMC, 1988.

Blumenson, Martin, "Can Official History Be Honest History?" *Military Affairs* 25 (Winter 1963): 153–61.

———. "Why Military History? To Analyse the Past, Discover the Present." *Army* 25 (January 1975): 33–37.

Bond, Brian. *The Victorian Army and the Staff College, 1854–1914*. London: Eyre Methuen, 1972.

———. *Liddell Hart: A Study of His Military Thought*. London: Cassell, 1977.

———, ed. *The First World War and British Military History*. Oxford: Clarendon Press, 1991.

Chambers, John Whiteclay, II. "The New Military History: Myth and Reality." [conference review essay]. *Journal of Military History* 55, no. 3 (July 1991): 395–406.

Charters, David A. "From Palestine to Northern Ireland: British Adaptation to Low Intensity Operations." In David A. Charters and Maurice Tugwell, eds., *Armies in Low-Intensity Conflict: A Comparative Analysis*. London: Brassey's, 1989, pp. 169–249.

Coffman, Edward M. "The New American Military History." *Military Affairs* 48 (January 1984): 1–5.

Cohen, Eliot A., and John Gooch. *Military Misfortunes: The Anatomy of Failure in War*. New York: Free Press, 1990.

Conn, Stetson. "The Pursuit of Military History." *Military Affairs* 30 (Spring 1966): 1–8.

Cooling, Benjamin Franklin, III. "Military History for the Military Professional." *Parameters* 1 (Winter 1972): 28–35.

Dastrup, Boyd L. *The U.S. Army Command and General Staff College: A Centennial History*. Ft. Leavenworth, KS: USAC and GSC, 1981.

Douglas, W.A.B. "Filling Gaps in the Military Past: Recent Developments in Canadian Official History." *Journal of Canadian Studies* 19, no. 3 (Autumn 1984): 112–24.

Eller, Rear Adm. Ernest M., USN (Ret.). "The Navy's Historians." *United States Naval Institute Proceedings* 89 (April 1963): 96–109.

Finney, Robert T. *History of the Air Corps Tactical School, 1920–1940*. USAF Historical Studies no. 100. Montgomery, AL: Air University, 1951.

French, David. " 'Official but Not History'? Sir James Edmonds and the Official History of the Great War." *RUSI Journal* 131, no. 1 (March 1986): 58–63.

Fussell, Paul. "The Real War, 1939–1945." *Atlantic Monthly*, August 1989, pp. 32–48.

Futrell, R. F. *Ideas, Concepts, Doctrine: Basic Thinking in the USAF, 1907–1984*. 2 vols. Maxwell Air Force Base, AL: Air University Press, 1989.

Gilbert, Felix. "From Clausewitz to Delbrück and Hintze: Achievements and Failures of Military History." *Journal of Strategic Studies* 3 (December 1980): 11–20.

Gooch, John. "Clio and Mars: The Use and Abuse of Military History." *Journal of Strategic Studies* 3 (December 1980); 21–36.

Greenfield, Kent Roberts. *The Historian and the Army*. New Brunswick, NJ: Rutgers University Press, Port Washington, NY: Kennikat Press, 1954.

Grove, Eric J. "Introduction and Notes." In Julian S. Corbett, *Some Principles of Maritime Strategy*. Annapolis, MD: Naval Institute Press, 1988, pp. xi-xlv.

Handel, Michael I., ed. *Clausewitz and Modern Strategy*. London: Frank Cass, 1986.

Helfers, M. C. "The United States Army's History of World War II." *Military Affairs* 19 (Spring 1955): 32–36.

Higginbotham, Don. "American Historians and the Military History of the American Revolution." *American Historical Review* 70 (1964): 18–34.

Higham, Robin, ed. *Official Histories: Essays and Bibliographies from Around the World*. Manhattan, KS: Kansas State University Library, 1970.

———. *A Guide to the Sources of British Military History*. Berkeley, Calif.: University of California Press, 1971.

———. ed., *A Guide to the Sources of United States Military History*. (Hamden, CT: Archon, 1975).

Higham, Robin and Donald J. Mrozek. *A Guide to the Sources of Military History: Supplements*. Archon, 1981, 1986, 1991.

Howard, Michael. *The Lessons of History*. Oxford: Oxford University Press, 1991.

———. "The Use and Abuse of Military History." [1961 lecture to the RUSI]. Reprinted in *The Causes of Wars and Other Essays*, 2nd ed. Cambridge, MA: Harvard University Press, 1984, pp. 188–97.

Hyatt, A.M.J. "Military Studies in Canada: An Overview." *Revue Internationale d'Histoire Militaire* 54 (1982): 328–49.

Jeffery, Keith. "Intelligence and Counter-Insurgency Operations: Some Reflections on the British Experience." *Intelligence and National Security* 2, no. 1 (January 1987): 118–49.

Jessup, Col. John E., and Robert W. Coakley, eds. *A Guide to the Study and Use of Military History*. Washington, DC: Center of Military History, U.S. Army, 1979.

Jordan, Gerald, ed. *British Military History: A Supplement to Robin Higham's "Guide to the Sources."* New York: Garland, 1988.

Karsten, Peter. *The Naval Aristocracy: The Golden Age of Annapolis and the Emergence of Modern American Navalism*. New York: Collier-Macmillan and the Free Press, 1972.

———. "The 'New' American Military History: A Map of the Territory, Explored and Unexplored." *American Quarterly* 36 (Summer 1984): 389–418.

Keegan, John. *The Face of Battle*. London: Jonathan Cape, 1976.

———. *The Mask of Command*. New York: Viking, 1987.

Kleber, Brooks E. "History and Military Education: The U.S. Army." *Military Affairs* 42 (October 1978): 136–41.

Kohn, Richard H. "The Social History of the American Soldier: A Review and Prospectus for Research." *American Historical Review* 86 (June 1981): 553–67.

Loughrey, K. A. "A Letter to My Brigadier—An Essay on Formal Training in Military History as a Necessary Part of Officer Development." *Defense Force Journal* 40 (May-June 1983): 56–60.

Luvaas, Jay. *The Education of an Army: British Military Thought, 1815–1940*. Chicago: University of Chicago Press, 1964.

Mahon, John K. "Teaching and Research in Military History in the United States." *Historian* 27 (February 1965): 170–84.

Matloff, Maurice. "Government and Public History: The Army." *Public Historian* 2 (Spring 1980): 43–51.

———. "The Present State and Future Directions of Military History." *Army Historian* 2 (Winter 1984): 7–11.

Mearsheimer, John. *Liddell Hart and the Weight of History*. Ithaca, N.Y.: Cornell, 1989.

Millett, Allan R. "Military History and the Professional Officer." *Marine Corps Gazette* 51 (April 1967): 51.

———. "The Study of American Military History in the United States." *Military Affairs* 41 (April 1977): 58–61.

———, and Murray Williamson. "Lessons of War." *National Interest* 14 (Winter 1988–89): 83–95.

Millis, Walter. *Military History*. Service Centre for Teachers of History Publication no. 39. (Washington, DC: American Historical Association, 1961, pp. 1–18.

Milner, Marc. "Reflections on the State of Canadian Army History in the Two World Wars." *Acadiensis* 18, no. 2 (Spring 1989): 135–50.

Mockaitis, Thomas R. *British Counterinsurgency, 1919–1960*. London: Macmillan, 1990.

Morgan, William James, and Joyce L. Leonhart. *A History of the Naval Historical Center and the Dudley Knox Center for Naval History*. Washington, DC: Naval Historical Foundation, 1983.

Morrison, James L., Jr. *"The Best School in the World": West Point, the Pre–Civil War Years, 1833–1866*. Kent, OH: Kent State University Press, 1986.

Nenninger, Timothy K. *Leavenworth Schools and the Old Army: Education, Professionalism, and the Officer Corps of the United States Army, 1881–1918*. Westport, CT: Greenwood Press, 1978.

Nye, Roger H. "The Army Historians: Who Are They?" *Army Historian* 1 (Fall 1983): 6–8.

Paret, Peter. "The History of War." *Daedalus* 100 (Spring 1971): 376–96.

———, ed. *Makers of Modern Strategy from Machiavelli to the Nuclear Age*. Princeton, NJ: Princeton University Press, 1986.

Paschall, J. Rod. "The Army Historian and Combat Developments." *Army Historian* 5 (Fall 1984): 5–6.

Possony, Stefan T., and Dale O. Smith. "The Utility of Military History." *Military Affairs* 22 (Winter 1958–59): 216–18.

Preston, R. A. *Canada's RMC: A History of the Royal Military College*. Toronto: University of Toronto Press, 1969.

———. "MARCOM Education: Is It a Break with the Tradition?" In W.A.B. Douglas, ed., *The RCN in Transition*. Vancouver, BC: University of British Columbia Press, 1988, pp. 61–89.

———. "Perspectives in History of Military Education and Professionalism." In Lt. Col. Harry Borowski, USAF, ed., *The Harmon Memorial Lectures in Military History, 1959–1987*. Washington, DC: Office of Air Force History, pp. 269–301.

Reardon, Carol. *Soldiers and Scholars: The U.S. Army and the Uses of Military History, 1865–1920*. Lawrence, KS: University Press of Kansas, 1990.

Reid, Brian Holden. *J.F.C. Fuller: Military Thinker*. London: Macmillan, 1987.

Sandler, Stanley. "History and the Military." *Military Review* 52 (January 1972): 26–31.

———. "The Army's Civilian Historians." *Perspectives: American Historical Association Newsletter* 24 (1986): 20–22.

Schurman, D. M. *The Education of a Navy: The Development of British Naval Strategic Thought*. London: Cassell, 1965.

———. *Julian S. Corbett, 1854–1922: Historian of British Maritime Policy from Drake to Jellicoe*. London: Royal Historical Society, 1981.

———. "Historical Strategy in Large and Small Navies." In W.A.B. Douglas, ed., *The RCN in Transition, 1910–1985*. Vancouver, BC: University of British Columbia Press, 1988.

"Service Historians in the Gulf War." *Headquarters Gazette* (Annapolis, Md.: Society for Military History) 3, no.1, (Spring 1991): 3.

Shy, John. "The American Military Experience: History and Learning." *Journal of Interdisciplinary History* 1 (Winter 1971): 205–28.

Skaggs, David Curtis. "Michael Howard and the Dimensions of Military History." *Military Affairs* 49 (October 1985): 179–83.

Spector, Ronald H. "Getting Down to the Nitty-Gritty: Official History and the American Experience in Vietnam." *Military Affairs* 38 (February 1974): 11–12.

———. *Professors of War: The Naval War College and the Development of the Naval Profession*. Newport, RI: Naval War College Press, 1977.

Spiller, Roger J. "The Tenth Imperative." *Military Review* 69 (April 1989): 2–13.

Stacey, C. P. "The Life and Hard Times of an Official Historian." *Canadian Historical Review* 51 (March 1970): 21–47.
———. *A Date with History*. Ottawa: Deneau, 1983.
Strauss, Barry S., and Josiah Ober. *The Anatomy of Error: Ancient Military Disasters and Their Lessons for Modern Strategists*. New York: St. Martin's Press, 1990.
Stuart, Reginald C. "War, Society, and the 'New' Military History of the United States." *Canadian Review of American Studies* 7, no. 1 (Spring 1977): 1–10.
Trask, David F. "The New Military History and Army Historians." *Army Historian* 5 (Fall 1984): 7–10.
Travers, Tim. *The Killing Ground: The British Army, The Western Front and the Emergence of Modern Warfare, 1900–1918*. London: Allen and Unwin, 1987.
———. "Allies in Conflict: The British and Canadian Official Historians and the Real Story of Second Ypres (1915)." *Journal of Contemporary History* 24 (1989): 301–25.
United States. Department of the Army. *The Writing of American Military History: A Guide*. Pamphlet No. 20–200. Washington, DC: Department of the Army, 1951.
———. Department of the Army. Ad Hoc Committee on the Army Need for the Study of Military History. *Report and Recommendations*. 4 vols. Manhattan, KS: *Military Affairs* and Kansas State University, 1971.
Vlahos, Michael. *The Blue Sword: The Naval War College and the American Mission, 1919–1941*. Newport, RI: Naval War College Press, 1980.
"What Is Military History?" *History Today* 34 (December 1984): 5–13.
Wickham, Gen. John A., Jr. "The Professional Soldier and History." *Army Historian* 4 (Summer 1984): 1–2.
Wright, Robert K. "Clio in Combat: The Evolution of the Military History Detachments." *Army Historian* 6 (Winter 1985): 3–6.

Index

About the Contributors

IAN BECKETT is Senior Lecturer in War Studies at the Royal Military Academy, Sandhurst, United Kingdom.

DAVID A. CHARTERS is Director of the Centre for Conflict Studies, University of New Brunswick, Canada.

W.A.B. DOUGLAS is Director, Directorate of History, Department of National Defence, Canada.

ROLAND G. FOERSTER is Director for Historical Education and Information in the Military History Bureau of the German Armed Forces.

ANNE N. FOREMAN is Undersecretary of the United States Air Force.

DOMINICK GRAHAM is Professor Emeritus of Military History at the University of New Brunswick, Canada.

DONALD E. GRAVES is a historian at the Directorate of History, Department of National Defence, Canada.

ERIC GROVE is a freelance naval historian and Visiting Lecturer at the Royal Naval College, Greenwich, United Kingdom.

DON HIGGINBOTHAM is Professor of History at the University of North Carolina at Chapel Hill.

ROBIN HIGHAM is Professor of History at Kansas State University.

KEITH JEFFERY is Lecturer in History at the University of Ulster, United Kingdom.

DAVID R. JONES is a Secretary of the Navy Fellow in the Department of Strategy at the U.S. Naval War College.

RICHARD H. KOHN is Associate Professor of History at the University of North Carolina at Chapel Hill and former Chief of (U.S.) Air Force History.

BILL McANDREW is a historian in the Directorate of History, Department of National Defence, Canada.

ALLAN R. MILLETT is Professor of History and Associate Director of the Mershon Center at Ohio State University.

MARC MILNER is Associate Professor of History and Director of the Military and Strategic Studies Programme at the University of New Brunswick, Canada.

DONALD M. SCHURMAN is Professor Emeritus of History at the Royal Military College of Canada.

TIM TRAVERS is Professor of History at the University of Calgary, Canada.

J. BRENT WILSON is Senior Researcher at the Centre for Conflict Studies, University of New Brunswick, Canada.